AUSTIN

AUSTIN

THE COMPLETE GUIDE TO TEXAS' CAPITAL CITY

BY RICHARD ZELADE

TexasMonthlyPress

Texas Monthly Press, Inc.
P. O. Box 1569
Austin, Texas 78767

A   B   C   D   E   F   G   H

Library of Congress Cataloging in Publication Data

Zelade, Richard, 1953–
    Austin, the most complete guide to Texas' capital city.

    Includes index.
    1. Austin (Tex.)—Description—Guide-books.   I. Title.
F394.A93Z44   1984   917.64'31   84-8505
ISBN 0-932012-69-8

Text design by Terry Toler
Cover design by Hixo, Inc.

To Will, and to Baylor: "This sign X was on his forehead, This star * was over him, He tried to be his brother's keeper and failed, and hid himself under the name of the Lone Palm Tree."

CONTENTS

★★

ACKNOWLEDGMENTS

Thanks to the staffs of the Barker Texas History Center, Austin–Travis County Collection, my parents Irv and Mary, Sally Archibald, Marianne Simmons, Dana Scragg, Bruce Safely, Hannah Overton, Darrell Kirkland, John and Malou, Hernando Merino, Laszlo Ravasz, Marilyn Calabrese, Barbara Rodriguez, Dan Okrent, Scott Lubeck, Candi Vernon, and Barbara Burnham for their help and inspiration; and to Mudstone, for just being herself.

Richard Zelade
June 1984

INTRODUCTION

Austin is—in a word—*exciting*. An exciting city, the most exciting in Texas. Boosters love to describe Austin as "a city of urban sophistication in a livable small-town package." Preservationists decry the imminent "Houstonization" of their beloved city. Both sides are right.

Nobody is going to mistake the densely wooded hills of central "old" Austin for Houston or Dallas. Possums and armadillos still wreak havoc in Tarrytown, Hyde Park, Travis Heights, and Blackshear neighborhood yards. Austin probably loses more trees to live-oak blight each year than to condo blight. Most developers like to brag about all the trees they save. But anyone who has crawled along Highways IH 35, 183 North, or 290 West, or Ben White Boulevard or even Brodie Lane during the rush hours, past fresh-faced tilt-wall shopping center after center, knows what all the Houstonization hoopla is about.

Except for a few lapses during its childhood and adolescence, Austin has always been a city on the grow, doubling in size roughly every twenty years. That growth has been slow, steady, and for the most part graceful over the years, until now. Few of us really understand the parameters and consequences of Austin's current boom. We hear the predictions of long-range planners who foresee one continuous urban thread linking San Antonio and Austin by the year 2001 and, after that, our metroplex to Dallas and Fort Worth. We hear the experts' words, in terms of "municipal utility districts" and "planned communities," but do we really understand the reality implicit in those phrases, all the forthcoming McFajita joints and Vista Buena subdivisions?

Austin is both gateway and capital of Texas's most beautiful region— the Hill Country—and it seems that everybody who doesn't already live here would like to. But the Hill Country (Austin included) is much more delicate an ecosystem than most folks realize. It can comfortably accommodate a certain density of people, and those capabilities may vary drastically from acre to acre. Most of the controversy is over how much is "comfortable."

That Austin will grow is inevitable; the recent landing of the highly prized Microelectronics and Computer Technology Corporation (MCC) is as telling a trophy as any. And this is really where everyone gets excited. Some people are thrilled (mostly the ones who stand to make money off it or who want to move here); most would like to see the growth "controlled" (whatever that is). Some still believe it can be stopped. But everybody is excited.

At best, Austin stands to become the city (and we do mean *city*) that just about every other city in the country would like to be like: the champion of clean water, clean air, lots of trees and parks, beautiful people and beautiful buildings, Barton Springs and Old Pecan Street, no traffic jams. At worst, we could become another Silicon Valley: tree-pretty on the outside, but with streets choked and life waters tainted by urban runoff and leaks from "clean industry."

But that is the future, and who can predict that? Here and now, Austin is just plain exciting, alive, and fun—whether you live here or are just visiting.

★★★

SYMBOLS USED IN THIS BOOK

RESTAURANT GUIDE
The following symbols indicate the cost of a typical meal for one person, exclusive of drinks, tax, and tip:

$: under $7
$$: $7–$17
$$$: $17–$25
$$$$: over $25

WHEELCHAIR ACCESSIBILITY SYMBOLS
W   This place is accessible to persons in wheelchairs; the entrance is at least 32 inches wide and there are no more than two steps at the entrance. Not all facilities (rest rooms, elevators, etc.) are accesssible, however.

W variable.   This place is accessible only in part.

W+   This place and all its major facilities are accessible.

No symbol.   This place is accessible only with great difficulty or not at all.

CREDIT CARDS
AE	American Express
CB	Carte Blanche
DC	Diners Club
MC	MasterCard
V	Visa
Cr.	All major credit cards
No cr.	No credit cards

BAR
The word "bar" at the end of a restaurant listing indicates that the establishment serves liquor and mixed drinks.

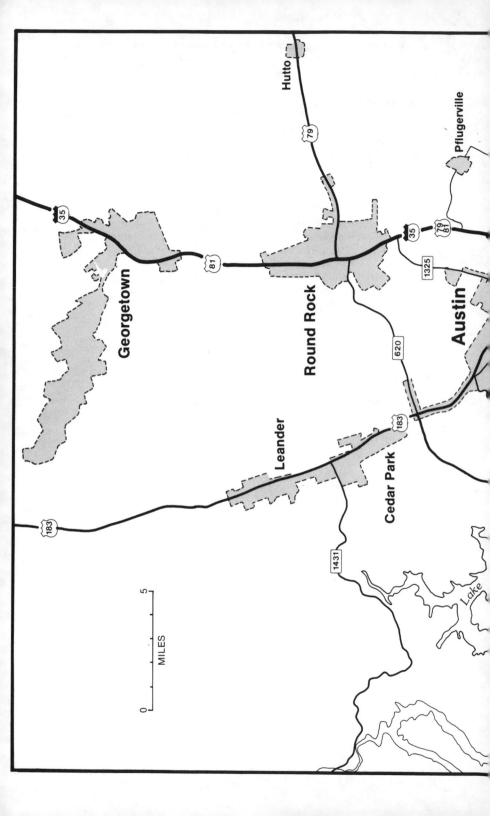

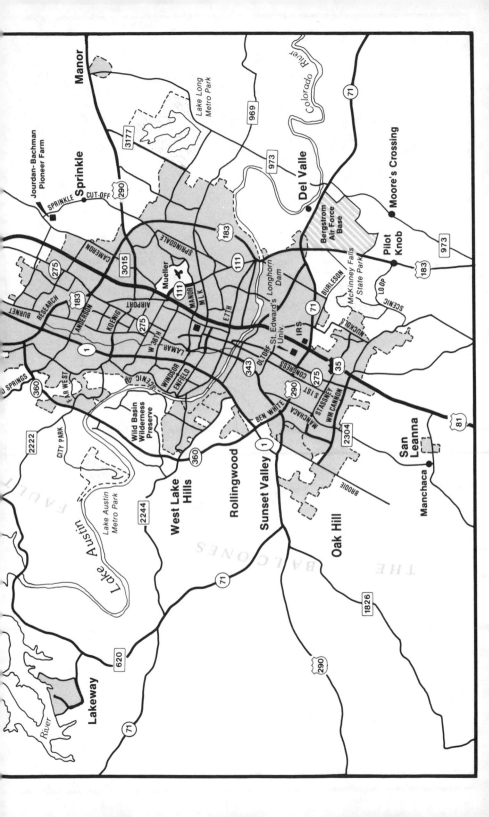

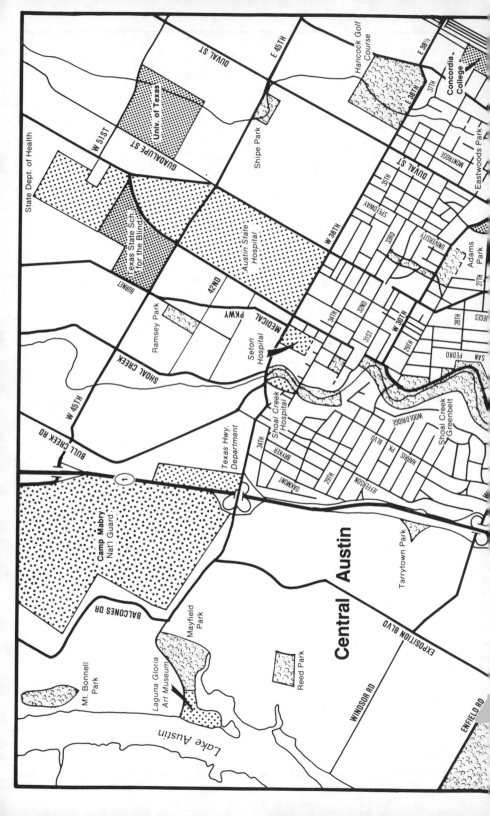

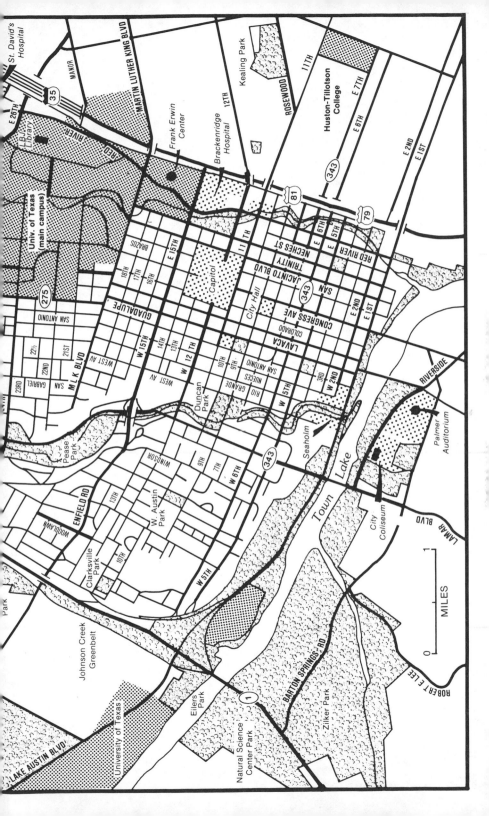

GENERAL INFORMATION

There's a lot to see and do and know about Austin, and just about as many publications to tell you how to do it. These are the tomes in print or otherwise easily obtained, as well as periodical publications to keep you abreast of what's going on. If you want to know more, particularly about Austin's history, head for the Austin Public Library's Austin History Center.

★★★

BOOKS

ALPHONSE IN AUSTIN
Selected and translated by Katherine Hart
Waterloo Press
Austin
$6.50
Learn about life in early Austin through the vainglorious eyes of Alphonse Dubois de Saligny, chargé d'affaires to the Republic of Texas and hero of the Pig War. (See History.) Excerpts of his letters back home.

AN AUSTIN ALBUM
Edited by Audray Bateman
Encino Press

Austin
$17.50
Newspaper clippings, photos, and ephemera from the past that depict, as graphically as possible across the span of years, life as it has been lived in Austin since the days of the republic. Features the famous, infamous, and not-famous.

AUSTIN: A HISTORICAL PORTRAIT
By Larry Willoughby
The Donning Co.
Norfolk, Virginia
$16.95
Hundreds of maps, photos, and illustrations with descriptive captions that capture the character of Austin, from the early days right through the last days of the Armadillo World Headquarters.

AUSTIN ORIGINALS: CHATS WITH COLORFUL CHARACTERS
Photos and text by Robyn Turner
Paramount Publishing Co.
Amarillo
$19.95
Special people make Austin a special town, good folks like Charlie Dunn, Ken Threadgill, Mary Faulk Koock, Robert Shaw. A couple dozen of the best are within these pages, captured in print and photographs.

AUSTIN, THE PAST STILL PRESENT
Text by Sue Brandt McBee. Illustrated by Virginia Erickson
The Austin Heritage Society
Austin
$8.95
A sampler of historical and architecturally important buildings to be found, alive and well, in Austin. Pioneer log cabins, workingmen's homes, Greek Revival mansions, and Victorian extravaganzas have been captured in sketches accompanied by stories of the people who built them, lived in them, or otherwise made them famous.

THE AUSTIN RUNNER'S BOOK
By Steve Hoppes
C&M Publications
Austin
$5.95
The Austin Runner's Book contains maps and descriptions of trails, tracks, and country runs in and around Austin, as well as information on the Austin Runner's Club and scheduled races. Profiles of eight Austin runners include training schedules and race results.

AN AUSTIN SKETCHBOOK
By Tony Crosby
Encino Press
Austin
$12.50
Sketches of and commentary on nearly three dozen notable surviving

and recently departed buildings from nineteenth-century Austin—both private residences and downtown business houses.

AUSTIN AND TRAVIS COUNTY: A PICTORIAL HISTORY,1839–1939
By the staff of the Austin–Travis County Collection, Austin Public Library, with text by Katherine Hart
Waterloo Press
Austin
$17.50
Two hundred sixty photographs and illustrations. For twenty-five years the Austin–Travis County Collection has been collecting and preserving pictures of the people, buildings, streets, and events of this part of Central Texas. The best book of its kind about Austin.

BUYING, RENTING, AND BORROWING IN TEXAS
By H. Clyde Farrell and Paul Kens
Texas Consumer Association
Austin
$6.95
Published by the Texas Consumer Association, this book raises and answers day-to-day consumer questions, translating legalese into everyday language. It speaks directly to those who are buying, renting, or borrowing for personal or family purposes. Handy reference for landlords and businessmen.

ELLIE RUCKER'S ALMANAC
By Ellie Rucker
Austin American-Statesman
Austin
$7.95
Several hundred of the most frequently asked questions from Ellie Rucker's daily column in the *Austin American-Statesman*. Includes many of the most-requested recipes from popular area restaurants.

EPITOME OF MY LIFE
By Major Buck Walton
Waterloo Press
Austin
$5
Civil War veteran and Austinite Buck Walton set down these freewheeling reminiscences about life in the Confederate Army in 1914, in the sunset of his life.

HISTORIC AUSTIN
The Heritage Society of Austin, Inc.
Austin
$2.50
This collection of six walking and five driving tours around Austin features more than two hundred significant homes and buildings. The city has been divided into eleven areas, and each tour features the area's

notable structures, giving building name, address, date of construction, and other pertinent historical and architectural information. Many photos. The tours have been designed to provide a glimpse into the rich, diversified heritage of each area, as well as an overview of each area's impact on the early development of Austin. Well worth the price.

HISTORY OF TRAVIS COUNTY AND AUSTIN, 1839–1899
By Mary Starr Barkley
Austin Printing Co.
Austin
$20
Provides valuable insight into the lives of those who laid the foundations of Austin and Travis County. The author covers all facets of life. A bit quirky in style and organization, nonetheless interesting.

HOW THE CRITTERS CREATED TEXAS
By Francis Edward Abernethy. Illustrated by Ben Sargent
Ellen C. Temple
Austin
$8.95
Folklorist Abernethy and Pulitzer Prize–winning cartoonist Sargent combine to present this creation tale handed down by the Alabama-Coushatta Indians of East Texas. The critters, floating on a raft "somewhere between Austin and Lampasas," combine forces to create and sculpt the state of Texas. Good, entertaining book for kids.

19TH CENTURY AUSTIN
Text by Katherine Hart
American Heritage Foundation
Austin
$1
Using pictures and maps from the Austin–Travis County Collection, this little paperback contains pictures of currently standing nineteenth-century buildings, as well as the dear departed. Also useful and unique is the index of nineteenth-century structures still standing in 1970, by street and block number. A good buy.

THE PARENT'S GUIDE TO AUSTIN
By Linda Crowell and Maryanne Mariotti
C&M Publications
Austin
$5.95
More than two hundred pages of information on child-care centers, schools, and youth activities in the Austin area. Categories include summer camps, sports, clubs, art, music and dance, social services, adoption agencies, and information for parents of adolescents in trouble. Also a chapter for new Austinites.

PEASE PORRIDGE HOT
Annotated by Katherine Hart
Waterloo Press

Austin
$4.50

Recipes, household hints, and home remedies of the Pease family. Elisha M. Pease was governor of Texas 1853–1857 and 1867–1869.

THE PET'S GUIDE TO AUSTIN
By David A. Nelson, D. V. M. and Peggy Vlerebome
C&M Publications
Austin
$5.95

Includes questions and answers on animal health and behavior, first-aid instructions, and a directory of Austin-area veterinarians. Special section for small children, as well as chapters on travel, exercise, ordinances, pet owners' and breeders' organizations, and information on buying purebred dogs and cats. Illustrated by Ben Sargent, 1982 Pulitzer Prize–winner for editorial cartoons.

RIDING THROUGH CENTRAL TEXAS: 22 CYCLE EXCURSIONS
By Richard Zelade
Violet Crown Press
Austin
$5.95

A collection of twenty-two trips in and around Austin and surrounding counties. Suitable for the armchair traveler and Sunday driver, as well as cyclist. Trips take you along the area's scenic back roads, providing an entertaining and insightful commentary on points of interest along the way.

SHOP AUSTIN
Hann Publications
Austin
$3.95

A 100-plus–page guide to goods and services in the Austin area, including Oak Hill, Round Rock, Cedar Park, and the Lake Travis area. More than five hundred categories are included. In most cases, the five lowest prices available are listed.

SIERRA CLUB GUIDE TO OUTDOORS AUSTIN
Sierra Club Lone Star Chapter and Austin Natural Science
Association
Austin
$5

If it's outdoors in or around Austin, it's in this slim volume. Naturally, swimming holes come first. Descriptions are brief, but very specific about how to get there, terrain and crowds to expect, and any hazards. Other sections cover tubing, skin diving, canoeing, sailing, hiking, nature photography, birding, caving, rock climbing, camping, and more. Maps of Austin's network of city parks, pools, tennis courts, and trails.

TEXAS
By Patricia Sharpe and Robert S. Weddle
Texas Monthly Press
Austin
$11.95

The most authoritative guide to all of Texas, useful to traveler, new-comer, and lifelong resident. Hundreds of entertainment, dining, and hotel listings. Available at bookstores, or order by writing Texas Monthly Press, P. O. Box 1569, Austin 78767. ($13.95 includes postage, handling, and tax.)

TEXAS ANTIQUE DIRECTORY AND ATLAS
By Jack Troe
The Troe Company
Austin
$2

Lists antique shops in Texas by geographical area. Cities and towns within each area are listed alphabetically, and shop listings are also al-phabetical. Locator maps are used, and major cities are broken down into smaller areas with maps.

TEXAS! LIVE THE LEGEND
Travel and Information Division, State Department of Highways and Public Transportation, Austin
Free

Large-format paperback that lists nearly four hundred Texas cities and towns, along with general information about each, places to see, camp, and otherwise recreate. Austin's star attractions are chronicled, as are those of surrounding towns. Other sections cover state parks, lakes, state and national forests, flora and fauna, and Mexico. Lots of color photos, and best of all, it's free. Available at the Tourist Informa-tion Center in the Capitol building or by writing the agency at P. O. Box 5064, Austin, Texas 78763.

THE UNIVERSITY OF TEXAS: A PICTORIAL ACCOUNT OF ITS FIRST CENTURY
By Margaret Berry
University of Texas Press
Austin
$25

A century's worth of photos, more than a thousand in all, of stu-dents, regents, professors, activities (official and otherwise), buildings, football heros, and more. The UT book to end all UT books.

THE WATERLOO SCRAPBOOK
By Katherine Hart
Waterloo Press
Austin
Six volumes, $2.50–3.50 each

"The Waterloo Scrapbook" has been a weekly column in the *Austin American-Statesman* for more than fifteen years. Written by the Austin–

Travis County Collection's curator, the column looks at life in Austin with a strong historical perspective. Katherine Hart, lifetime Austin resident, began the column in 1968, and the articles have been reprinted in book form, six volumes in all, for the years 1968 to 1975.

★★★

MAGAZINES

AUSTIN BUSINESS EXECUTIVE
1606 American Bank Tower, Austin 78701
478-4068
Monthly
$15/yr.
Business in Austin these days is definitely big, and getting bigger; two publications now serve the Austin and Central Texas business community. This is the slicker of the two, a glossy full-color number. Articles and features of interest to upscale business types.

AUSTIN BUSINESS JOURNAL
815 Brazos, Austin 78701
474-5481
Biweekly
$15/yr.
Just as it says. Self-proclaimed "source for business information in Central Texas." Serves the business community of Austin and Central Texas with business news, columns, features. Subscription perks like free copy of 1983–84 *Texas Legislative Handbook*.

AUSTIN CHRONICLE
P. O. Box 49066, Austin 78765
473-8995
Biweekly
Free
The James Dean of Austin media. Most complete club listings in town, along with popular music, art, literature, live show and record reviews, movie reviews, and food and restaurant reviews, in a trendy, personalized risk-taking tabloid format. Its editors have proclaimed that the *Chronicle* "should be reborn every issue." Sometimes it works, sometimes it doesn't. Distributed at restaurants, clubs, bookstores.

AUSTIN CONVENTION NEWS
119 E. 6th, Austin 78701
479-0573
Monthly
Free
For the conventioneer, tourist, and newcomer to Austin. Austin and UT maps, restaurants, entertainment, shopping, points-of-interest listings, convention news.

AUSTIN HOMES AND GARDENS
1800 Rio Grande, Austin 78701
474-7666
Monthly
$12/yr.
Glossy full color monthly catering to wealthy Austin homeowners and those who wish to be.

AUSTIN'S KALEIDOSCOPE
P. O. Box 4368, Austin 78765
458-4271
Quarterly
Free
Brought to you by the folks who publish *Austin Magazine*; of primary interest to newcomers and visitors. Calendar of events, points of interest, restaurant and club listings, recreation, newcomer information, house hunting and hotel/motel listings, accompanied by features on the Austin lifestyle. Distributed at hotels, restaurants, businesses, and the like.

AUSTIN LIVING
1805 Rutherford, Austin 78754
837-3534
Bimonthly
Free
Aimed at newcomers and homebuyers and focusing on real-estate developments, condominiums, and apartments, *Living* includes maps and facts about Austin, as well as things to see and do. Distributed at airports, restaurants, banks.

AUSTIN MAGAZINE
P. O. Box 4368, Austin 78765
478-9383
Monthly
$14/yr.
Official publication of the Austin Chamber of Commerce, "dedicated to telling the story of Austin and its people." Glossy, full color. Combination of business news and general-interest articles, inevitably upbeat. Extensive restaurant and event listings.

KEY: THIS MONTH IN AUSTIN
3636 Bee Caves Rd., Austin 78765
327-7244
Monthly
Free
Yet another dining, shopping, entertainment, places-to-see guide to Austin. Similar in format to other magazines published by parent company across the country. Distributed at restaurants, hotels, banks, etc.

TEXAS HIGHWAYS
P. O. Box 5016, Austin 78763

Monthly
$10/yr.
Each month, *Texas Highways* takes you to well-known and not-so-well-known attractions across the state: parks, scenic places, historic spots. Beautiful color pictures and an excellent monthly calendar of events around the state, conveniently divided into regions. A good buy.

TEXAS MONTHLY
P. O. Box 1569, Austin 78767
Monthly
$18/yr.
Texas's premier magazine is located in Austin and provides up-to-date monthly restaurant, entertainment, sports, arts, and special-events listings for Austin and Texas's other major cities.

TEXAS PARKS AND WILDLIFE
4200 Smith School Rd., Austin 78744
Monthly
$8/yr.
Just as the name implies. Excellent color photography by some of Texas's finest. State publication, and like *Texas Highways* a good buy.

THIRD COAST
P. O. Box 592, Austin 78767
472-2016
Monthly
$12/yr.
Third Coast bills itself as "the magazine of Austin." Although it does cover an increasingly wide range of interests, 3C still appeals primarily to young Austinites (ages twenty to forty-five), being fresh, sharp, ever-so-witty, ever-so-good-looking, always in black-and-white, stylish, exciting, and cool, while also managing to be analytical and in-depth on subjects that the local daily seems afraid to touch.

★★
NEWSPAPERS

AUSTIN AMERICAN-STATESMAN
166 E. Riverside
445-4040
$6.50/mo.
Austin's only daily, unless you count the *Daily Texan* and *USA Today*. The *American-Statesman* aims to satisfy the average Austin reader, whoever that is. Some call him Joe Six-Pack; regardless of what you might call him, this editorial policy translates to a "soft" newspaper: long on entertainment and "people" pieces, short on the hard stuff. If you want good state and national coverage, go with one of the Houston or Dallas papers. Even the *Daily Texan* offers more in-depth national and world coverage at times than does the *American-Statesman*. The appearance of *USA Today*, although it is not exactly an Austin paper, has sparked a bit of life in the *Statesman*. Most Austinites seem to read the *Statesman* "despite," rather than "because." What's the alternative?

AUSTIN LIGHT
100 N. Interregional, Austin 78701
477-5833
Weekly
$12.50/yr.
     Weekly community tabloid serving the inner city. Business, entertainment, city, and state news with a Mexican-American slant.

CAPITAL CITY ARGUS
1704 E. 12th, Austin 78767
476-0211
Weekly
Free
     Community weekly; local news, features, sports, columns aimed at east Austin and the black community.

DAILY TEXAN
Drawer D, University Station, Austin 78712
471-5244
$24.00/semester
     Student newspaper at the University of Texas, published Monday through Friday. Acclaimed as one of the country's best college newspapers, it is nonetheless still a college newspaper, in which aspiring young journalists attempt to learn the trade. And it shows. Still, it is the best paper to read for UT news, and sometimes for state, national, and world stories, since the *Texan* often runs more of its UPI wire copy than the *American-Statesman* does its AP copy.

THE VILLAGER
1151 1/2 San Bernard, Austin 78702
476-0082
Weekly
Free
     A community service weekly. Local news, features, sports, public-service announcements, columns aimed at east Austin. Distributed at local stores and restaurants. Home subscription $7.50/yr.

★★
MISCELLANEOUS PUBLICATIONS

AROUND AUSTIN COMMUNITY CALENDAR
Assistance League of Austin
327-0242
$4
     This community calendar has seventeen months of comprehensive listings of local events and community organizations. Recipes and artwork by local high-school students flesh it out. Available at most local bookstores.

AUSTIN GUIDE
825 W. 11th, Austin 78701
474-2742
Bimonthly
Free

Aimed at visitors and newcomers to Austin. Events, restaurant and club listings, plus nuts-and-bolts information like how and where to get driver's licenses and utility service and when you can legally buy booze. Good map of greater Austin. Distributed at airports, hotels, restaurants, businesses.

CALENDAR OF TEXAS EVENTS
Travel and Information Division, State Department of Highways and Public Transportation, P. O. Box 5064, Austin 78763
Free

This six-month calendar lists what's going on all over the state, such as fairs, homecomings, fiddlers' contests, wildflower trails, balloon races, rattlesnake roundups, as well as the ubiquitous chili cookoff. Available at the Tourist Information Center in the Capitol building as well.

CELEBRATE TEXAS
High Flight Publishing
Argyle, TX 76226
Annual
About $6

A hardbound guide to things to do, see, and eat in Austin. Distributed at local hotels for use by guests. Personal copies available at some local bookstores, hotel desks, and gift shops.

A DRIVING TOUR OF AUSTIN
Austin Chamber of Commerce
478-9383
Free

This illustrated pamphlet takes you on a well-mapped driving tour of Austin's principal attractions. Barton Springs, the Capitol, the UT Tower, Mt. Bonnell, and all the rest of Austin's must-sees are along the route. Available from the Chamber of Commerce and most of the other visitors' centers in town.

1887 MAP OF AUSTIN
Waterloo Press
Austin
$4.50

Reprint, in the original colors, of Augustus Koch's 1887 map of Austin. Not everything was black and white and gray back then. He also took the time to draw puffing engines on the railroad tracks, all of the buildings, and nearly all the trees in town on this fascinating map. And many of the buildings standing then are still here today, surprisingly.

Aside from any historical interest it might hold for you, it just looks good hanging on the wall.

A GUIDE TO THE LEGISLATURE
League of Women Voters of Texas
1212 Guadalupe
472-1100
Free

Each legislative year, the league compiles this handy visitors' guide to the hurly-burly world of the Texas Legislature, down to the House and Senate seating charts and committee assignments. Included are all the correct phone and office numbers and a handy map of the Capitol complex that shows each building by name.

SENIOR DISCOUNT DIRECTORY
Adult Services Council
1100 W. 1st
476-1974
Free

Directory booklet listing more than one hundred local businesses that offer discounts to senior citizens. Airlines, auto repair, fishing accessories, pet shops, restaurants, and therapy are among the headings. Phone numbers, addresses, and as complete a description of the discount offer as possible is given for each business. Available from the Adult Services Council or at the Old Bakery and Emporium information desk.

TEXAS CAPITOL GUIDE
Travel and Information Division, State Department of Highways and Public Transportation
Capitol Tourist Information Center, South Foyer
Free

Pamphlet with maps, facts, commentary, and lots of color photos to guide you through the statehouse itself, plus a convenient photo map of Capitol Hill with all buildings and statues well marked and identified. The Tourist Information Center is open seven days a week, 8–5.

GETTING HELP

★★
NUMBERS TO CALL

There are many agencies in Austin to call on for help, whether for an emergency, mental health problem, consumer complaint, or general information. It is impossible to list them all, but we have included most of the important ones.

Note that the City of Austin will have a new phone system installed in September 1984, allowing direct-dial access to more agencies than we have indicated here. Some numbers listed here may change at that time.

GENERAL

EMERGENCY
911

The number to call when you need the Fire Department, Police or Sheriff's Department, or emergency medical help. Teletypewriter numbers for the deaf: Fire 472-1516; Police 480-2911.

PERSONAL PROBLEMS
472-HELP

Crisis Intervention Hotline is a twenty-four-hour hotline to help you cope with personal problems. Counseling in suicide prevention, rape crises, depression, drug abuse, and child abuse. Counselors can help solve other problems by giving information about other useful local agencies. Teletypewriter number for the deaf: 929-3410.

POISON CONTROL CENTER
478-4490

A twenty-four-hour service that gives information on how to deal with poisonings and drug interactions.

WEATHER SERVICE RECORDED FORECAST
476-7736

AGRICULTURE

TRAVIS COUNTY AGRICULTURAL EXTENSION COUNTY AGENTS
473-9600

Information on horticulture, livestock, crops.

ALCOHOLISM

AA—ALCOHOLICS ANONYMOUS
451-3071

Twenty-four-hour answering service.

AL-ANON FAMILY GROUP
441-8591

ALCOHOLISM INFORMATION CENTER
(Austin Council on Alcoholism)
454-7627

Free services to Travis County residents include screening and referral, educational presentation, and informational library.

AUSTIN–TRAVIS COUNTY ALCOHOL COUNSELING SERVICES
473-9540, 473-9533

MENTAL HEALTH/MENTAL RETARDATION OF AUSTIN AND TRAVIS COUNTY (MHMR)
447-4141

ANIMALS

ANIMAL CONTROL
(Dangerous or stray)
469-2024

ANIMAL CARE
Travis County Humane Society
478-9325
   Open daily; provides a shelter for healthy animals, helps with adoption of dogs and cats.

DEAD ANIMAL REMOVAL
477-6511

EMERGENCY ANIMAL CLINIC
5129 Cameron Rd.
459-4336
   For small-animal emergencies occurring when regular veterinary clinics are closed (nights and weekends).

WILDLIFE RESCUE INC.
472-9453
   Picks up and rehabilitates injured wild animals to return them to the wild.

ARSON

ARSON HOTLINE
476-2876

CHILDREN

CHILD ABUSE HOTLINE
1-800-252-5400
   Twenty-four-hour toll-free number. Use this number also to report adult abuse and abuse of the handicapped.

AUSTIN CHILD GUIDANCE AND EVALUATION CENTER
476-6015

CHILDREN'S PROTECTIVE SERVICES
834-0034
   Adoption services, foster care, emergency shelter.

HELPING HANDS
480-5010
Designed to help children who are lost or in trouble. Participants in this program operated jointly by the community and the Austin Police Department display "Helping Hand" signs on the fronts of their houses, as a signal to children that this is a safe place to come for help.

CONSUMER COMPLAINTS

BETTER BUSINESS BUREAU
476-6943
Keeps complaint record of Austin businesses and helps consumers file complaints.

TEXAS ATTORNEY GENERAL CONSUMER PROTECTION DIVISION
475-3288

CRIME

CRIME STOPPERS
472-8477
To report a crime or give related information about one without giving your name, call this Police Department number.

DRUG ABUSE

MHMR—AUSTIN/TRAVIS COUNTY
447-4141

AUSTIN DRUG AND ALCOHOL ABUSE PROGRAM
458-6361

TEXANS' WAR ON DRUGS
459-1231
Drug abuse research and education.

EMPLOYMENT

AUSTIN WOMEN'S CENTER
472-3775
This nonprofit organization maintains a job bank with hundreds of jobs in dozens of fields for women who are seeking employment.

INTERNAL REVENUE SERVICE JOBS
477-5627

Since Austin hosts a regional IRS Service Center, there are always several hundred seasonal jobs available here during the tax season.

TEXAS EMPLOYMENT COMMISSION
478-8734

Three branches around town offer free job placement, counseling, and testing.

FAMILY

CHILD AND FAMILY SERVICE
2001 Chicon
478-1648

This nonprofit United Way agency provides family counseling, marriage counseling, consumer credit counseling, family life education, teenage parenting services, and a violence diversion network.

GARBAGE

CITY PUBLIC WORKS DEPARTMENT
477-6511, ext. 2640

Garbage and brush collection, dead animal removal.

HEALTH

TEL-MED HEALTH INFORMATION SERVICE
472-4113

The Austin Public Library, Travis County Medical Society, United Way, and PARD Senior Aides Program provide this handy service. Tel-Med is a collection of tape-recorded health and medical messages that have been carefully selected to help you remain healthy, recognize signs of an early illness, adjust to a serious illness. Subjects range from arthritis to foot care, male and female problems to child care. Each tape has been prepared with the help of local physicians to ensure accuracy. You can pick up a list of the tapes offered at your local library. Tel-Med is a seven-day-a-week service, but not twenty-four-hour. Hours are the same as those for the Central Library downtown.

HOME ECONOMICS

TRAVIS COUNTY AGRICULTURAL EXTENSION AGENTS
473-9600

HOUSING

AUSTIN APARTMENT ASSOCIATION
474-1294

This association of apartment owners, managers, and related service businesses offers mediation services in landlord-tenant disputes, but not legal advice.

AUSTIN TENANTS' COUNCIL
1619 E. 1st
474-1961

Provides information and technical assistance to Austin and Travis County residents on all areas of tenant-landlord relations. ATC also offers the Rental Repair Assistance Program and the Mobile Tool Library to those tenants and landlords who qualify. The phone is difficult to get through during business hours (Monday through Thursday, 9–1). It's best to leave a message on the machine after hours.

CONSUMER PROTECTION DIVISION, ATTORNEY GENERAL'S OFFICE
475-3288

Enforces the Deceptive Trade Practices Act, which sometimes applies to the security deposit.

INFORMATION

CARPOOLING INFORMATION
477-5663

Information on the city's Ride Share Program.

CITY NEIGHBORHOOD ASSISTANCE OFFICE
480-9711

This city service directs you to the proper city agency.

COUNTY INFORMATION
473-9020

Refers you to the appropriate county government department.

ENERGY CONSERVATION INFORMATION
477-6511, ext. 2880

City of Austin number for consumer information on electricity, heating, air conditioning, etc. The number to call concerning the city's energy rebate for purchasing energy-efficient appliances is 440-0400.

FEDERAL INFORMATION CENTER
472-5494

Information on federal government agencies.

FLOOD PLAIN INFORMATION
United States Geological Survey
300 E. 8th, 6th floor (library)
This department has maps with flood-plain information, and they will help individuals who *come by in person* determine if they live in a flood plain. They will not advise you over the phone. Bring a city map with you.

FLOODING OF CREEKS INFORMATION—CITY
Watershed Management Division, Public Works Department
477-6511, ext. 2524 for general information
During emergencies the Emergency Operations Center (ext. 2883) has up-to-date information on conditions. To make a complaint, call the Drainage Complaint Investigator, Street and Bridge Division, ext. 2631.

FLOODING OF CREEKS INFORMATION—COUNTY
County Hydrologist's Office
473-9122

GAY LINE
477-6699
Recorded message that gives phone numbers and addresses of gay services and organizations in Austin and San Marcos.

SENIOR CITIZENS INFORMATION AND REFERRAL
451-0106

SOLAR INDEX
441-2706
Sponsored by the city Office of Energy Conservation and Renewable Resources and Cole Solar Systems Inc. Designed to make consumers aware of the energy-saving potential of solar energy equipment.

STATE INFORMATION—GOVERNOR'S CITIZEN ASSISTANCE OFFICE
1-800-252-9600
Provides information on state agencies. Toll-free number. Local number 475-6774.

STREET INFORMATION
477-6511, ext. 2545
You can call the Public Works Department, Street and Bridge Division, at this number for information on new streets not yet on maps or to find out for whom or what a street is named.

TAX INFORMATION—FEDERAL
472-1974
Provided by the Internal Revenue Service.

TAX INFORMATION—STATE
1-800-252-5555
The state comptroller's office operates this toll-free number.

UNITED WAY
472-6267 (office)
472-HELP (information and referrals)
Provides information and referrals concerning social service agencies in Austin and Travis County.

UNIVERSITY OF TEXAS INFORMATION
471-3434
This is the number of UT-Austin's main switchboard.

LEGAL

LAWYER REFERRAL SERVICE OF THE TRAVIS COUNTY BAR ASSOCIATION
472-8303
This twenty-four-hour service is a nonprofit corporation for people who don't have a lawyer and suddenly find themselves needing one. Nominal fee for first consultation.

LEGAL AID SOCIETY OF CENTRAL TEXAS
476-7244
Offers legal services in civil cases at no charge for eligible, low-income persons.

TEL-LAW LEGAL INFORMATION SERVICE
478-5010
Monday through Thursday, 9–9, Friday and Saturday 9–6, Sunday noon–6
Tel-Law, designed to help the layperson understand and use the justice system in Texas, is sponsored by the Travis County Bar Association, the State Bar of Texas, Austin Public Library, the United Way, and the City of Austin. It provides general legal information at no cost. Each tape has been prepared and reviewed by Texas lawyers to ensure its accuracy, and each is in straightforward, easy-to-understand language. Just call the Tel-Law operator and request the number of the tape you want to hear. Tape index is available at all Austin Public Library branches.

MEDICAL AND HEALTH SERVICES

On September 6, 1881, the voters of Texas chose Austin as the site of the "main" University of Texas campus. On the same ballot, they chose Galveston, then Texas's largest city, as the location of the university's Medical Branch. And it has remained that way ever since. Austin's eight local hospitals and numerous special health services offer health care equal to that of any other comparably sized city, but the medical centers, medical schools, and teaching hospitals that seem to accumulate around state capitals and major universities have stayed out of Austin.

BRACKENRIDGE HOSPITAL
601 E. 15th
Central West
476-6461
This is Austin's full-service hospital, with a fully staffed twenty-four-hour emergency room. It was massively upgraded in 1978 to incorporate state-of-the-art emergency equipment and procedures. The hospital has recently moved into new quarters adjacent to the old building.

The hospital also maintains a speakers' bureau, which provides knowledgeable speakers on a variety of medical subjects to local organizations.

SETON MEDICAL CENTER
1201 W. 38th, near Lamar
Central West
459-2121
Seton offers low-cost health education classes and seminars through its Good Health School. (See Revelation.)

SHOAL CREEK HOSPITAL
3501 Mills near Seton Medical Center
Central West
452-0361
This private psychiatric hospital specializes in the treatment of drug and alcohol problems and is a good source of information on these problems.

PUBLIC TRANSPORTATION

AUSTIN TRANSIT SYSTEM
385-6860
In addition to the regular city bus system, the Armadillo Express loops between Palmer Auditorium and 18th and Congress. Buses decked out as trolleys carry passengers to and through downtown Austin every ten minutes Monday through Friday 7–7 from intersections marked with catchy 'Dillo signs. Park free at Palmer Auditorium and ride for 25¢. Call the Austin Transit System at the number above for additional or up-to-date hours of operation.

RAPE

RAPE CRISIS CENTER
472-RAPE
A rape-crisis counseling and referral service.

SENIOR CITIZENS

MEALS ON WHEELS
474-6416
Delivers hot meals to homebound and disabled senior citizens.

SENIOR PROGRAMS
477-6511, ext. 2856
The Austin Parks and Recreation Department offers a great variety of programs and services for people fifty years and older. Several Actvity Centers are located around town, providing a variety of arts and crafts classes and special events. More than a dozen additional Senior Centers scattered around Travis County and Austin provide lunch, social activities, and educational, referral, and counseling programs for anyone sixty years of age or older.

The Senior Aides Program, Experience Unlimited, and the Senior Job Factory are all programs designed to utilize the knowledge, skills, and talents of senior citizens.

VOTER REGISTRATION

COUNTY TAX ASSESSOR-COLLECTOR'S OFFICE
473-9473

WOMEN

AUSTIN WOMEN'S CENTER
472-3775
The Women's Center is a nonprofit community-based organization that offers information and referral, employment services, and low-cost classes and workshops in a wide range of subjects.

CENTER FOR BATTERED WOMEN
472-4878
Temporary shelter, counseling, and referrals for victims of family violence.

WOMEN'S REFERRAL CENTER
2404 Rio Grande
476-6878
The center has free pregnancy testing as well as counseling and information on birth control, pregnancy, alternatives, venereal disease and sexuality, and referrals to other sources.

★★★
COMMUNITY ORGANIZATIONS

As a center for higher education, Austin has long attracted special people with special and diverse interests. This fact is borne out by the incredible number of clubs and community organizations that exist in Austin. This cross-section of organizations is just the tip of the iceberg; the iceberg itself consists of four file drawers full of club and organization listings maintained by the Austin History Center. (See Libraries.) This is the only place in town to go if you're looking to find a club to match your interest, be it political, social, or activity-oriented.

In cases where an organization does not have an office, we have listed the address or phone number of a contact person who can provide more information about club meetings and activities. Remember that almost all of these organizations are volunteer groups, so the contact person may change frequently. Many of the clubs have regular meeting times and places, which we have listed wherever possible; but since they too are subject to change without notice, it's best to check with the contact person to verify details.

AUSTIN AMATEUR RADIO CLUB
Claude Green, Jr.
282-1820
P. O. Box 13472, Austin 78711
This is a general-interest radio club (not CB), oriented toward public service. Besides participating in the Central Texas Weathernet (which is activated in times of severe weather), the club provides communications support for all sorts of public events at no cost. The club meets the second Tuesday of each month at Luby's Cafeteria, 2233 N. Loop.

AUSTIN AREA GARDEN COUNCIL
Gladys Hudnall
453-8142
The Austin Area Garden Council serves as parent group to most local gardening clubs; approximately forty affiliate clubs belong to the council. The council's main purpose is to maintain and support the Austin Area Garden Center in Zilker Park, which is a joint project with the city Parks and Recreation Department. The council sponsors programs at the center for member clubs and the general public and can refer you to specialty clubs. The council puts on Florarama each May (see Calendar of Events) and also takes part in Zilker Park's annual YuleFest. Any garden-related club can join if their purposes are similar to the council's, and council meetings are held on the second Tuesday of each month September through May at the Austin Area Garden Center in Zilker Park, 2200 Barton Springs Road.

AUSTIN AREA QUILT GUILD
Erica Rogala
266-1279   or
Mary Redus

282-1421
807 W. 31st., Austin 78765

The guild exists to foster and promote the art of fine quilting, whether traditional or modern. It sponsors a quilt show every two years featuring quilts by members. The organization as a whole meets the first Monday of the month at the Central Library, 800 Guadalupe. Smaller groups— "Quilt Bees"—meet every week to work and exchange ideas.

AUSTIN BANJO CLUB
Duke Waggoner
451-3379

The Austin Banjo Club consists of people who enjoy *four*-string banjo music—the sing-along banjo music of the 1890s and early 1900s—not country-western or bluegrass banjo, although the club has some five-string members. Beginners are welcome, and club members are willing to teach the novitiate. Club members play around a lot, mostly at nursing homes and events like Laguna Gloria's Fiesta. The club meets every Monday at the E-Z Travel Motor Hotel, 9106 N. IH 35.

AUSTIN BONSAI SOCIETY
Don Rehberg
442-9397

This club carries on the fine Japanese art of bonsai, the growing of dwarfed, ornamentally shaped trees in small shallow pots. The society holds a show every April (the third or fourth weekend) at the Austin Area Garden Center. Once a year, a different bonsai master comes to Austin to conduct workshops. Meetings are the second Wednesday of each month at the Austin Area Garden Center in Zilker Park.

AUSTIN CACTUS AND SUCCULENT SOCIETY
454-9836, 495-7214

If you have been cursed with a brown thumb, this might be the club for you. About all you have to do is remember to water your cacti whenever it rains in El Paso. Of course, if you like pretty flowers you may water them more often. The society meets the third Thursday of each month at the Zilker Garden Center.

AUSTIN CHARRO ASSOCIATION
Daniel Peña, Sr.
243-0689
404 Bastrop Highway, Austin 78741

The Austin Charro Association exists to bring to Austin the traditional Mexican sport of *charrearia* in its purest form. *Charrearia* is the sport of rodeo, Mexican style, and differs in execution from its American cousin. Each *charreada*, or rodeo, consists of nine events, and the *charros* compete as teams against each other. The Austin team competes with teams from other cities during the summer. Home *charreadas* are held in the club's "Lienzo Charro," located on Farm Road 812, southeast of Austin. They are open to the public. Club members also put on a number of exhibitions around the area each year featuring *charreada* events. *Floreo de riata*—trick roping—is one of the most popular. Meetings are the first Wednesday of the month, usually at 404 Bastrop Highway.

AUSTIN ETHNIC HISTORY ASSOCIATION
Will Howard
477-8238
708 W. 30th, Austin 78705

This association is a confederation of independent ethnic groups that have banded together to perpetuate and celebrate ethnic differences and harmonies. The association maintains a speakers' bureau, in case your group would like to learn about things like Afghan weaving and Czech cooking. The association also sponsors a citywide Cultural Heritage Essay Contest (in conjunction with the Austin Independent School District) and the annual Austin Folk Festival (see Schedule of Events). The association meets the third Thursday of January, March, May, July, August, and October at the Saengerrunde Hall, 1607 San Jacinto.

AUSTIN FIDDLE CLUB
Olaf Riewe
926-3783

The Austin Fiddle Club is made up of folks who get together to play old-time Texas fiddle music—reels, breakdowns, hornpipes. These are not old fiddlers; they just play old music. Novices are welcome, but lessons aren't given. Everyone just plays, and members learn from each other. The club meets every Tuesday at the Friends Meeting House, 3104 Washington Square.

AUSTIN ORGANIC GARDENERS
Josephine Huntley
478-1025

Just as the name says; members learn and practice gardening techniques that do not employ petrochemical fertilizers and insecticides. The second-largest gardening club in town. Members range from apartment gardeners to professionals with twelve-acre truck gardens. The club sponsors field trips to organic farms and buys supplies in bulk, so that members may buy at reduced prices. Meetings are the second Monday of each month (except December) at the Austin Area Garden Center in Zilker Park.

AUSTIN SIERRA CLUB
478-1264

As you might expect, Austin's Sierra Club is an active one, sponsoring a variety of outdoor activities in and around Central Texas: canoeing, backpacking, and day hikes among them. All activities are open to the public. The Sierra Club meets the first Tuesday of each month at the Unitarian Church, 4700 Grover.

AUSTIN RING #60, INTERNATIONAL BROTHERHOOD OF MAGICIANS
Judy Wilkes
837-4752

If you've always wondered how the rabbit got into the hat in the first place, this is the club for you. Anybody with an interest in the fine arts of illusion and deception is welcome to join, and Austinites from all walks of life have. Meetings are the first Tuesday of each month.

AUSTIN SQUARE AND ROUND DANCE ASSOCIATION
Dick and Shirley Macken
451-1853

There are more square- and round-dance clubs in and around Austin than you can shake that bootie at. Most of them belong to this umbrella organization, which is a good place to start if you want to learn how to dance but don't know where to go.

AUSTIN STAMP CLUB
Allen Kerr
452-2875
1424 Westmoor, Austin 78723

The Austin Stamp Club's big event of the season is its annual Stamp Show, which is usually held the first weekend in March. The rest of the year members hear guest speakers, see slide shows, trade stamps, or bid on them at club auctions. A monthly newsletter is published. Meetings are the first and third Tuesdays of the month, at the Howson Branch Library, 2500 Exposition.

AUSTIN THUNDERBIRD OWNERS
Elaine Hughes
255-1506

Unlike some of the other car clubs in town, the T'bird Owners club is a family one—wives and children are included in the various activities, such as road rallies and picnics. The club specializes in the preservation and restoration of 1955 through 1957 Thunderbirds. Members' cars carry the dignitaries in the AquaFest Land Parade each year. The club meets the third Saturday of each month; meeting places vary.

AUSTIN WRITERS LEAGUE
Debbie Stedman
444-9379

The Austin Writers League was formed in response to the need for support among freelance writers in Austin. The more than three hundred members run the gamut from fiction and poetry writers to non-fiction (travel and high-tech) writers. Meetings are the third Thursday of each month at Execucom, 3410 Far West Boulevard. In addition to monthly programs that respond to member needs, the league sponsors a series of seminars, twice a year, that cover topics such as copyright, taxes, writing, and word processing.

CAPITOL CAMERA CLUB
Carl Heather
452-8486

This is a contest-oriented club. Print and slide competitions are held once a month throughout the year. One meeting each month is dedicated to the contest, and the other meeting is a program. The Camera

Club meets the first and third Tuesdays of each month; call for meeting location.

CAPITOL CITY COIN CLUB
Harry Barnette
442-2546
P. O. Box 33159, Austin 78764
This is a general-interest coin club, open to anyone who is interested in numismatics. The club sponsors an annual coin show each spring; dates differ from year to year. Meetings are the third Thursday of each month at the County Courthouse, fourth floor, 261st District Courtroom.

CENTRAL TEXAS COMPUTER ASSOCIATION
Neal Grice
441-8815
Unlike most other computer clubs in town, Central Texas Computer Association is a general-interest club. (Most others are devoted to a single brand or type.) Presentations at the monthly meetings are on general computer topics. The club has an ongoing group-purchase plan, which enables members to buy hardware at reduced prices. Many of the members also belong to specialized clubs, and you can find out more about them here. Meetings are on the fourth Monday of each month at the Central Library, 800 Guadalupe.

COLOR COMPUTER CLUB
Neal Grice
441-8815
There are an incredible number of specialty computer clubs in Austin. For example, the Color Computer Club is specifically an organization for users of the Radio Shack Color Computer. Club members learn how to use it, keep abreast of new software applications as they become available. Through the ongoing group purchase plan, they can buy equipment at reduced prices. The club meets the first Monday of each month at the Central Library, 800 Guadalupe.

COLORADO RIVER WALKERS
Jim Essler
477-4314
P. O. Box 13051, Austin 78711
The River Walkers are members of the American Volkssports Association, which promotes family sports like walking, swimming, and biking. The River Walkers specialize in just that. The club puts on fall and spring walks, the proceeds going to a local charity. Meetings usually involve a guest speaker or a short program and then a walk through a nearby park. The Walkers meet the third Monday of each month at the Howson Branch Library, 2500 Exposition.

DAMN YANKEES CLUB
P. O. Box 26942, Austin 78755
The Damn Yankees Club is a nonprofit social/cultural organization in

Austin for transplanted Yankees and friendly Texans. Newcomers are welcome, as are those who have lived here for a length of time. "Meetings" are every Friday at Birraporetti's, 905 Barton Springs Road, starting at 5:30 (happy hour). The club prefers that you write for further information, so no phone number is given.

LEAGUE OF UNITED CHICANO ARTISTS/LUChA
1619 E. 1st
477-5770
LUChA is an organization of Chicano and Chicana artists dedicated to the advancement and promotion of Chicano visual arts. It puts on a number of exhibitions yearly through the Museo del Barrio. (See Museums.)

PARENTS WITHOUT PARTNERS
Gloria Pinion
459-5573 (days)   or
Gayle White
453-0006
PWP is a group for the single parent who enjoys activities with other single parents. Custody is not required. Functions are for members only, and there are many, just about every day of the week. Examples are dances, bridge games, dining, and roller skating. Attendance at a friendship orientation meeting is required. PWP maintains a three-faceted program of family, educational, and social activities, equally balanced.

SOCIETY FOR CREATIVE ANACHRONISM, AUSTIN BARONY
Hal Simon
452-4608   or
Martha George
482-8453
If you've ever driven by Waterloo Park on Sunday afternoon and seen what appears to be King Arthur's Court in full swing, then you've seen the Society for Creative Anachronism in action. Besides engaging in generic creative anachronism á la the Middle Ages, the society promotes activities such as calligraphy, dancing, and beer brewing. The society meets every Sunday at Waterloo Park (Red River at E. 15th) at 1:30.

W. H. PASSON HISTORICAL SOCIETY
Don Nesby
472-0174
The society's purpose is to discover what the black experience has been in Austin and Travis County and to record, preserve, and publicize the black community's role in local history. The society works closely with the Carver Museum (see Museums), schools, and other local groups that would like to know more about black history. The society stresses the importance of providing positive role models for young blacks, and it has more than two hundred members. General

meetings are held as announced, except for the annual meeting, which is always on Juneteenth. Project groups meet more often.

WEAVERS AND SPINNERS SOCIETY OF AUSTIN
Marjorie Erwin
442-0159
2402 Deerfoot Trail, Austin 78704
The Weavers and Spinners Society is a nonprofit organization that includes artisans working in all forms of fiber. Annual dues are $10 and include things such as the society's newsletter and use of its equipment and materials. Program meetings are the second Thursday of each month; spinning groups meet all other Thursdays at the Dougherty Cultural Arts Center.

WELCOME TO AUSTIN CLUB
Pauline Smith
250-8750
This is a club for newcomers to Austin. It meets the fourth Tuesday of each month at Wyatt's Cafeteria, 910 W. Anderson Lane.

★★

LIBRARIES

Visitors flock to Austin from the rest of Texas and the world to enjoy the multifaceted pleasures of our parks, our Capitol, our nightlife, our Mexican food, our libraries. Now, libraries are not on the cutting edge of fun for most people, but Austin's media collections are certainly prominent among the many jewels of our crown. Readers and researchers have possibilities open to them in Austin as nowhere else in Texas or the world. After all, how many other cities—Texan or otherwise—can claim both a Gutenberg Bible and the world's first photograph?

The Zavala State Archives and Library notwithstanding, the University of Texas General Libraries system is king of the heap; it currently contains around five million volumes, making it the eighth-largest academic library center in the United States. Nineteen libraries make up the system. Writers and researchers from all over the world come to pore through the university's incredible special collections. Allied with, though not a part of, the university's library system is the Johnson Presidential Library, which is operated by the National Archives and Records Service.

Despite being overshadowed by its glittering big brothers, and despite being plagued by budget cutbacks, the Austin Public Library system does quite well by itself. Its books-per-capita ratio ranks alongside that of the Dallas system as the highest among the state's major cities. The Central Library and seventeen (soon to be eighteen) well-scattered branches serve all parts of the city.

AUSTIN HISTORY CENTER
(Also known as the Austin–Travis County Collection)
810 Guadalupe at W. 9th
Central West
472-5433
Monday through Thursday 9–9, Friday and Saturday 9–6, Sunday 12–6
W

As befits a collection of its quality, the Austin History Center of the Austin Public Library is housed in the city's most graceful library building, Art Deco's rendition of the Renaissance Revival, the "Old Main" library. The building is now called the Austin History Center and has recently been restored. Although the collection's official name is now the Austin History Center, most natives still call it by the original name, the Austin–Travis County Collection. Since the collection's creation in 1955, its archivists have pursued an aggressive policy of gathering and preserving everything ever recorded in or about Austin, making it invaluable to the Austin-oriented researcher. Local newspaper files and photo archives are among its strong suits. If you need to look through the 1840 census records, the 1931 Austin High Maroons yearbook, or the 1872 City Directory, this is the place to come.

Several exhibits are up at any given time. Barton Springs through the years, the University of Texas centennial, and Austin weddings from the past are among recent shows.

A number of books about Austin have been written and illustrated with the help of the Austin History Center; many of them have been published by the related Waterloo Press. (See For Your Information.)

AUSTIN PUBLIC LIBRARY
800 Guadalupe at W. 8th (Main Branch)
Central West
472-5433
Monday through Thursday 9–9, Friday and Saturday 9–6, Sunday 12–6
W

The Austin Public Library is more than just a repository for books of various sizes and subjects. It is also adult education, business information, childrens' services, consumer aids, film showings, legal and medical information, large-print books, museums, puppet shows, and story times. You can check out art prints and record albums, or study for your G. E. D. Community clubs and organizations make extensive use of the central and branch libraries' meetings rooms.

The collection itself is well-rounded and extensive. Crown jewel of the system is the Austin History Center next door. Call the Central Library at 472-9454 for hours of branch libraries.

BARKER TEXAS HISTORY CENTER
Sid Richardson Hall 2.109, Red River and Manor, adjacent to LBJ
Library
University/Central West
471-5961
Monday through Saturday 8-5
W

The Barker Texas History Center is the single most important re-source center in existence for the study of the historical development of Texas. The Texas Collection has 120,000 volumes of Texana (the most extensive anywhere); the Archives and Manuscripts unit has more than four miles worth, including the Bexar Archives and the papers of Moses and Stephen Austin. The Texas Newspaper and Non-Textual Records Unit features approximately 2000 Texas newspapers published since 1829, as well as the Dime Novel Collection.

Because most of the Barker Center materials are rare and unique, it is a closed-stack library. The center is open, however, to anyone agreeing to abide by the official rules and regulations. (See also Museums.)

BENSON LATIN AMERICAN COLLECTION
Sid Richardson Hall 1.109, Red River and Manor, adjacent to LBJ
Library
University/Central West
471-3818
Open seven days; call for hours
W

With nearly half a million volumes, the Benson Latin American Col-lection is one of the most important libraries on Latin America in the world. The collection also includes thousands of maps, newspapers, and archival materials. It is an ongoing collection; the library currently receives thirty or more daily and weekly Spanish-language newspapers from all over the Americas. Visitors are welcome to use the library and its resources, but because of the unique and delicate nature of much of the material, users are required to abide by the Benson Collection's careful rules.

HARRY RANSOM HUMANITIES RESEARCH CENTER
Harry Ransom Center, W. 21st and Guadalupe
University/Central West
471-9111
Monday through Friday 9–5, Saturday 9–noon
W

The Humanities Research Center is as telling a testimony as can be found anywhere to the power of money lavishly spent. In the last twenty years the university has put together a rare book and manu-script library scarcely equaled in the world. Scholars from around the globe have come to burrow through its millions of components. It has notable collections in English, American, and French literature, iconography, theater arts, and photography. How many other libraries in the world can boast of a Gutenberg Bible and the world's first photograph in the same building? Exhibits from this massive collection are on display in the HRHRC and in the university's Academic Center. (See Museums.)

LORENZO DE ZAVALA STATE ARCHIVES AND LIBRARY
1201 Brazos, on the Capitol grounds
Central West
475-2445
Monday through Friday 8–5; Genealogy Section also open Saturday 8–5
W

The state library is the official collection of archival books and documents dealing with all phases of Texas history. Most visitors are here to pore through the Genealogy Section. (See also Museums.)

LYNDON B. JOHNSON LIBRARY
2313 Red River near E. 23rd
Parking on Red River between Manor and E. 26th
University/Central West
482-5136
Open seven days 9–5
W+

The LBJ Library houses all of the important papers of Lyndon Baines Johnson, thirty-sixth president of the United States. It contains all of the unimportant materials, too. If the president ever doodled it, chances are it rests in here. Most visitors content themselves with exploring the museum, but they cannot altogether avoid the archives, which frame the hollow core of the library, up and up and up for four stories, clad in thousands of identical imperial red boxes.

LBJ wanted this rich archive of manuscripts and audiovisual records to become an important, well-used research center. The library has generated some headlines over the years, but LBJ would not have liked all of them; Robert Caro and Ronnie Dugger made extensive use of his archives. It's really pretty easy to get a library card to use the place; the most important thing you need is a good reason.

PERRY CASTANEDA LIBRARY
Speedway at 21st
University/Central West
471-3813
Open seven days; call for hours
W

The "main" library on the University of Texas campus, with almost 1.7 million volumes. (It can hold 3.25 million.) The entrance floor service desks are the places to go if you have "How do I use?" and "Where do I go?" questions about the UT library system. The information resources of UT libraries are generally available for on-site public use

without charge. By depositing $15 (refundable) at the PCL, and paying
a $2 annual ID card fee, a Texas resident may obtain a courtesy bor-
rower's card for borrowing unrestricted materials in person.

University officials claim that the PCL building's Texoid shape is
purely coincidental.

TARLTON LAW LIBRARY
University of Texas School of Law
727 E. 26th
Central West
471-7726
Open seven days, 8 a.m.–10 p.m.
Free
W

The Tarlton Law Library is quite impressive, if only by virtue of its
size (fifth largest collection in the country) and facilities (best in the
country). But there is icing on this cake, or as one employee puts it,
"We live in a museum." This library-museum houses much of the considerable collections of Law School alumnus Elton M. Hyder, Jr., and
his wife Martha: legal art, objets d'art, antiques, furniture, kilims (Middle Eastern rugs), plants, art books—about seven hundred pieces in all.
You can spend a long time in here; all six floors and the stairwells are
full. The Rare Book Room (sixth floor) contains the collected papers of
Judge Tom C. Clark, the only UT Law School alumnus ever to serve on
the United States Supreme Court.

★★★

MILITARY

No one would ever call Austin a military town; in fact, some guides to
Austin omit mention of Bergstrom Air Force Base and Camp Mabry
altogether. Although the military does not fuel the local economy the
way it does in San Antonio, it does contribute its fair share—Bergstrom
in particular. Actually, Austin is much more a "military" town than most
of us give it credit for. It's just that most of the work is done by civilians
filling defense department contracts, at firms such as Tracor and Lock-
heed and UT's Balcones Research Center.

BERGSTROM AIR FORCE BASE
Texas Hwy. 71 East, just east of US Hwy. 183
Southeast
479-4100 (switchboard)
W variable

Bergstrom Air Force Base was constructed during the summer of
1942, on the south side of the Colorado River. Originally called Del
Valle Army Air Base, it was renamed shortly thereafter to honor Captain J. A. Bergstrom, the first Austin casualty of World War II.

The city cleared the 3000-acre tract and leased it to the government at
a dollar a year. The army put in the improvements, and the understanding was that the facility would revert to the city after the war. But

government leaders changed their minds, and Bergstrom became an important station of the Strategic Air Command, then the Tactical Air Command. In 1968 Bergstrom became headquarters for the 12th Air Force.

Approximately 5000 active-duty personnel are currently based at Bergstrom; the host unit is the 67th Tactical Reconnaissance Wing, which takes reconnaissance photographs and trains pilots for this particular mission. It operates separately from the 12th Air Force.

Escorted tours can be arranged for schools and groups, and the base has an annual open house, AeroFest, in conjunction with AquaFest in early August. The actual date varies from year to year, depending on when the base can secure the services of the famous Flying Thunderbirds.

CAMP MABRY
W. 35th at MoPac
Central West
465-5001

All that most people ever see of Camp Mabry are the rows and rows of limestone-walled equipment sheds that run alongside MoPac. They know it has something to do with the army. It is in fact home of the Texas Guard—an amalgam of the Texas Army National Guard, Texas Air National Guard, and the Texas State Guard.

Named for W. H. Mabry, adjutant general of Texas during the 1890s, the camp was established in 1892 as a summer encampment for the Texas Volunteer Guard. Local citizens donated the land. During the following years they were entertained by annual sham battles staged by the guard.

Camp Mabry became a federal camp and training center during World War I and again during World War II. Parts of the original grounds became MoPac, the United States Army Reserve Armory, and Camp Hubbard, a division of the Texas Highway Department.

Camp Mabry serves as headquarters for the 49th Armored Division (Lone-Star Division). The camp welcomes visitors and gives bus tours. In April 1983, racers from the United States Olympic Cycling Training Camp set a new national fifty-mile race record time here (although the time may not be official). Camp Mabry also has an important stained-glass chapel: the Lt. Gen. Thomas P. Bishop Texas Guard All-Faith Chapel, built in 1976.

CALENDAR

Austin is a city of diverse and interesting people, a fact mirrored in the abundance of annual events put on by and for Austinites. Here are some of the prominent happenings for each month. We haven't usually given specific dates, because they vary from year to year. If this list isn't complete enough for you, the Chamber of Commerce publishes an excellent quarterly free calendar of local events.

JANUARY

GOLDEN GLOVES BOXING TOURNAMENT
Pan-American Recreation Center, 2100 E. 3rd
Central East
444-6601
Usually midmonth, four days midweek
About $3–10
W
Winners in this district contest go on to compete in the San Antonio regionals, then state and national Golden Gloves championships.

AUSTIN BOAT, SPORT, AND MOTORCYCLE SHOW
Palmer Auditorium, Riverside at S. 1st
Southwest
478-9383
Usually third weekend in January, Thursday through Sunday
About $2 adults, 50¢ children 12 and under
W

MARCH

LAMME'S CHOCOLATE-DIPPED STRAWBERRIES
Various locations
Spring

Several times each spring (usually) and just before Easter (almost always), this local candy maker frenziedly dips berry after fresh strawberry into melted dark chocolate, while thousands of equally frenzied Austinites await their arrival on the counters. Dates are announced in the paper and on television—no phone calls, please—and they're all gone in three or four days.

MARDI-GRAS
Congress Avenue; various locations
Central
Weekend before beginning of Lent
Free
W

The annual Austin Mardi Gras celebration provides a unique alternative to its New Orleans counterpart, beginning on the weekend before "Fat Tuesday." The citywide festivities include a coronation ball and culminate in a full-fledged parade down Congress Avenue.

KITE-FLYING CONTEST
Zilker Park
Southwest
477-6511
Usually second Saturday
Free
W

Just as the name says: prizes are awarded in a variety of categories, with the emphasis on fun. About the only requirements are that you make your own kite and that it be able to fly.

CAPITOL 10,000
Downtown
445-3500
Usually second Sunday
Entry fee; spectators free
W

Just since 1978, this footrace has become an Austin institution, draw-ing more than 20,000 official competitors and goodness knows how many more hangers-on and spectators. Traditionally the race starts downtown, heads west towards Lake Austin, then returns east to a finish at Auditorium Shores.

AUSTIN–TRAVIS COUNTY LIVESTOCK SHOW AND RODEO
Texas Heritage and Exposition Center, 7311 Decker Ln.
928-3710
Usually fourth week in March, ten days
Admission to some events
W
Livestock and agricultural exhibits, auction, horse racing, a carnival, national country-and-western singing stars every night, a barbeque cookoff, a children's barn, and of course the rodeo are on the schedule of events. Brand-new facilities in 1984 are a great improvement over the former, cramped City Coliseum quarters.

MARCH AND APRIL

EASTER EGGSTRAVAGANZA
Symphony Square, 1101 Red River at 11th
Central West
476-5662
Easter weekend
Adults $2, children $1. Bring two eggs per child.
The program is somewhat different each year, but the Eggstrava-ganza always includes lots of live music and entertainment (like jug-glers and mimes), in addition to the traditional egg roll.

APRIL

TEXAS RELAYS
Memorial Stadium, University of Texas, San Jacinto at Manor Rd.
University/Central West
471-3931, 471-7437
Usually first weekend in April, Friday and Saturday
Admission
W partial
One of the oldest and best track meets around, featuring some of the best high-school and college track and field athletes in the world.

PIONEER FARM'S TRADITIONAL MUSIC FESTIVAL
Jourdan-Bachman Pioneer Farm, 11418 Sprinkle Cut-off Rd.
Far Northeast
837-1215

Usually first or second Sunday of April
Adults about $3; children 3–12 $1; under 3, free
W
"A celebration of Central Texas' cultural heritage," featuring old-time fiddlers, mariachis, bluegrass, old- and new-style folk music, gospel singing, and square dancing.

HIGHLAND LAKES BLUEBONNET TRAIL
Austin, Marble Falls, Buchanan Dam, Burnet, Llano, Kingsland
478-9383
Usually two weekends in April, Saturday and Sunday
Free
Besides the beautiful roadside wildflower displays on the highways between towns, this event features arts and crafts shows in each community, as well as a golf tournament and old-time fiddlers' contests.

INTERNATIONAL CULTURES WEEK
Texas Union, University of Texas
University/Central West
471-5651
Date, even month, may vary year to year
Admission to some events
W
Each year the Texas Union focuses on three countries for its International Cultures Week. Arts, crafts, and food from each country are featured. Visual and performing arts predominate. The week is meant to be educational as well as fun, in order to create a better understanding of our many world neighbors.

SAFARI
Austin Nature Center, 2416 Barton Springs Rd.
Southwest
Usually last full weekend in April, Saturday and Sunday
Adults $2, children 50¢, includes free shuttle ride from parking area
W partial
Annual fund-raiser for the Austin Nature Center, whose programs include the Pioneer Farm and Nature Center Annex. Among Safari's diversions are continuous live entertainment, exhibits, workshops, demonstrations, games, refreshments, and nature. When they tell you to take a hike, do it. Dozens of footpaths lace the center's eighty-acre preserve in west Zilker Park, and during Sarafi you never know who or what you might see along the way.

LEGENDS OF GOLF TOURNAMENT
Onion Creek Golf Course, IH 35 South
Far South
282-4430
Usually last week
About $10 per day
W

Just as the name implies, the tournament features some of the great-est names in golf history and lots of other celebrities to boot. First and foremost among the "old-timers" tourneys. The first three days are de-voted to practice and special events; the tournament takes place on the final four days.

EEYORE'S BIRTHDAY
Pease Park, on Parkway off W. 12th
Central West
Usually last Friday afternoon in April
Free
W

Brigadoon meets Babylon here on the banks of Shoal Creek one after-noon each spring, all in honor of Pooh Bear's *pobrecito amigo*. If you have ever wondered where all the hippies went, well, they're all here for about six crazy hours, and they're bringing their kids along, too. Eeyore's is about as close as Austin gets to the "good old days" these days.

MAY

FLORARAMA
Austin Area Garden Center, Zilker Park, 2200 Barton Springs Rd.
Southwest
477-8672
Usually first weekend in May
About $1
W

Besides being nationally accredited and the city's largest flower show of the year, Florarama is the Austin Area Garden Council's one big fund-raising event of the year. Anyone can enter, even those who do not belong to the council or member clubs. Entertainment, food, and booths that hawk everything from statues and pottery to John Deere tractors abound; the only requirement is that it be garden-related. This is the only weekend of the year that admission is charged to enter the beautiful Garden Center grounds, which is the reason why it's free the rest of the year.

O. HENRY PUN-OFF
O. Henry Museum, 409 E. 5th at Neches
Central West
472-1903
Usually first Sunday in May
Free
W

The rules are few, but competitors must preregister. The punning starts at 2 p.m. in the backyard and goes from there.

CINCO DE MAYO
Fiesta Gardens, 2101 Bergman
Central East
477-9096
May 4 and 5
About $3 adults; children and senior citizens $1
W

Mexican Independence Day is celebrated with all the trimmings, including a menudo cookoff. Special children's program on the morning of the fifth.

OLD PECAN STREET SPRING ARTS FESTIVAL
E. 6th between Congress and Red River
Central
472-1971
First weekend, Saturday and Sunday
Free
W variable

Austin's heartbeat street revels in its very existence for two days each May, managing to celebrate spring and benefit some local artists at the same time. Music, street performers, specialty foods, arts and crafts, and children's events are set up inside and out.

PRCA-TRAVIS COUNTY SHERIFF'S POSSE RODEO
Sheriff's Posse Arena, US Hwy. 183 South
Far Southeast
243-2026
Usually midmonth
About $5

FIESTA LAGUNA GLORIA
Laguna Gloria Art Museum, 3809 W. 35th at the end of Old Bull Creek Rd.
Central West
458-8191
Usually third weekend, Saturday and Sunday
About $3 adults; children 12 and younger $1
W

For one frenzied weekend a year, the spacious, genteel Laguna Gloria grounds are obscured by thousands of Austin art patrons. They enjoy ethnic food, mariachis, jugglers, a children's fiesta, free parking and shuttle bus, and, oh yes, *art*—more than two hundred artists, along with an art auction. Proceeds are donated by the Women's Art Guild to the Laguna Gloria Art Museum.

SPECIAL OLYMPICS STATE TRACK AND FIELD MEET
Memorial Stadium, University of Texas, San Jacinto at Manor
University/Central West
453-7236
Usually last week in May, Wednesday through Friday
W

Mentally retarded athletes from across the state come here to compete and to qualify for the national Special Olympics meet. The competition is spirited, and everyone comes away a winner.

JUNE

JUNETEENTH CELEBRATION
Rosewood Park, 2300 Rosewood Ave.; other locations
East
472-6838
June 19
Free
W
Juneteenth is Emancipation Day in Texas; on June 19, 1865, Major
General Gordon Granger took command of Galveston and officially proclaimed that all slaves in the state were free. This date—"Juneteenth"—
has been celebrated ever since. After falling into disfavor for some
years, Juneteenth is regaining its popularity. Juneteenth in Austin starts
with a grand parade, followed by an equally grand celebration at Rosewood Park. Softball and basketball tournaments, music, and lots of soul
food and barbeque are among the highlights.

JUNE THROUGH AUGUST

THIRTEEN FRIDAYS AT SYMPHONY SQUARE
Symphony Square Amphitheater, 1101 Red River at 11th
Central
476-6090
Every Friday evening
About $2.50–5
W
Big band, gospel, folk music, and jazz acts.

CATCH A RISING STAR
Symphony Square Amphitheater, 1101 Red River at 11th
Central
476-6090
Every Saturday evening
About $4
W
Jazz and rock bands.

CLASSICAL SUNSET SERIES
Symphony Square Amphitheater, 1101 Red River at 11th
Central
476-6090
Every Sunday evening
About $2.50
W
Classical ensembles.

JULY

AUSTIN SYMPHONY JULY 4TH CONCERT
Auditorium Shores, Riverside at S. Congress
Central
476-6064
July 4
Free
W

JULY 4TH FIREWORKS DISPLAY
Town Lake Shores
Central
478-5666
July 4, evening
Free
W
Bring your own blanket or lounge chair, refreshments, and a bit of patience; attendance is such that you'll have to get here a little early for a convenient parking spot and a plot of grassy lakeside. But don't let that deter you. Dusk's violet crown complements the dazzling pyrotechnics perfectly.

AUGUST

AUSTIN AQUA FESTIVAL
Auditorium Shores, Riverside at S. 1st; various locations
Central
472-5664, 472-5699
Usually first two weeks in August
Some events free; separate admission to other events; reduced charge with purchase of Skipper Pin (call for information)
W variable
A citywide celebration of summer, sunshine, water, and other Austin attractions. Includes a land parade on Congress, a water parade on Town Lake, and—the main draw—more than a week's worth of ethnic nights on the shores of Town Lake. And athletic events? Literally the whole shootin' match, plus figure skating and hockey.

SEPTEMBER

SERTOMA ARTS AND CRAFTS FAIR
Palmer Auditorium, Riverside at S. 1st, and Auditorium Shores
Central
836-1010, ext. 216
Usually third or fourth weekend in September

$1.50
W
Indoor and outdoor shows; one admission entitles you to attend both.

ETHNIC FOLK FESTIVAL
Fiesta Gardens, 2101 Bergman
East
477-6511, ext. 2737
Usually last weekend in September
About $2 adults, 50¢ children; 3-day pin for $1.50
W
Food, dancing, and entertainment headline this celebration of Austin's multicultural heritage.

OCTOBER

BRONZE GLOVES BOXING TOURNAMENT
South Austin Recreation Center, 1100 Cumberland
South
444-6601
Usually midmonth, 3 days midweek
About $3–5
W
Local amateur boxing tournament.

FALL FESTIVAL
Jourdan-Bachman Pioneer Farm, 11418 Sprinkle Cut-off Rd.
Far Northeast
837-1215
Usually third Sunday
About $2 adults; $1 children 3–12; 3 and under free
W variable
Interpretive exhibits and activities demonstrating the daily lives of pioneers.

HALLOWEEN ON 6TH STREET
October 31
This event is not sponsored by anyone, produced by anyone, or for the benefit of anybody else (at least not yet). Halloween is Austin's gayest holiday of the year, especially on Old Pecan Street, when for one night *all* the inmates of the San Antonio Zoo and Alice's Wonderland descend on us thicker than pixie dust for a giant street and sidewalk party.

OCTOBER THROUGH MAY

AUSTIN SYMPHONY
Performing Arts Center, University of Texas, 23rd at E. Campus Dr.

University/Central West
476-6064
Monthly, Friday and Saturday; weekends vary
Season tickets $30–90
Individual performances $4.50–13
W

Conductor Sung Kwak leads the Austin Symphony. An annual "Pops" concert is held each May at Palmer Auditorium, and the symphony performs two free summertime concerts in city parks. Dates and locations vary; call for specific dates and places.

NOVEMBER

AUSTIN ARTISTS HARVEST
Palmer Auditorium, Riverside at S. 1st
Southwest
478-9383
Usually first weekend, Saturday and Sunday
Free
W

More than two hundred local exhibitors, sponsored by the Tourism Department of the Austin Chamber of Commerce. Visa, MasterCard accepted. Many arts and crafts demonstrations.

HIGHLAND LAKES ARTS AND CRAFTS TRAIL
Austin, Burnet, Buchanan Dam, Marble Falls, Llano, Kingsland
478-9383
Usually first weekend in November, Saturday and Sunday
Free

Each community along the trail offers an arts and crafts fair, along with the usual refreshments, door prizes, music, crafts demonstrations, and bazaars. The drive itself is worth the trip, as the usually colorful Hill Country autumn nears its zenith.

DECEMBER

LIGHTING OF THE TREE
Zilker Park
Southwest
477-6511, ext. 2580
Usually first Sunday
Free
W

The "world's largest man-made Christmas tree" is actually one of Austin's venerable moonlight towers, festooned with thousands of bright Christmas lights. But the effect is spectacular and visible for several miles. The light switch is flipped on at dusk and is accompanied by caroling and other musical activities.

HANDEL'S *MESSIAH*
Performing Arts Center, University of Texas, 23rd and E. Campus Dr.
University/Central West
451-2224
Early December
Admission
W

CANDLELIGHT CHRISTMAS
Symphony Square, 1101 Red River at 11th
Central
476-6064
Usually first full weekend in December
Free
W

One day a year is set aside at Symphony Square especially for the celebration of Christmas. Tree trimming, caroling, and other musical presentations are among the festivities.

ARMADILLO CHRISTMAS BAZAAR
Cherry Creek Plaza, Stassney and Manchaca
Southwest
447-1605
Usually December 10–24
Admission $1.50
W

The Armadillo World Headquarters may be gone, but a piece of it continues every Christmas, in the form of this distinctive, popular Christmas shopping bazaar. Originally held at the Headquarters, it has been at Cherry Creek Plaza for the last several years. What you choose from is a variety of handcrafted and imported products, some useful, some frivolous, some tasteful, some weird. Live music nightly by Austin's best bands, and beverages, both soft and fermented, make an interesting experience more enjoyable. And no matter what, you almost always find something you can't go home without.

YULEFEST—ZILKER TRAIL OF LIGHTS
Zilker Park
Southwest
477-6511, ext. 2580
Follows Lighting of the Tree Ceremony
Free
W

A different Christmas theme every year, but always lots of entertainment and Christmas cheer in Santa's Village. A drive-through display, the Zilker Trail of Lights includes the Austin Garden Center. A shuttle bus runs back and forth from Palmer Auditorium.

HISTORY

★★
HISTORY

In the year 182— Stephen F. Austin, Daniel Boone, Davy Crockett, Ed Morris, Ponce de Leon, and Ben Thompson, together with other prominent citizens, while navigating the Colorado River in a canal boat, stopped to feed the mule and tap a fresh buffalo skin of kourmiss at the foot of what is now known in the guide book as Congress avenue.

Those were early times in Texas.

After lunch the explorers took a fresh chew of jerked Indian and went ashore.

Suddenly an idea struck Stephen F. Austin, and he was too generous a man to conceal it.

"Boys," he said, "let's start a town site here and call it Austin."

"Just as you say," they all replied.

Then they got a gun and killed off all the Indians between the lunatic asylum and the river, and laid out Austin.

It has been laid out ever since."

Not every grain sifts true in this story of creation written in the *Roll-*

ing Stone in 1894 or 1895 by noted historian and onetime Austinite O. Henry, but of all the histories of the Capitol City written over the years, his is both the shortest and the most entertaining.

Now that you are possessed of the basic facts of Austin's noble history, you are free to move on to greener chapters; but as long as you're here, why not stay for the details?

Austin did not actually begin with Stephen F., although he did endow the city with its shortest and most enduring moniker. We can only speculate what the original settlers called the place when they moved here fifteen or sixteen thousand years ago. We can only speculate who they were. Whoever they were, they swam at Barton Springs, admired the view from Mt. Bonnell, and crossed Town Lake about where we do now. They were calling themselves *Tickanwatic*, "those most like humans," by 1709. That year their Chief Cantona encountered Spanish army captain Pedro Aguirre and company in the woods near present-day St. Edward's University. They were hunting the Colorado and the Tejas; he was hunting deer, but the "Tonkawas" would do nicely. Cantona and Aguirre exchanged hows and whys and promised to write each other, and then the Spaniards headed back for the Rio Grande. Thus went the white man's first visit to Austin.

The Spaniards had liked what little they had seen of south Austin, and they came back in 1730 to build a mission at Barton Springs. But they moved back to San Antonio the next year. So Those Most Like Humans had the Place Most Like Austin to themselves again for the next hundred years, until the enterprising Jake Harrell set up his tent at the corner of 1st and Congress in 1838. He built a log cabin and stockade very soon thereafter. Those Most Like Humans were not the most gracious neighbors. But Harrell persevered. He knew he had found the soft thing; there were just a few thorns and arrows to be removed. And it wasn't long before other Damn Yankees joined him, and they decided to call their stand "Waterloo," which was either in recognition of what they were going to do to Those Most Like Humans or in homage to that town in Iowa most near Cedar Falls.

At the height of the tourist season that fall, vice-president of the Republic of Texas Mirabeau B. Lamar visited Harrell and Waterloo, because he had heard that the buffalo were running on Congress. (Pardon—what was to *become* Congress; we keep getting ahead of ourselves.) Rising early the next morning, Lamar had only to step out into Harrell's front yard to pick his target. Congress Avenue and the rest of downtown Waterloo were teeming with buffalo. Lamar barely had time to load his gun before he brought down a museum specimen, somewhere between the Greyhound Station and the statehouse on the hill. Hiking to the top of Capitol Hill, looking down to the sparkling Colorado flush from the fall rains, Lamar was impressed. He was moved to grandiloquence. "This," he pronounced, "should be the seat of future empire." Signet and Harlequin versions of this story have Lamar's right foot resting on his kill, which had fallen about where the Seal of the Republic of Texas rests now. Lamar would have liked that version.

Mirabeau Bonaparte Lamar was a man whose dreams were as grandiose as his name. The poet-soldier from Georgia succeeded Sam the Raven, the hero of San Jacinto, as president of the poverty-stricken Republic of Texas a month or two after his historic 1838 hunt at Waterloo. A special government commission had recently been appointed to select a site for the permanent capital of the republic, and Lamar recommended that the commissioners examine Waterloo firsthand. They did, and chose their site accordingly, although the deadly yellow-fever plague, which was just then abating in Houston, might have had something to do with their choice.

The commission's report of April 1839 dutifully pointed out Waterloo's fine water and empirically strategic location before finally waxing rhapsodic on her curvatures. "The imagination of even the romantic will not be disappointed on viewing the valley of the Colorado, and the fertile and gracefully undulating woodlands and luxurious prairies at a distance from it. The most sceptical will not doubt its healthiness, and the citizen's bosom must swell with honest pride when standing in the portico of the Capitol of his Country he looks abroad upon a region worthy only of being the home of the brave and free."

Work on the new capital began in May 1839; and while Lamar was sowing the seeds of his future empire down in the bayou city of his greatest political enemy, Edwin Waller was knocking up Texas's first official capital city. The first lot sales were held on August 1, 1839. Three hundred and one lots sold that day for a total of $182,585. Then, as now, Congress Avenue at 6th was the primest of locations. The Scarbrough lot was high seller that day at $2800.

Natural beauty notwithstanding, Waller and his two hundred laborers did not have an easy time of it. Building materials and provisions were scarce, and they were laboring in the vicious heat of the Texas summer. The Tonkawas and their bully cousins the Comanches were expressing reluctance at giving way to the new order; meanwhile, the Houston faction was busy accentuating the negative and denigrating the positive aspects of life in Austin.

Lamar was eager to get settled in his seat of empire, and so he, his cabinet, and fifty wagons' worth of paperwork arrived here on October 17, 1839. They were greeted by one hotel and enough log cabins to house the major branches of government. The president's house and the Capitol had been whitewashed for the occasion. Sam Houston's house had not been. The opposition's leader plotted, schemed, and otherwise lived in a dirt-floored shanty on Congress.

The Indians were not impressed by the president's stand in his seat of empire. As one resident wrote, "The Indians are stalking through the streets at night with impunity. They are as thick as hops around the mountains in this vicinity, and occasionally they knock over a poor fellow and take his hair." Most congressmen did not take leave of their boarding-house citadels after sundown. The Capitol was surrounded by a stockade until 1845.

By 1840 Austin had 856 citizens and two newspapers. By 1841 it had survived its first brush with high culture. "Count" Jean Peter Isidore Alphonse de Saligny, the king of France's chargé d'affaires to the republic, had swept into town the year before and immediately begun building what we now call the French Legation. It was the most luxurious house, horse barn, or office building in Austin.

Saligny was a young man of high taste, hot temper, few scruples, and even less tact. He was in fact not a count, or anything else noble. He soon made a name for himself in Austin, passing counterfeit bills, neglecting his own bills, and fighting the Pig War with neighbor and ex-landlord Richard Bullock.

After declining to settle his bill with the hosteler Bullock, Saligny moved in next door to the Bullock complex at 6th and Congress. Soon thereafter, Saligny began to complain that Bullock's pigs were making hash out of his garden and fodder out of his linens and official papers. In retaliation, Saligny ordered his manservant to make bacon out of every porker he could lay his hands on. Bullock raised the stakes by thrashing the servant and promising to do the same to Saligny.

Upset at this grave affront to His Majesty's corporate dignity, Saligny asked the republic to punish Bullock, posthaste. The republic demurred, citing due process of law. The republic and Saligny were already on bad terms.

Outraged, yet quick to recognize a convenient opportunity to duck his creditors, Saligny personally broke official diplomatic relations with the republic and flew the coop for Louisiana. He stayed in "that which Louis stands on" for a year, constantly warning the Texians of the consequences they were going to face.

The French government harbored no such countenances, though for the record it supported Saligny. A compromise was cooked up that left egg on neither face, and Saligny returned to Texas in 1842. He served off and on as chargé until 1845, when Texas annexed the United States.

There wasn't much in Austin for Saligny to come home to in 1842, so he didn't. One of Santa Anna's divisions had decided to vacation in San Antonio that spring and looked poised to move on to Barton Springs for the summer. That was enough for Sam the Raven, who was president again; and in March 1842 he ordered the men of government to congregate S. P. Q. R. in the town of his name.

Realizing that, then as now, paperwork is truly the heart of government, Austinites formed a vigilante committee and placed the state archives under armed guard so that they too did not flee to Houston. Tiring of this division of power by the advent of 1842, Sir Sam de Jacinto sent a company of rangers to retrieve the papers. He stressed that blood was not to be shed in their liberation. The rangers sneaked into town under cover of darkness, impressed the papers, and stole away—but not before being spied by the insomniac Mrs. Angeline Eberly, who fired the city's warning cannon. The next day, New Year's 1843, the Austin vigilantes trailed the scions of Sam to their camp near Round Rock and re-expropriated the scrolls of democracy. The archives' bipedal alter egos finally rejoined them here in 1844, when the capital officially returned from Washington-on-the-Brazos. But even this was a temporary state of affairs until the vox populi of Texas sentenced Austin to a life term in 1850. That year Austin counted a meagre 629 souls. Even New Braunfels was bigger. By 1860 the Austin host measured 3494. In the meantime, John Grenninger had invented barbed wire (See First, Biggest, Best); but the significance of these events should not be linked. Certainly the building and respective inhabitants of the new limestone Capitol, the governor's mansion, and the state lunatic asylum had contributed to this sixfold increase. Santa Anna was busy chewing Chiclets with Mr. Adams and Harriet Beechnut Stowe in the Big Apple, and the last of the outlying redskins were now pushing up hops. And so Austin braced itself for the success that must now surely come its way.

But along came the abolishioner president, and in the spring of 1861 the vox populi of Texas and the South was unleashed again. Austin and Travis County chipped in their two cents' worth on the losing side, but the newly crowned Confederate administration didn't hold it against our capital citizens. Quite the contrary; the Rebs set up a cap and cartridge factory in the old Supreme Court building, built a cannon foundry on the banks of Waller Creek, and cut down the great grove of elms and live oaks atop College Hill in order not to build a fortress, about where the UT Tower now grows. Drovers freighted goods down to Brownsville, secreted Mexican oranges in their wagons, and sold them back in Austin at a toadskin per.

As the curtain fell on the Glorious Rebellion, the Confederate government in Texas scattered like dust in the wind, and Austin was left to sift for itself until the Damn Yankees arrived to instruct the vanquished rebels in the finer points of reconstructive democracy. In the meantime there occurred the State Treasury Robbery of June 11, 1865. (See Mysteries and Fantasies.)

General George A. Custer arrived to save the day in November 1865. Soon he had established residence at the old Blind Institute and "bullpens" on Shoal Creek. Austin's marshall Ben Thompson (see Noshes and Nebbishes) and many other reconstructing rebels passed the time of day and night in Custer's al fresco detention and mud-bath resort.

But in the middle of this political atonality, Austin finally stepped into the modern, reach-out-and-touch-someone age, when the first telegraph line began tapping out condolences and compliments in October 1865. The steam cars came in December 1871, a Christmas present come a couple of days early. It has been empirically insinuated that there is no God and no free brunch; you could not convince Austinites of either. During the first years rubberneckers flocked to the station for no other reason than to bear witness to the smoky departures and arrivals. Why, the cost of lumber got sawed in half in less than a month after the railroad's arrival in Austin, as did practically everything else not grown, forged, or quarried more than a flagstop out of town. The honeymoon of this age brought on by the iron horse lasted about six months. By May 1872 the faithful were complaining about price-gouging and kickbacks, and life had settled down merely to a new and improved level of normalcy, one of Sears and Roebuck and Sunday excursions and flagstone sidewalks and ice-cold beer.

Now that the necessities of life were assured, Austinites began to thirst after its luxuries. A dam across the Colorado River, they figured, would solve just about every problem the railroad and the restitution of a Democratic administration hadn't. Austinites were not fazed by the fact that no greater feat of its type had yet been constructed in Texas or in the world at large; they were just tired of digging out of the mud after every flood and having to crank their own ice cream.

So in 1890, the vox of Austin spoke in favor of a million-dollar bond issue to finance the dam's construction. Upon its completion in 1893, the dam enjoyed the immediate respect and adulation of all. Had it been able to take the oath of office, the dam could have been elected governor. This lunch hadn't been free, but at least it was going to pay for itself through production of household electricity and unlimited industrial power. Austin was going to become an industrial oasis. The dam broke in 1900 (see Flotsam and Jetsam), and despite several rebuilding attempts, and because of several more washouts, it was not successfully rebuilt until 1940. By that time, Austin had outgrown the dam, which had finally gotten a name—Tom Miller—after the mayor of the same name.

Austin did not grow into the industrial epicenter the dam's instigators dreamed it would. It settled down instead to a comfortable, dignified life as majordomo to the state's legal heart and collegial mind. About the heaviest that Austin industry got was the AusTex Chili and Tamale Factory. (See First, Biggest, Best.)

Nonetheless, Austin, the government, and the university have all gotten bigger together. When putting down a history of Austin, one can only put off mention of the Universitatus Primerus et Pluribus Unum de Texas for so long. In this case, three-quarters of a century is long enough. This particular gleam in Mirabeau's eye became reality in 1839, when the Congress of the Republic ordered a site set aside for the establishment of a "university of the first class" and then granted their child a generous 115,000-acre dowry. According to the tradition of the times, Congress decided that popular vote should decide the site. The election was set for September 6, 1881. And guess what?

Building commenced in the fall of '82. Classes commenced the following fall. They have commenced every fall since, and the buildings now threaten to outnumber the students on campus.

Graduated UT students (let's leave the bureaucrats out of this for now) who couldn't bear to leave the city of Barton Springs and Scholz Garten have contributed as much as any other collective body to Austin's steady growth over the years.

Then, in 1967, Tracor established an outpost in this industrial wilderness: electronics on the new frontier, major industry American style. IBM and Texas Instruments soon joined Tracor in the noble, glorious and enriching task of harnessing Austin's vast and virginal resources, in the name of continued American economic dominance. MCC and Motorola and most of the rest of the siliconized world are hot on their heels. And it has been that way ever since.

★★★
A BUFFET HISTORY OF AUSTIN

It is well and good that we know the important history and facts of Austin: that it was a favorite Indian watering hole before M. Bonaparte Lamar expropriated it in 1838 in the name of future seats of empire; that it became the capital of the only nation ever to lapse into United Statehood; that Austin is the home of Barton Springs and Matt's El Rancho.

Austin is unique; things have transpired here that could have happened nowhere else: things that have forever altered the quality of life in Austin, things that betray some essential characteristic of life here, things that are merely humorous.

Things: acts of God and acts of man, pain and joy, crazy schemes and brilliant ideas, ignominious failures and untrammeled successes. All of these things have been threaded into the rich and complex fabric that is Austin; unfortunately, many of them have passed from the public consciousness over the years.

It's time here and now to revive some of these slumbering Austin tidbits, so we will all be able to appreciate our dear old city a bit more— or if for no other reason, to gird our conversational loins for tomorrow night's cocktail party.

Herewith then, and caveat reader: *A Buffet History of Austin*, conveniently serialized.

1883
Everyone complains about the size of government these days, but back in 1883, city councilmen outnumbered the cops twenty-four to twelve. A common joke that year was that it was "easier to find an alderman than a policeman in Austin."

1908
The Driskill Hotel lobby has hosted many grand comings-out and goings-on over the years, but on April 16, 1908, the Driskill lobby was the site of a pitched gun battle between two prominent lawyers.

Austin Bar Association president John Dowell and San Antonio attorney Mason Williams had been at each other's legal throats for several months over a small ranch in Williamson County. The day before the shooting, Dowell had upped the ante by seeking to have Williams disbarred from the practice of law. The trial had been postponed until 2 p.m. the sixteenth.

But at one that afternoon, Dowell strode into the Driskill lobby armed with a double-barreled shotgun and revolver. The lobby was filled with lingerers from lunch. Among them was Mason Williams. Dowell winged him with the first blast as Williams entered the lobby from the bar. Williams dodged behind a pillar, as did Dowell, and the rest of the room cleared out. Williams drew his pistol, and they traded volleys back and forth until disarmed. Neither was seriously wounded.

1911

As any visitor will tell you, Austin is an easy town to get lost in. One reason why is Austin's crazy-quilt pattern of streets. When you take a look at a map, at the core of Austin—that square of blocks bordered by 1st Street, IH 35, Martin Luther King Boulevard, and West Avenue—you see order: rectangles and right angles. But outside this tidy core, you note that the courses of these precise streets begin to run awry. For example: E. 12th tacks off sharply to the north, E. 11th slightly to the south. This begat all sorts of filler streets—Cotton, Rosewood, and New York—to flesh out the widening void. It was 1911 before the city found out that its streets were missing the mark as they radiated out. The city's engineering department sent surveying parties out to battle the problem, but as you can see, they didn't exactly win the war. They never figured out how the streets came to stray from the true line of the right angle.

1912

The chickens were penned up in Austin in 1912, and hundreds of city women sighed in relief. Local women's clubs and societies had campaigned for years to get the city's chickens cooped up. They were tired of having their flower beds and gardens ravaged by visiting foghorns and leghorns. With the fryers penned, one local paper was able to report that women of all the clubs and societies "are digging flowerbeds with a sense of security."

1913

The Texas Legislature has never enjoyed much of a reputation, but one thing we've always been able to count on is a legislature that is seldom able to agree on anything, save when to adjourn for lunch and for the day. In February 1913, though, both the House and Senate were of one mind. They wanted to get the hell out of Austin as quickly as possible. Two of their colleagues had just died of meningitis, and they feared like fates. Officially the senators and representatives cut out with the blessings of their presiding officers, but it was noted that most came to that morning's session with overcoats and grips in hand. And only a few days earlier they had vowed to stay in Austin for months, if that's how long it was going to take to pass the legislation they had deemed necessary.

"Appalled by the spectre of threatened death," one reporter wrote with a tinge of scorn, "most of the lawmakers had but one desire—to get away, and at once. Merger bills, constitutional amendments, road laws, factional differences, and 'crying needs' were forgotten. There was but one 'paramount issue' and no division. For once, the Legislature was a unit having one mind and that mind dominated by fear—a fear unreasoning and not to be removed." House Speaker Terrell and the two Travis County representatives stayed behind, to meet and adjoin for a few minutes each afternoon until March 5, when the solons were due to return. The few who remained declared the flight "absurd and entirely uncalled for."

In the summer of 1913, the Austin school system hired its first woman janitor, just in time to get Austin High ready for the fall term. Superintendent A. N. McCallum hailed it as a great advancement, noting that a female in that position was going to be invaluable and that her services would be of much benefit to the school.

1916
In 1916 the Travis County sheriff publicly dared Harry Houdini to escape from *his* jail. Houdini was on his way from San Antonio to Austin for a show at the Majestic. While in San Antonio, Houdini had escaped from a pair of handcuffs while suspended seventy-five feet in the air. The sheriff sniffed at his feat, saying that any number of his inmates could wriggle free of such bonds given enough time. If Houdini wanted a real challenge, he would be glad to set the contortionist up and then set him straight.

1917
You can complain about the blue laws today if you must, but just be glad you weren't here in 1917. That year the city and courts allowed only one gas station in town to be open on Sundays. Located at 4th and Brazos, the station was open to serve transients and only strict emergency cases of townspeople.

In 1917 champion shooter Ad "Dead-Eye Dick" Toepperwein came to Austin to teach aviation cadets at the U. S. School of Military Aeronautics how to use the shotgun in aerial combat. "The shotgun is rapidly becoming an intensely important weapon in modern warfare," Dead-Eye declared. "Not only is it used in the trenches for short range work in the field, but it is being used extensively from aeroplanes."

1918
Austin's first airport was in South Austin, just past St. Edward's University. Pilots don't much like the Austin airport now, and they didn't in 1918, either—all of which prompted the Chamber of Commerce and newspapers to urge all patriotic Austinites to show up on a particular Sunday at 8 a.m., armed with lunch, rake, shovel, or grubhoe and dressed in their best old clothes, in order to "help make this field the safest, the best, and most inviting in the country with our fliers."

The plea was in response to an incident wherein the propeller of a landing plane sucked a fist-sized limestone rock up through its tender canvas belly.

1920
Fearing an outbreak of the dreaded bubonic plague, the mayor and City Council approved a bounty system on rats during the summer of 1920. Beginning July 19, the city promised to pay a nickel for each rat delivered to City Hospital between 8 and 9:30 each morning. The bounty applied only to rats caught within the city limits, and all rats

had to be tagged with the address and place caught.

In closing his proclamation to the citizens of Austin, health officer C. H. Brownlee, M. D., noted, "Aside from aiding in a most worthy and humanitarian cause, all those delivering rats at the City Hospital will be earning a neat little sum of money."

1924

In 1924 local attorney I. L. Peeler was talking up a constitutional amendment that would convert Austin into another District of Columbia and would also deprive Austinites of their right to vote. One reason that Peeler gave was that Austin voters habitually voted against the man elected as governor by the rest of the state, and that furthermore no one from Austin had ever been elected governor. This was inappropriate behavior on the part of a city constitutionally obligated to host the governor and his duly appointed hoardes.

1926

Suffering from white-line fever, the 1926 edition of the Exchange Club of Austin petitioned the city to paint a white line down the middle of Congress Avenue. The club gravely noted that traffic would be facilitated greatly by marking the middle of the street and requiring passing cars to stay on the proper side of the line. The council acceded to their wishes and has been defacing the streets of Austin ever since.

1928

In 1928 the Hay Fever Committee of the Chamber of Commerce campaigned for a city ordinance requiring all male cedar trees within the Austin city limits to be cut down. The committee believed that this grandly scaled exorcism would go far in relieving the suffering of hay-fever victims. The Hay Fever Committee ended its campaign when the Travis County Medical Society declined to endorse the proposed ordinance.

★★★

ONE MAN'S MEAT IS ANOTHER MAN'S POISON: VIEWS OF AUSTIN OVER THE YEARS

JAMES S. JONES
Indian Fighter
1838

"I have just returned from Waterloo, the contemplated new seat of government. . . . It is the most beautiful and sublime scene. . . . Rome itself with all its famous hills could not surpass the natural scenery of Waterloo."

E. CHANDLER
Huckster
1840

"The climate and soil of the Colorado we conceive to be as well if not better, calculated for the cultivation of the vine and silk, as any portion of the North American continent."

GEORGE W. BONNELL
Mountain namesake
1840
"Like the ancient city of Rome, Austin is built upon seven hills, and it is impossible to conceive of a more beautiful and lovely situation."

WILLIAM BOLLAERT
Professional traveler
1843
"It is difficult to give a full and just description of this spot with its surrounding scenery. If Rome was celebrated in song for her 'seven hills,' Austin may well boast of her 'thousand mounds.'"

DR. FERDINAND ROEMER
Father of Texas geology
1845
"As to beauty of location, I should prefer Austin to all other Texas inland cities, excepting New Braunfels and San Antonio." (He was plagued by bedbugs later that night, the first time he had encountered them in Texas.)

RUTHERFORD B. HAYES
Fourteenth president of the United States
1847
"Austin is an inconsiderable village on the Colorado, with large expectations . . . not more than one or two passable buildings in the city . . . gaming and drinking very abounding in all quarters."

AGNES WENDE
Bricklayer's wife
1854
"Everything is very expensive here. I live at the krick and not in town and have to pay a monthly rent of $6 for a little house of room and a stable. But I prefer this to a dwelling for half the rent because it is only a few steps to the water and Wende is close to the Capitol. . . . In town, apart from the creek, nearly all the people have to buy water. The town stands on sandy soil but the environment is very fertile and the farms are better here."

FREDERICK LAW OLMSTED
Traveler
1854
"Austin has a fine situation up on the left bank of the Colorado. Had it not been the Capitol of the state, and a sort of bourne to which we had looked forward for a temporary rest, it still would have struck us as

the pleasantest place we had seen in Texas. It reminds one somewhat of Washington; Washington, en petit, seen through a reversed glass.

"There is a very remarkable number of drinking and gambling shops, but not one book store."

JULIEN SIDNEY DEVEREAUX
State legislator
1855

"Austin is the most artificial city or town I have seen. I have not seen a bale of cotton, vegetables of any kind except a few Yankee onions that sell for 20 cents a pound. What few turnips and cabbage that was alive in the country have been swept clean by the grasshoppers and also what wheat that has been sowed. I don't see what inducement people have to move here and pay high prices for land."

GALVESTON NEWS
1877

"Austin . . . is justly noted for the culture and refinement of its society, the enterprise of its people, the beauty of its situation, the charm of its climate and the delightful natural scenery by which it is surrounded. Austin is a delightful place for winter residence for people from the North who suffer from pulmonary diseases and bronchial and catarrhal affections."

CHICAGO ILLUSTRATED GRAPHIC NEWS
1887

"The city of Austin, Texas . . . has been pronounced by tourists who have travelled extensively, to be one of the loveliest locations for an attractive city within their observation . . . a town resembling in miniature, Washington City, except that Austin is superior in picturesque scenery, healthfulness, and beauty of natural surroundings."

O. HENRY (WILL PORTER)
Short-story writer
1884

"Town is fearfully dull, except for the frequent raids of the Servant Girl Annihilators, who make things lively during the dead hours of the night [see Mysteries and Fantasies]; if it were not for them, items of interest would be very scarce, as you may see by the *Statesman*."

J. T. BRACKENRIDGE
Banker
1890s

"None who have ever seen and known, as was written of Florence, can forsake Austin."

BERTON BALEY
Famous newspaper poet
1922

"Well, I think that Austin is unnecessarily dirty.

"Of course, you've got to have water and light and those things—I don't mean that: but what's the use of trying to make a thing ugly when it can be made beautiful. I think that beauty is a darn sight more important than the practical things. San Antonio is more of the ideal city."

FORTUNE MAGAZINE
1979
"Austin is what many a U. S. city longs to be—compact and cultivated. It has style."

★★
FIRST ★ BIGGEST ★ BEST

BARBED WIRE
First in the world
John Grenninger unleashed this bane of fat men and livestock on the world in 1857, when he veiled his garden on Waller Creek with long strands of iron wire that had been twisted around sharp little snips of iron wire. He had fabricated the barbed wire in the iron foundry where he worked, so as to protect his watermelon crop from fleet-of-foot light-fingerers. City marshall Ben Thompson, late in his illustrious career, confided that he had ripped his pants on the barbs of Grenninger's dilemma. Grenninger was murdered in 1862, but you shouldn't make any connections. A dusky man axed him for his money. With Ben murder was strictly for fun. The first patent for barbed wire wasn't issued until 1867.

BREAD
Biggest loaf in the world
In 1912 Austinite A. S. Newburg baked the world's biggest loaf of bread: 162 pounds heavy, 10 feet long, 18 inches wide by 18 inches high. The loaf took one hour to bake and could supply 162 families for one day, or one family for 162 days. Newburg had previously baked two other world's largest breads.

CITY CHARTER
Most perfect
The city-manager charter written in 1924, which provided for our present form of city government, was called "the most perfect city manager charter ever written in the United States" by one prominent authority.

DINNER PARTY
Biggest in Texas and by extension the world
Pappy Lee O'Daniel invited every last Texan to attend an inaugural dinner at the Mansion in honor of his second term as governor in 1941. Twenty thousand people took him up on the invite. The Mansion grounds and nearby streets served as dining room. The guests de-

voured 19,000 pounds of barbeque, 1000 pounds of potato salad, 1300 pounds each of pickles and onions. Thirty-two thousand cups of coffee were sweetened with 1000 pounds of sugar.

ICE CREAM
Biggest factory in Texas
Clay Jones bought a seventeen-horsepower steam engine in 1878, and soon he was top banana in Texas ice cream, churning out 250 gallons of it a day. He sold it wholesale as well as retail in his own Congress Avenue parlor.

OLDEST PROFESSION
First U. S. City to bust up
Mayor Alexander Wooldridge caught a fit of morality one day just before World War I and called in his city marshall Will Morris to do something about it. "Morris," he says, "I'm thinking about doing something that's never been done before in the United States—I'm going to break up the red-light district."

A couple of weeks later, Morris visited each madam personally so as to read them a letter from the mayor, in which he informed the matrons that they had twenty days to move before they would be forcibly ejected from the premises. But as a carrot, Sir Wooldridge also promised to find honorable employment for any lady of the night who wished to take leave of her sinful ways.

All but one madam had moved by the required date, and the last did soon after. Wooldridge's invitation to salvation went unanswered, though. All the ladies resurfaced soon after, scattered all over Austin now, instead of within their former tidy scarlet ghetto.

PICNIC
Biggest in Texas and by extension the world
Pappy Lee actually took it easy with his 1941 dinner party. He had celebrated his 1939 inauguration with a picnic for 60,000 in UT's Memorial Stadium.

POWER PLANT
Biggest in Texas
In 1933 Austin had the largest municipally owned water, light, and power plant in Texas.

STREET
Widest in the world
Congress Avenue was once the widest street in the world, about three times wider than it is now. It replaced a small creek, incidentally.

East Avenue was also once touted as the widest street in Texas, laid out to be 200 feet wide, in contrast to Congress' 120 feet. One early twentieth-century plan called for it to be refined into a divided boulevard with park areas in the median strip. Today East Avenue is an IH 35 frontage road.

STRIKE
Texas's first labor
In 1885 stonecutters quarrying stone for our present state Capitol struck when a transient, who refused to join their union, hired on at a dollar a day less than the union men and then did more work. "Brock" was the offender's name. Union cutters threatened to walk out of the Oak Hill Quarry (now Convict Hill) if Brock was allowed to stay. Brock stood his ground, and the strike was on.

TAMALE FACTORY
Biggest in the U. S.
In 1911 Austin's Austex Chili Factory had the only tamale-making machine in the country, which had been invented here in the factory. Peppers for the chili were grown south of town. During the 1930s and 1940s Austex operated the nation's largest chili con carne and tamale canning factory here.

TELEPHONE CONVERSATION
First in the South
Many years ago, in 1924, veteran telegrapher W. A. Pillow confided to a local reporter that the first telephone conversation in Texas and probably the South had been conducted between the telegraph office at 6th and Congress and Dr. Clark's store at St. Elmo, about six or seven miles south.

Professor Sebe Sneed, an electricity enthusiast, had recently borrowed two magnetos from a Massachusetts friend. He and a couple of telegraph company men went down to Clark's store and threw a wire over the telegraph wire, thereby connecting a phone at Clark's with one already installed at the office downtown. Brother Ben Pillow was back at the city office with a few friends.

It was a quiet Sunday afternoon, so hot and dry that several buckets of water had to be poured onto the bundle of copper wire buried a foot or two underground to form a "ground" connection. Pillow described the ensuing conversation as perfect, "individual voices being easily recognized."

A preacher's young daughter sang "Almost Persuaded" down at the St. Elmo end, and "all listeners were fully persuaded that the telephone was a wonderful invention."

Pillow recollected that the newspaper ran an article the next day, but unfortunately he couldn't remember the date, the year, or the singer's name.

URNITE
First in the world
Surely you've heard of urnite, everybody's heard of urnite—hasn't he? C. F. Paul of Austin invented the stuff during the Roaring Twenties.

Urnite is a synthetic stone, with all the good looks of white marble but lighter and cheaper.

An urnite factory was built here in 1927 to manufacture urnite urns, benches, tables, fountains, birdbaths, and God knows what else. It was reported by the papers later that year that several prominent Austin businessmen—among them an undertaker, a car dealer, and a drug- gist—had purchased urnite articles.

WATER SYSTEM
Best in America

In 1926 Al Skinner, representative of the National Pitometer Com- pany of Chicago, pronounced, "Austin has the finest filter plant in the country." He qualified his declaration by saying that he had inspected all the waterworks plants in the United States, and that the Austin water-treatment plant was ahead of anything else he had seen in con- struction and architecture.

FIRST IN AUSTIN

FIRST AIRPLANE LANDING

On October 20, 1911, Cal Rodgers—flying the first successful cross- America trip—landed in Austin. Will T. Caswell induced him to land here as part of a scheme to promote Caswell's new subdivision in north Austin (just beyond Hyde Park). Thirty-nine hundred Austinites were on hand to greet Rodgers, who had hopped here from Waco in one hour and forty minutes. On this leg as well as all the others, Rodgers followed the railroad tracks and otherwise relied on a compass for directions.

Courageous Cal took off for San Antonio an hour and a half later, pausing long enough to circle the Capitol dome twice before crash- landing at Kyle.

Rodgers finally made it to the Pacific, but once there he crashed into San Diego Bay and drowned. The plane now rests in the Smithsonian.

FIRST BLUE LAWS

Austin's first blue laws took effect in 1870, and churches became the only places open for business on Sunday. And while they were at it, city fathers outlawed boxing matches, bear and bull fights, and kite flying. They put leashes on every goat, horse, mule, and sheep, and almost every cow (milk cows excepted).

FIRST COLD BEER

Life has been a little easier in Austin ever since that fateful day in the spring of 1877 when cold beer first arrived in Austin, as faithfully re- ported by the *Statesman*:

"The International Depot was a scene of life and activity yesterday

forenoon, many people having been attracted there to see the first re-
frigerating beer car ever brought to Austin. . . . The ceiling, floor, and
sides of the car are all double, and the ceiling and walls are interlaid
with India rubber which makes it almost airtight. The car was filled
with keg and bottled beer for Mssrs. Brueggerhoff and Heidenheimer,
and these gentlemen had a keg tapped and having taken the precaution
to have dozens of glasses convenient they were inviting people up to
sample the beer."

FIRST ICE CREAM

Reconstruction may have brought Yankee Carpetbaggers to Austin,
but like every cloud with a silver lining, it also brought ice cream to
town, in 1869. 'Twas a great occasion for socializing, young and old.

On June 15, 1869, the *Daily Republican* announced, "Charles W.
Ohrndorf has just fitted up an ice cream saloon, where he will keep ice
cream and lemonade at all hours of the day." A great number of other
ice cream saloons soon followed.

FIRST OIL

They don't call it the *Austin* Chalk for nothing, you know. Oil was
first discovered here back in 1883, just three miles east of the present
Travis County Courthouse. Workers digging a water well struck black
gold at 600 feet; they plugged the hole in disgust. In 1915 a group
of local entrepreneurs attempted to revive the Radam Well, as it was
known, in hopes of striking natural gas.

The first drilling attempts had come much earlier, though, in the
spring of 1872. That March a group of investors from Austin bought ten
acres in what is now Pease Park, on the west shore of Shoal Creek, for
the express purpose of finding oil. They gave up after striking coal at
the depth of 14 feet.

FIRST PAVED STREET

Austin's streets were first paved with brick, and the initial honors
were performed on Congress Avenue, on January 2, 1905.

FIRST TRAIN

Austin's most anxiously awaited gift the Christmas of 1871 was its
first train. Citizens talked of nothing else; the general excitement was
scarcely believable. But, just like every train you've ever waited for, this
one was two hours late. No matter; the cannons roared anyway, and
everyone assembled at the Capitol for a grand reception, supper, and
cotillion. The Senate and House chambers were thrown open for dancing, and supper tables were set up in the basement. More than a thousand Austinites attended.

FIRST SEWER

Now who do you think would get the first sewer service in Austin?
His Nibs's private line ran from the Mansion straight down to Town
Lake ("the River," back then) sometime in the 1880s.

FIRST SKYSCRAPERS

It is fitting that Austin's first skyscrapers stand directly across the street from each other at Austin's choicest crossroads: 6th and Congress.

Construction on the eight-story Scarbrough Building (southwest corner) commenced in February 1910, making it Austin's first skyscraper. So new was this beast to the Texan mentality that in announcing plans for the new structure, the *Austin Statesman* felt compelled to explain: "The building is of a type known as a steel frame building, all weight being carried by the steel frame work and the floors being formed of a reinforced concrete slab, with finish floor laid on top of the slab."

The Scarbrough Building remained Austin's tallest skyscraper for only a few months, however, because Major George Washington Littlefield was charging hard at Lem Scarbrough's heels with his slightly taller "business home." The Littlefield Building (northeast corner) opened in 1911 and was described by *Statesman* pundit Milton Everett: "It is perhaps the most costly building of its size and kind to be found in any city of the commercial importance of Austin in the United States; nothing in Texas can begin to compare with it. It is a "made-to-order" building from sub-cellar to roof garden, even the steel girders and other massive steel parts, which in most buildings of this kind are of stock forms, measurements, and designs, in this instance were specially manufactured for the Littlefield Building. Not a stick of wood has been used in its framework or walls, and in this respect, it rivals the ancient palace of the Mayas, which is said to have fallen after centuries by the decay of the single wooden beam used in its construction."

Everett waxed further: "The construction of the Littlefield Building marks the closing of the provincial or town era of the city of Austin and the beginning of the metropolitan or city era of this place. It is the fore-runner of other improvements and its success in a financial way will encourage other citizens to believe that Austin has a future that will warrant them in making improvements and encourage its early development." His prose was accompanied by a lavish architect's rendition of the building and its immediate street-level environs; and it's interesting to note that among all the pedestrians, horses, buggies, and streetcars there is nary an automobile.

Legend has it that the eighth story of both the Scarbrough and Littlefield Buildings was tacked on at the last minute, as each builder learned of the other's plans—hence the cornice that interrupts the transition from seventh to eighth story on each structure. True or not, Littlefield cemented his claim on "Austin's tallest" title in 1915, when he added an extra story, thereby obliterating the building's delightful and popular Japanese roof garden. But because of his efforts, Littlefield was able to boast briefly of owning the tallest building between New Orleans and San Francisco.

Both these first-generation cloud crackers were eclipsed in 1929 by the elegant Gothic Revival Norwood Building (114 W. 7th). The Norwood also made history as the first skyscraper in America to have an integrally designed air-conditioning system. And all this time the Capitol, seconded by the Tower, stood well above the commercial fray downtown, queen of the Austin skyline. But then along came 1984 and One American Center (northwest corner). Ethics of height and Woolworth's aside, it is the classiest 'scraper to hunker downtown since the Norwood. It can be said that One American Center marks the end of a leisurely chapter in the life of our beloved city and the beginning of another: the biggest and busiest yet.

FIRST TELEPHONE

Austin's first telephone lines appeared on June 1, 1881, linking the Police Station, Miller's Livery Stable, Bremond's store, Forster and Co. Bank, and Ben Thompson's house. The biggest problem encountered in installing this system was finding suitable poles; they ended up using thirty-five-foot cedar poles.

Just for the record, Austin didn't get its first telegraph line until *after* the Civil War, October 1865 to be exact.

FIRST DRINKING WATER

Austin's first drinking water was hauled in whiskey barrels up from the Colorado River, selling for 25¢ per.

FIRST INFORMALITY

The first recorded sighting of informality, for which Austin is justly famous, was made sometime during the 1880s, when it became unfashionable for Austinites to wear hats.

★★★

MYSTERIES AND FANTASIES

MYSTERIES

THE SERVANT GIRL ANNIHILATOR

Ranking up there with London's Jack the Ripper is Austin's own Servant Girl Annihilator. For two years, a maddened axman roamed the darkened streets of the Violet Crown City, searching for the victims of his trade—domestics, working girls—who were invariably hacked to death while sleeping. Altogether, thirteen Austin girls fell prey to this, the unkindest cut of all, the last on Christmas Day 1885. And like Jack the Ripper, the Annihilator's identity has never been unmasked.

THE ENGLER MURDERS

It was just the start of another hotter-than-hell Del Valle August day in 1925, until the visitors stepped across the threshold of Charles

Engler's spacious home. Then they found the bullet-riddled bodies of the prosperous farmer, wife Augusta, and pretty twenty-five-year-old foster daughter Emma. There was no apparent motive.

The sheriff's department "went fishing" with a couple of suspects but didn't catch a thing. So desperate were the white-hats for a nibble that they resorted to the use of a then-new and controversial drug—scopolamine—for the first time in Travis County. Most of us know scopolamine as truth serum.

A related story has one of the suspect's wives cornering him while "under the influence." "What I want to know," she demands of him, "is—have you always been true to me?" His answer is not known.

The case was still alive thirteen years later when *True Detective Mysteries* magazine retold the grisly story and then offered a thousand-dollar reward for information leading to the arrest and conviction of the killer. The reward was eventually withdrawn, and no perpetrator or motive has ever surfaced.

WHAT HAPPENED TO THE GIRAFFE?

"The first and only Giraffe to be ever exhibited in Texas," trumpeted the advertisements during the early fall of 1880. The Greatest Show on Earth was stretching its neck all the way out in promoting its newest mysterious strange attraction, fresh from the depths of darkest Africa.

A full complement of rubberneckers and starry-eyed children were waiting for the great Barnum & Bailey gypsy train as it chugged in from Houston. This greeting committee didn't exactly get what they came for, but they got their money's worth; Giraffe looked and smelled a dead-ringer for a land-locked mackerel, and had since Brenham.

The roustabouts were looking forward to a big barbeque until a public-spirited citizen decided that the children of Austin would not walk away from the circus disappointed. He engrossed the carcass and engaged the services of Mr. Lesterget, Austin's most popular butcher. Lesterget promptly and scientifically skinned the hide and in turn presented it to the local tanner, who performed his peculiar ablutions, and bequeathed the hide to the local taxidermist, who restuffed it to original specs.

Suitably remodeled, *Giraffa camelopardalis* was now ready for the carnival midway, where it could be viewed by the general public for the modest sum of 15¢. (So much for public spirit.) Folks paid the price, gazed upon its remnant beatification, and left, muttering that they had seen it all now.

Being as this particular mother lode played out rather quickly, the giraffe's proprietors/agents offered it up for sale or trade for city property. It sure beats the hell out of a wooden Indian, they suggested to prospective clients. That done, what could those hucksters then possibly do for an encore?

We do not know. We don't even know whether they actually ever managed to palm their four-legged skyscraper off on some cubic rube, much less what ultimately happened to the long-necked pawn in this story. But we can be sure of one thing: an eighteen-foot mercerized giraffe doesn't just gambol off into the sunset one evening, never to be seen again.

PATERNITY AND THE GODDESS

Of her divinity, there is no question. Of her paternity, there is.

Some say she is a mail-order bride, some say E. E. Meyers of Chicago had designs on her, still others swear that an unknown sculptor—probably Belgian—shaped her, struck her, then shipped her off to Austin, where her pieces were assembled in February 1888 on the Capitol grounds.

What we do know of the Goddess of Liberty atop our statehouse dome is that she is sixteen feet tall, built like a warship, and otherwise every bit as statuesque now as she was a hundred years ago.

THE STONE ON THE STEPS

Louis Francke had a powerful thirst, and he was determined to do something about it. A day's labor in the vineyards of the public weal often does that to a man. But at that particular hour of the afternoon, he and his pocketbook weren't on speaking terms. *Pero no es importante*; Fayette County's representative to the Texas Legislature just quick-stepped down the statehouse hall to the sergeant-at-arms's office, where he pocketed his per diem and travel pittances.

Thus armed, he maneuvered down Capitol Hill, down Congress Avenue, hellbent on fulfillment, past the Blue Ruin, past the Last Chance, finally turning into an anonymous little watering hole just the wrong side of the End of the World, where the beer was cold and the talk cheap. He drank his fill, and as there was no lobbyist present to pick up the tab, Francke whipped out a fiver and shoved all but a nickel back in his pocket.

Then he steered back up Congress to Capitol Hill. The black hills to the west were clutching at their violet crowns. Climbing the dark statehouse steps, Francke was ambushed by a pair of deadly swift shadows, who stove in his skull with a large rock. They lightened his pockets and tossed the corpse down the steps before disappearing forever into the night.

Quite a few people had noticed two strange men lounging on the Capitol steps late that afternoon, February 19, 1873, and a grocer recollected selling them some beers, but they were never apprehended.

TREASURY ROBBERY

There was no law to speak of then, save what the citizens could muster up. Lee had surrendered two months ago, Pendleton Murrah had faded into Mexico, General Gordon Granger USA's triumphant entry into Galveston on Juneteenth was still a week away. There was no moon, either.

All in all, a perfect time to strike, that particular Sunday night, June 11, 1865.

The forty-odd brigands, turncoats, bushwhackers, and other assorted scalawags stole into town at a fashionably late hour and up darkened Congress Avenue to Capitol Hill, to the old Treasury building, which stood to the right of the old corncrib-cum-pumpkin Capitol building.

Some stayed outside as lookouts, while the others battered down the doors and proceeded to smash open the safe.

The drummer of the local militia company dicovered the break-in and started to beat a call to arms on his drum. Within minutes, fifteen armed men were marching on the Treasury. Gunfire erupted as the minutemen encountered the lookouts; the militia stood their ground, the outlaws ran. The good guys entered the building with guns blazing, not that it did much harm; only one robber bit the dust. The others escaped into the inky night, some towards Mt. Bonnell, others to the south. No one knew exactly how much they got away with—best estimate was about twenty grand—but much of what they left with was dropped along the roadside as they scurried for cover.

The militiamen found the treasury-room floor knee-deep in silver and gold coins, but neither they, nor anyone else, ever found any of the midnight raiders.

FANTASIES

BURIED TREASURE

The pestilence brought on by the lure of buried treasure seems to be a universal affliction, and Austin has certainly been no exception to the rule.

We have long been possessed of all the right ingredients: skulking Indians, vulnerable Spanish gold trains, skulking bushwhackers, a vulnerable state treasury, skulking robbers, vulnerable bank vaults—you get the picture—multiplied by a multitude of limestone cubbyholes in which to stash the swag.

A buried-treasure map once fell into Will Porter's hands. According to the map, the hoard seemed to rest somewhere in Pease Park. Porter and company hoisted shovels and lanterns one night soon thereafter, and set about retrieving it. These two-legged moles resolved that they would either have the treasure or be standing in the streets of Shanghai by dawn.

Would have, but for the inhuman shriek and accompanying scream that frightened them off. A few hours later, early risers found a state hospital inmate sitting on the edge of the hole with a spade in his hands. They all wondered how he could have dug such a deep hole in so short a time.

Every bit as infectious as the buried-treasure bug is Diamond Fever. Diamond Fever was wreaking havoc around here by 1869, sending countless citizens out into hills in search of bits of crystalline allotrope of carbon.

The *Gazette* observed: "Everybody in Austin will soon have his pocket full of rocks. The search for diamonds is unabated. During the rain, we saw individuals hunting with umbrellas over their heads. We are fearful that digging will commence soon, and that our beautiful city will be undermined."

Another account read: "For some time past, people of all sorts—officers, clerks, white boys and black ones—have been seen roving over our gravelly hills, with their eyes intently fixed upon the ground as if in search of something lost. They are looking for Austin diamonds, not yet found, but they may be—who knows? What they do find are small pieces of crystalized quartz, very hard, hard enough to cut common glass."

★★

NOSHES AND NEBBISHES

FRANK T. BINGAMAN

Austin piano repairman of the early twentieth century. Built world's first "novelty string band"—a machine that played eight different stringed instruments at once, operated by one man. His shop was at 1005 Congress.

COLONEL RICHARD CARMICHAEL

Austin's Colonel Carmichael piloted the first American B-29 to be shot down over Japan in World War II.

M. H. CROCKETT

Father of Texas spinach. In between bites of your next spinach-with-ranch salad, remember to thank him.

Born in Manor and educated in Austin, Crockett greened to spinach during the early years of this century. As a UT student, Crockett began in 1907 to ship out sugar barrels full of his spinach, one or two at a time to far-off markets like St. Louis and Chicago. Although his test runs proved successful, a legion of skeptics told him that spinach could not successfully be grown and shipped such a long way, on so large a scale. He proved them wrong. Through perseverance, Crockett built Austin into the spinach capital of Texas, the country's second-largest spinach shipping point, behind only Norfolk, Virginia. By 1922 Crockett was considered the country's leading spinach authority, and by 1928 he was one of the country's biggest growers.

JOHN W. BRADY

When you come to the subject of falls from grace, it's hard to match the unfortunate plunge of Judge John W. Brady.

A prominent Austin legal fixture and appellate court judge, Brady found himself on the wrong side of the bar on November 10, 1929, arrested for the murder of young Lehlia Highsmith, a Supreme Court stenographer. She had been stabbed to death with a pocketknife on the steps of her E. 10th Street residence the night before, after the Baylor-Texas football game. Brady and Miss Highsmith had been seen at a postgame party together. The arrest rocked the city, and over the next several years produced nearly as many headlines as the dam.

Brady pleaded innocent, by way of an accident that occurred as he was scuffling with an unknown assailant. At his trial, an endless string of his friends and peers, prominent bankers and lawyers, testified that they felt Brady had "lost his mind" due to excessive drinking. The respected pillar of society was in fact a bootleg boozehound and guilty of some of the pleasures that usually accompanied the illicit hooch. This wild life provided Brady with his second line of defense, that his actions were brought about by a recurrent mental disorder brought on by alcohol abuse.

The first trial ended in a mistrial. The next jury convicted him. He served two years before being paroled on July 1, 1932. In her infinite mercy, Governor Ma Ferguson restored his full civil rights the very next year.

CAMELS

Back in 1855 the Pentagon was not above borrowing foreign technology when it thought the imports could get the job done. The job at hand was finding a fast and efficient means of travel through the Great Southwest Desert, which in those days started somewhere between Rosie's Tamale Factory and Paleface Park. The borrowed technology was camels from the Middle East. Nearly three dozen of the spitting ruminants were collected from the region and dispatched to Central Texas, where most of them were to spend the rest of their lives. Forty more reinforcements arrived shortly thereafter, and the lot of them settled down on Verde Creek in Kerr County.

The camels and their jockeys in blue first visited Austin in 1858, and it was while these cud-chewing ships of the desert were docked for the night in South Austin that a herd of cattle sighted them and promptly stampeded.

The camels returned to Austin as civilians in June 1872, on their way to pastures south of town owned by local lawyer Bethel Coopwood. Coopwood had just set up a camel mail and express service from Austin to Mexico City. Coopwood boasted that he could make San Antonio in less than five hours, camel-bound.

The scheme didn't float, and so the humped creatures passed into the possession of Austin's Dr. M. A. Taylor. (He had loaned Coopwood $10,000 to establish the camel express.) Taylor kept them in what is now Tarrytown and loaned them out for all sorts of parades and special events before selling off the grizzled survivors to an itinerant circus.

CRICKETS

Austinites expect and welcome autumn as overdue relief from the long hot summer. And just as surely as we expect the cool evenings and golden leaves of fall, we expect and brace ourselves for the annual autumnal Austin cricket invasion. Central Texas crickets have been coming to Austin to make their winter homes for as long as anyone can remember. The invasion proper is always preceded for several days by scattered reconnaissance buzzlegs. Generally the critters hop for the great canyons of downtown, their sidewalks and cavernous openings; but in good years they will visit you in your home, too.

One of the great invasions of all time was in 1915. Billions of crickets blanketed the city. Wagonloads of them were hauled away day after day. Austin became famous all over Texas and the immediate South as *the* fall resort for crickets. One observer noted further: "Had the cricket invasion been purposely advertised, it is probable that hundreds of tourists would have come to Austin to see the unusual sight and their trip to the state capital would not have been wasted."

GEORGE ARMSTRONG CUSTER

Colonel Custer came to Texas already a war hero, commander of a cavalry division sent to occupy Texas in April 1865. He moved his troops to Austin that fall to prop up the state's Reconstruction government. Only twenty-six and already vainglorious, Custer, his wife and family took as their headquarters the old Blind Institute (now a part of the UT campus and restored to its original appearance). They fell into the Austin lifestyle immediately, picnicking and camping at Mt. Bonnell, Seiders Springs, and Pease Park. Custer liked Pease Park and its stretch of Shoal Creek so much that he built his "bull pens" here; and when thirty-five of his men died with a fever, he buried them here. After a flood in the 1880s washed up some of the bodies, they were exhumed and moved to a national cemetery in Washington.

The Custers left Austin in 1866, so that George might further pursue his career as Indian killer.

E. J. DAVIS

Spare a kind thought for Davis, Texas's most despised citizen. Though his memory is now fading from the Texas mentality, E. J. Davis, governor of Texas from 1870 to 1874, still stands as our most universally disliked Texan.

As Texas's first Republican governor (and its only one for more than a hundred years—a U. S. record!), Davis plunged his party into a hundred-year abyss and caused one prominent state historian to write, "Certainly the name of no Texan has gone down to posterity so hated as his."

Florida-born and Texas-raised, Davis was a district judge by the start of the Civil War. He ran as a delegate to the state Secession Convention, but was defeated. Friends attribute his alienation to the rebel cause to that defeat. As a union officer, he attacked Laredo (unsuccessfully) in 1864. He finished the war a brigadier general. As state constitutional-convention delegate and president, he hewed the radical Republican line: disenfranchisement of ex-rebels and unrestricted Negro suffrage. He also led the movement that nearly split Texas into three states.

As governor he was a martinet and absolutely devoid of political tact. His friends could do nothing wrong, his opponents nothing right. Impeccably bred and personally honest, Davis nonetheless surrounded himself with unprincipled opportunists who took full advantage of their posts. He also dissolved the already legendary Texas Rangers in favor of his own prominently black State Police.

Soundly defeated by Democrat Richard Coke in the 1873 governor's race, Davis refused to give up office when his time came due in January 1874. He called the election law unconstitutional. For a few days that month, the old Capitol building housed two administrations: downstairs sat the Republicans, guarded by Negro militia. The Democrats were upstairs. Davis telegraphed President Grant for military assistance but was refused. On January 17 Davis waved the white flag and retired.

He stayed on in Austin, in his fashionable east Austin residence, practicing law and serving as the state's chief Republican until his death in 1883. Although he ran for office several more times after 1874, he was always ignominiously defeated. Davis is buried on the State Cemetery's prestigious high knoll, alongside the likes of Stephen F. Austin, Bigfoot Wallace, and Albert Sidney Johnston; his graceful obelisk memorial is the cemetery's tallest monument. Davis's brother saw to that.

CHARLEY LOCKHART

Forty-five inches tall, Charley Lockhart of Austin was the shortest man ever to serve as state treasurer. He was also the shortest state treasurer in the United States at the time. He served from 1931 to 1941. Lockhart was succeeded by Jesse James, who in turn begat Warren G. Harding.

THE MICROBE KILLER

Medical "miracles" aren't as common these days as they were a hundred years ago. Austin was the birthplace of at least one of these miracles—the Microbe Killer—invented by William Radam. This was during the 1880s, while the Prussian emigrant was running a feed store and successful commercial nursery. It was not an easy task. Radam suffered from a variety of ailments, and his health was generally poor. He sought cures everywhere, experiencing the successive failures of other folks' miracles.

Then Radam flashed on something: if he was smart enough to invent substances that killed blight, fungi, and microbes on his plants without killing the plants, he could surely do the same thing to the "minute but evil creatures" torturing him. After a year of experimenting, Radam had his Microbe Killer.

He drank large doses of it for six months, by which time he felt and proclaimed himself a new man. Naturally, Radam felt that if it had cured him, the Microbe Killer could certainly do the same for the rest of mankind, ridding the world of most all its diseases, inconsequential and otherwise. By 1890 the Killer was being made in a string of factories that stretched from coast to coast. It cost 5¢ a gallon to make and sold for $3 a jug.

No lot was ever exactly the same, but one analyst found a batch to be 99 percent water, a little red wine, and dashes of hydrochloric and sulfuric acids. Radam was able to move into a mansion on New York's Central Park, where he died in luxury in 1902. While in Austin, Radam built the Koppel Building, in 1888, at 322 Congress.

SOUTH AUSTIN

"Boston has her Dorchester Heights, New York has her Brooklyn Heights, and Austin has her South Austin Heights."—Frederick Cushman, 1910

Ever since there has been a Colorado River, we have had Austin and south Austin, although the city did not officially dip south of the river until the late 1880s, as it debated building the great dam. That original southside outpost, "the Eleventh Ward," consisted basically of the Texas School for the Deaf and Fairview Park, which was a 111-acre subdivision located across S. Congress Avenue from the Deaf School. The *Austin Statesman* had this to say about Fairview Park in 1888:

It occupies an altitude as exalted as that of the Goddess of Liberty, and commands a view of the entire city and surrounding country. Its topography and rural scenery is diversified at every turn. Here the gently sloping hill; there the sylvan dale, ornamented with groves of the stately pecan; here, a cluster of live oaks; there a group of juniper, hackberry or elm. This picturesque park belongs to a private individual, who has laid it off in convenient lots and drives. Water and gas pipes are laid through the park, and it is connected with the city by telephone.

These days, south Austin is celebrated by certain of the *Statesman*'s minions as "BubbaLand," a bucolic province where there's at least one chicken in every backyard, a car on blocks out front, and a bass boat on the side. Clichés do not spring up out of nowhere; but while south Austin has its fair share of Bubbas and K-Marts, so does Austin north of the river. And just as there are people who are proud to be from Brooklyn, there are lots of folks who are proud to be from south Austin.

So how did we get from sylvan glades to BubbaLand? South Austinites will say it's north Austin's fault. They've been saying that for
nearly a hundred years. The ink on the annexation papers was hardly
dry before southsiders began to complain of broken promises, about
lack of water, lights, fire hydrants, streets, and bridges. The water and
lights were working by 1910, but south Austin still considered itself a
stepchild, even Pollyanna southsiders like Frederick Cushman, who
wrote:

> When Austin is struck squarely astern by the tidal wave of pros-
> perity that the knowing ones tell us is coming, South Austin will
> put in her plea for recognition and she will get it, for our home city
> is a square dealer as well as a standpatter. South Austin will not
> rock the boat nor foul the oar, but will simply want the garment cut
> according to the cloth—and only when she receives a moity even
> of what her merits deserve, she will put on her gala attire. Her
> activities shall be such that the liveliest cakewalk comparatively
> will be as a spiritless shuffle.

Well, we doubt that gimme caps and mobile homes were the gala
attire that Cushman envisioned for south Austin, and if he could see
the traffic on Ben White these days, he'd probably move to Dime Box.
But now that the long-awaited tidal wave of prosperity is resolutely
kicking Austin in the behind, we'll see whether south Austin finally
gets its fair shake.

BEN THOMPSON

Ben Thompson had charisma and gall, which caused our most famous city marshall to be alternately adored and damned by the people
he served.

Thompson's origins are obscure. We know he was born in 1843 of
English parentage. Some say he was born in Lockhart. At any rate, he
moved with his parents to Austin shortly thereafter. Thompson first
bloodied his hands while still a shavetail teenager. He deliberately shot
and wounded a playmate. He was tried but not punished. Trained as a
printer, Ben soon abandoned the black-and-white world of Austin for
the blazing reds and golds of New Orleans. After killing a Frenchman
in a knife duel, he escaped back to Austin, where he took up the pur-
suits of printing and gambling. Then the war came. As a Confederate
soldier, Thompson killed or wounded several more men, and not nec-
essarily the enemy. After the war he went to Mexico to fight for the
Emperor Maximilian.

Returning to Austin after Max's demise, Ben spent his first two years
in jail, for a previous murder. Once free, he followed the action to Abilene, Kansas, where he gambled and kept a saloon. He worked as bully-
boy for the Santa Fe Railroad long enough to get a grubstake together,
and headed back to the gambling dens of Austin. He ran for the post of
city marshall but lost. He ran again and was elected. He was reelected
in 1881. While he served, major crime in Austin dropped to an all-time
low.

You didn't mess around with Ben. In 1876 he shot Mark Wilson, owner of the old Capitol Theatre, over some carelessly tossed fire-crackers. He once explained his shooting philosophy, in reference to a man whom he had shot three times, when the first shot got the job done. "The first shot was to make him fall, the second was a precaution in case the first did not finish him—it was to catch him as he fell, the third was to scare the gang in the saloon." Thompson was also a legendary shot. He once matched opinions and bullets with an Austin bartender. The tender fired at Ben and ducked behind his bar. Ben quickly calculated the barkeep's position and fired through the wooden bar panel, hitting the purveyor squarely in the head.

He closed up most of the town's gambling joints, save the handful he was interested in.

Keeping a town on the straight and narrow track is hard work, and nobody begrudged Ben when he had a little fun. Marshall Thompson sometimes took pleasure trips to San Antonio, and during an 1882 jaunt he killed prominent San Antonio gambler, politician, and theater-owner Jack Harris. It was another one of those legendary shots; Thompson couldn't see Harris. Jack was behind a door. Ben ricocheted his shot off a wall and into Harris's heart.

Acquitted after a trial that lasted many months, Thompson was welcomed back to Austin by a big parade and brass band. But he was no longer marshall. He had resigned during the trial.

As Ben Thompson, private citizen, he grew increasingly cantankerous. He would stop trains by driving his buggy across the tracks and pulling a gun on the engineer. Then he would summon an acquaintance from the platform to talk. When Ben was done talking—that might take half an hour—he would holster his hogleg, move his buggy, and wave the engineer on.

The legislature threatened to move the capital out of Austin unless Thompson was made to behave. He had, for instance, shot up a grand banquet of the Texas Cattle Raisers' Association convention. We don't know anymore exactly why he got mad at the cattlemen, but Ben didn't require much in the way of reasons.

The banquet was progressing quite nicely inside the dining room of a Congress Avenue hotel until Thompson strayed in. He wasted no time with words—preferring bullets—and began systematically to shoot the plates in front of the diners. A general stampede ensued.

Afterwards, one of the cowmen was describing the tableau: "You claim Ben Thompson is tough, huh? He got mad at our association but did he jump on the whole convention? No sir! He waited until he caught fifty or sixty of us off to ourselves."

He threatened to kill the *Austin Statesman* editor and a staff writer over remarks made in their paper about the outcome of the Jack Harris murder trial. The paper had said that Thompson should have hanged.

Three or four weeks later, Thompson and the notorious "King" Fischer strolled into the paper's office. They flipped through the clippings file for a minute and walked out. Ben and the King then tied one on and decided to rail it down to San Antonio. That was to be the most serious mistake Ben Thompson would ever make. A courteous, soft-spoken, gentle man when sober, he was both capricious and deadly when liquored up. The bigger the danger, the calmer Ben got.

The late Harris's theater partners, Mssrs. Sims and Foster, had earlier warned Thompson publicly never to set foot inside their auditorium again, or he would be killed. Thompson declared that he was just going to go down there to see if Sims and Foster had the nerve to make good on their threat. He said it a little too loud; someone jumped off the train at San Marcos or New Braunfels and wired ahead to San Antonio. Upon detraining, Thompson and Fischer jumped a hack and were at the theater doors ten minutes later. Five minutes after that they were both dead. Foster was, too. He had been hit by a stray bullet.

The successful ambush made all the papers. Some approved, some alased. The *Statesman* bitterly denounced San Antonio for liquidating one of Austin's most publicized citizens. Sixty-two vehicles made up his funeral procession, and his plot is marked by a simple, shaded marker in Oakwood Cemetery's old section.

Compadre Bat Masterson delivered Thompson's most telling epitaph: "It is doubtful, if in his time there was another man living who equalled him with a pistol in a life-and-death struggle."

W. A. A. WALLACE

"Bigfoot" Wallace moved to Austin in the spring of 1840 and stayed long enough to see the region's last buffalo run down Congress Avenue. Time to move on, he decided; people are getting too thick around here. But as was the case wherever he went, W. A. A. Wallace left his mark on Austin.

Folks called him "Big Bill" then. Soon after his arrival here, Big Bill fell in love with a winsome Austin belle and became engaged to marry her.

Thereafter, an epizootic of the gravest proportions broke out. Oakwood Cemetery—not yet one year old—began earning its keep, and even Big Bill himself came to lie at death's door. An old French woman nursed him back to health, but during his convalescence, all the hair on his head fell out. He was bald as a billiard ball. "A fine-pretty bridegroom I am," he mused, and he resolved to take to the mountains until his hair grew back.

Wallace made his stand on Mt. Bonnell, setting up camp and killing three bears his first week there. They were all very fat, which was very good, since Bill needed a lot of bear grease. He greased and massaged his bare noggin daily with the stuff, washing afterwards in the Colorado River with soap.

In time, a fine baby fuzz grew out, making him resemble a "young buzzard." But no real hair followed. Weeks passed, and Big Bill was increasingly filled with despair. But then it began to sprout out, first in scattered clumps, finally "thick as a horse's tail, like grass after a spring rain." And like Samson with his hair back, Big Bill began to get worked up about life again. His thoughts turned to love, and he decided to lope back into town to see his betrothed.

But just as he was breaking camp, a friend arrived from town with some news. "What do you think, Bill? Your sweetheart has gone and married another man." Bill was momentarily thunderstruck, but then his hackles rose: "I'm glad she's gone—a woman that can't wait till a man's hair grows out, I don't want." He never married.

Wallace earned his new nickname a couple of years later, in the prisons of Mexico. Captured during the Mier fiasco, Wallace found it impossible while in Mexico to buy ready-made shoes for his size 13 feet. He had to commission a Mexican cobbler to make him a pair. The cobbler christened him *Pata Grande*—"Bigfoot"—because he had asked the cobbler to make the shoes "at least two inches extra long for comfort's sake." His name was "Bigfoot" from then on.

★★

FLOTSAM AND JETSAM

MOST EXCITING WEEK IN AUSTIN
May 10–19, 1888
When our great granite statehouse was finally completed in 1888, it took more than a week to celebrate the fact properly. Each day was marked by a Grand Ball, parade, sham battle, or other exciting event. Dedication Day was May 16. Citizens were warned months in advance to be courteous to all the out-of-town guests and not to gouge them.

DARKEST MOMENT IN AUSTIN
April 7, 1900
"Austin has been visited by a great calamity. The granite dam has been destroyed, and the city stands without power, light, and water. The condition is the most serious that has ever confronted a Texas City. There was never a time in the history of our city when there was more real necessity for the citizens to stand together."—*Austin Statesman* editorial

PRETTIEST STREET IN AUSTIN
West Avenue
In 1918 E. C. Bartholomew, city councilman and West Avenue resident, officially proclaimed West Avenue to be the prettiest street in Austin, upon the paving of that road and the first night's lighting of the street's new ornamental lights. Block for block, the fourteen blocks of this, the westernmost of Austin's original streets, is still the prettiest of Austin thoroughfares. See for yourself.

BEST PIPE DREAM
We tend to take our local dams—Longhorn, Miller, and Mansfield— pretty much for granted these days, although we value quite highly the lakes they create, as evinced by AquaFest.

AquaFest is a grand celebration, an ambitious year-round undertaking. Yet even it pales in the face of a 1915 precursor, the *Texas Passion Play*, which was to feature the world's only water-played pipe organ, "played not by the hands of man, but by the waters of a river as they fell over a dam." That river was the Colorado, the dam was "The Dam," precursor to the present Tom Miller Dam.

A series of diapason organ pipes of the lowest note would be constructed at the foot of the dam (pieces of which lie visible just below Miller Dam), to take advantage of the falling waters. Because the "music" of the falling water was of a very fine, low note, the pitch of the pipes had to be low. The pipes were to be arranged in the same order as in a regular pipe organ, and placed in such a way that the water, as it fell over the dam, would run through the pipes. The organ was to be accompanied by a forty-four-piece human orchestra, whose tone evolved around the organ. A special piece of music was composed by Professor Frank Reed that had the water organ playing certain tones, while the other instruments played the rest.

Its inventors proclaimed to the public that "this is the first time in history that anything of this kind has ever been attempted, and owing to peculiar circumstances making this achievement possible, it will probably be the last time." Later on in the show, they announced, the water falling over the dam would "blaze with fire and flames," by means of special electronic effects.

But this grand spectacle had been built upon one, ultimately fatal, premise: that the great dam would be rebuilt in time for the *Passion Play*. It wasn't. By the time the dam was finished, twenty-five years later, "passion" had taken on a whole new meaning, and so had "play," for that matter.

TOURS

★★

TOUR AND GUIDE SERVICES

GUIDED TOURS

Lots of sights for us to see . . .
But sakes alive, I'm scared to drive!
Austin drivers make me cuss.
Honey, let's just take the bus.

AROUND AUSTIN
3305 Northland Dr., Suite 403, Austin 78731
452-3228
Monday through Thursday, 1 p.m., and by appointment
W

Around Austin prides itself on personalized service to both small groups and convention masses. You can take the standard tour of the city at the times given, or make up your own, from antique shops to zither-makers (call to make arrangements). Weekend Hill Country tours (six-person minimum) available. Will pick you up anywhere in Austin.

GRAY LINE OF AUSTIN
7115 Burnet Rd., No. 118, Austin 78757
459-1300; evenings 345-6810 or 836-2255
Seven days, 9:30 and 1:30
W
   Yellow Rose offers two daily guided tours of historic and scenic Austin. Approximate time is two and a half hours. Besides the standard city tour, they offer ten different specialty tours, including the LBJ Ranch, Austin Night Life, Shopping, and Mexican Fiesta. Shuttle service, bilingual guides, group rates.

COMMODORE'S PUP
Docked on Lake Austin
345-5220, 346-0011
Charter
W with difficulty
   This side-wheeler riverboat offers chartered cruises of Lake Austin. Food and entertainment optional. Thirty-person minimum, total capacity sixty. Write Carol Fowler, 6917 Greenshores Rd., Austin 78732.

LONE STAR RIVERBOAT
Hyatt Hotel dock
Southwest
327-1388
Public excursions May through early September; Wednesday, Friday, Saturday, Sunday 5 p.m.
About $6 adults, $4 children
   An old-fashioned paddle wheeler that offers scenic cruises on Town Lake. The public excursion lasts about an hour and a half, summer months only, on days listed. Charter service is available anytime. Capacity is 30–100 people. Public excursion reservations not necessary. Write 1839 Westlake Dr., Austin 78746.

RIVERBOAT COMMODORE
Docked on Lake Austin
346-0011, 346-7438
Charter
W with difficulty
   A large paddle wheeler offering chartered cruises of Lake Austin. Minimum 100 people. Food and entertainment optional. Write Marion Fowler, 6900 Greenshores Rd., Austin 78732.

★★

TOUR AIDS

AUSTIN CHAMBER OF COMMERCE TOURISM DEPARTMENT
901 W. Riverside, between Palmer Auditorium and City Coliseum

South
478-9383
Monday through Friday 9–5
   A tourist info supermarket, the Tourism Department of the Chamber
of Commerce is the first place to contact when planning a trip or a move
to Austin. You'll need a shopping cart to tote away all the brochures on
where to stay and what to do in the Austin and Highland Lakes area.
Even longtime Austinites will find things they didn't know from reading some of these pamphlets. The department staff provides travel
counseling and offers a variety of other services for large groups.

MEXICAN AMERICAN CHAMBER OF COMMERCE OF AUSTIN/
TRAVIS COUNTY
Littlefield Mall, 6th and Brazos
Central
476-7502
Monday through Friday 8:30–5:30
   The Mexican American Chamber of Commerce is Austin's information clearinghouse for Hispanic and Latin American conventions and
visitor development. Any travel agency, tour operator, wholesaler, or
tourism agency with Telex service can contact MACC directly and obtain tourism information. Bilingual staff.

TEXAS DEPARTMENT OF HIGHWAYS AND PUBLIC
TRANSPORTATION VISITOR CENTER
State Capitol, 11th and Congress
Parking on the southeast corner of 11th and Congress or north of the
Capitol in the 1500 block of Congress
Central
475-3070
Open seven days 8–4:30
W+
   The staff at the Visitor Center in the Capitol's south foyer can provide
information and advice on travel around Austin and the rest of the
state. The center also offers a wide selection of where-to and what-to
brochures on Austin and Central Texas.

THE OLD BAKERY AND EMPORIUM HOSPITALITY DESK
1006 Congress
Central West
477-5961
Monday through Friday 9–4
W
   Provides information, brochures, and advice on Austin-area attrac-
tions, as well as information on senior citizens' activities and services.
The Old Bakery is also open Saturday 10–3 during the months of June,
July, August, and December.

★★
OLD EAST AUSTIN DRIVING TOUR

Up to the wee dawn hours of the twentieth century, fashionable Austin lived amidst the lush meadows and gentle green hills east of Waller Creek: ex-governors, prominent bankers, leading tradesmen. But the great dam of 1893 changed all that. The lure of sparkling Lake McDonald (now Lake Austin) proved irresistible, and those lucky few who could afford to do so moved west towards the lake. Healthy land prices are nothing new in Austin; as far back as 1872, an acre at 6th and Shoal Creek sold for a cool millenary. The Swedish and German immigrant families who also settled east of Waller Creek have been slower to leave the area.

Black and Mexican-American families gradually replaced them, moving into the grand old Victorian mansions and charming gingerbread cottages instead of tearing them down; so old east Austin is still richly populated by these venerable old structures, whole blocks worth. They may not all be architectural masterpieces or famous, but they are becoming increasingly attractive to Austinites who desire to own, work in, or live in a piece of Austin's gracious Victorian past. Only a handful of the youngest children—now grown very old—from those long-ago families hang on in the old Swede Hill and Robertson Hill homesteads.

The trip properly begins at the corner of East Avenue (IH 35 South frontage road) and 1st (née Water) Street, the southeast corner of oldest Austin.

Proceed east on E. 1st to Canadian Street. Turn left on Canadian and drive to E. 7th. Turn left on E. 7th. You will turn right a few yards on San Marcos in order to reach the French Legation. From the French Legation, return to E. 7th and proceed the last block back to the IH 35 North frontage road, where the Old East Austin Tour ends.

PALM SCHOOL
700 E. 1st
1892

Otherwise known as the Tenth Ward School, this building served east-side students as such until 1970. Namesake Sir Swante Palm came to Texas a political refugee from Sweden in 1844. In 1866 the Swedish government appointed the by-then–sixteen-year Austin resident vice-consul to the United States. The Republic of Texas Arsenal first occupied the site, followed by an army post.

ROBERT E. RIFE HOUSE
900 E. 1st
ca. 1895

Once this spacious house stood proudly on the prestigious corner of Brushy Street and E. 1st. Now it stands dilapidating on the noisy corner of IH 35 and E. 1st. Most would call it an eyesore, and even the most diehard preservationists would have to agree with them. This was not always so. Once it was a source of public pride, appearing in booklets extolling the virtues of the good life in Austin, 1900 style. Perhaps it is already beyond restoration; if not, it has precious few years of grace left before it implodes under the burden of years of neglect.

MRS. H. V. FOX HOUSE
1000 E. 1st
ca. 1905

Except for the pink-grey asbestos siding, this big house is essentially intact. All the turned porch posts and gable and bracket gingerbread are still there, along with the roofline trim and lightning rods. This is definitely the death knell of the Victorian style; no turrets, arches, or cupolas.

SAM MCDONALD HOUSE
1010 E. 1st
ca. 1905

This little one-story frame cottage is saved from anonymity by its Classic Revival window framings and jigsaw-cut porch brackets.

MORELAND HOUSE
1301 E. 1st
1897

Charles B. Moreland was an Austin paint and wallpaper dealer who did well enough by it to build this two-story frame blend of Queen Anne, Eastlake, and Shingle styles. Tradition honors Moreland as a painter of the Lone Star in our present Capitol dome. The current, distinctive rust-with-green-and-yellow-accents color scheme is in fact of paint faithful to the original; Moreland used leftover paint from his store. Years later, he finally painted it white.

STAVELY-KUNZ HOUSE
1402 E. 1st
ca. 1877, 1897

The two-story limestone Queen Anne house you see out front was built about 1897; the little rock house attached to the back preceded it. Bryant O. Stavely was a farmer, fruit raiser, and real-estate investor. August Kunz, grocer and keeper of the bar at the Lone Star Saloon on E. 6th, bought it in 1897. Some of the original features have been removed. Restoration has been contemplated of late.

WOLF HOUSE
1602 E. 1st
c. 1900

Charles Wolf—"merchant, capitalist, real estate, money broker"—built this stately last gasp of the Victorian era. It bears a family resemblance to the similarly subdued Pierre Bremond House built in 1898. (See Bremond Block Tour.) Also on the site are a hothouse and family laundry. Members of the Wolf family lived here until 1954, and it was a part of the family estate until 1971.

HEADSPETH-SCHULZE HOUSE
1804 E. 1st
1894

J. B. Headspeth built houses for a living in Austin for more than forty years. This house was both shop and residence for him until 1900, when he sold it to daughter Helen and built a fresh one for him and the mis- sus. Its original looks have been muddied by subsequent additions and paint attacks, but the Headspeth House remains distinctly Victorian, with its wraparound porch, turret with carved finial, and sunburst ga- ble. The stained glass in the turret and the slender turned porch col- umns have withstood the slings and arrows of time.

PAN-AM PARK HILLSIDE THEATER MURAL
2100 E. 3rd, at Canadian

Aficionados of mural art find good pickings on the east side, and this is one of the best: bright, vivid, depicting the past, present, and possi- ble future of Mexico-America. It begins on the east wing of the stage and enwraps the theater clockwise. Some of the subsequent graffiti fits comfortably into the scheme of things; some doesn't. Don't miss the dragon's mouth opening to the southeast corner of the Zavala School. The theater actually fronts on E. 4th.

TEXAS STATE CEMETERY
E. 7th and Navasota
1851

This pleasant wooded glade is the final resting place of many famous Texans and Confederate veterans. The late General Edward Burleson first established eternal habitation here in 1851. He had few compan- ions until after the Civil War. As time wore on, the remains of numer- ous departed famous Texans were moved here, chief among them Stephen F. Austin. He has Bigfoot Wallace, among others, to keep him company. Works of art include Elisabet Ney's reclining marble figure of General Albert Sidney Johnston and Pompeo Coppini's bronze statues of Joanna Troutman and Stephen F. Austin.

GENARO BRIONES HOUSE
1204 E. 7th
1939

Briones was one of the best masons in Austin in his time. That skill is shown in the family residence, which he spent fourteen years building. The whole house is dressed in his fanciful stucco work, down to the eaves. He even made the unique lawn furniture out front. You'll have to slow down to appreciate this one. Briones patched up the UT Tower after Charlie Whitman's excesses up there in 1966.

FRENCH LEGATION
802 San Marcos
1841

The Robertsons were the first family proper to move into this Louisi- ana bayou–style home, taking up where Alphonse de Saligny never really left off. (Chances are he never lived here, fearing Indian attacks.) The embassy grounds numbered one-and-twenty acres then. The yard diminished over the years, but the house remained in the Robertson family until 1945, when the state bought it. The house is currently a museum, maintained by the Daughters of the Republic of Texas. (See also Museums.)

ROGERS-LYONS HOUSE
1001 E. 8th at San Marcos
1891
Railroad engineer Martin Rogers built this white-paintedbrick house for his family. The green shutters give it a romantic, New Orleans touch, which compleménts the French Legation just across San Marcos Street. Louis Lyons, prominent black businessman and unofficial mayor of E. 6th, bought it in 1943.

ROBERTSON HILL NEIGHBORHOOD
A good neighborhood to explore, with lots of Victorian-era cottages and even a few storefronts, adjacent to the Legation and Rogers-Lyons home. As you might guess from the name, this neighborhood consists of most of the French Legation's original twenty-one acres. Bounded by San Marcos Street (the Legation), E. 11th, Navasota (the State Cemetery), and E. 7th.

★★
WEST AUSTIN DRIVING TOUR

Beverly Hills, Newport News, Highland Park—all well-known enclaves of the well-to-do. Houston has its River Oaks; Austin has its Tarrytown. Stephen F. Austin wanted to live out here. Elisha M. Pease, Robert Redford, and the Savior of the Alamo actually did. John Hill, Allan Shivers, and Roy Butler still do. Although Austinites have lived out here amidst the first steps up the Balcones since the settlement's earliest days, Tarrytown and the rest of west Austin did not really begin to flesh out until after the great dam's completion in 1893. Greater Tarrytown (as defined and abused by the laws of the Sunday paper's "Houses for Sale" ads) is bounded roughly by W. 35th, Lake Austin Boulevard, Enfield, and the MoPac expressway (Loop 1).

But we are getting slightly ahead of ourselves. Even greater west Austin was first divided into a handful of great estates, such as Elisha M. Pease's 365-acre "Enfield." Between the end of Reconstruction and the advent of World War II, these prominent landowners and their descendants divided up and sold their holdings, giving rise to early, glitzy subdivisions: Edgemont, Pemberton Heights, Westfield. But all was not glitter and glory. Tucked away in the rises and ravines west of W. Lynn was Clarksville, a community of freedmen and their families that began during the waning days of Reconstruction. MoPac took a chunk out of the Clarksville neighborhood, and young white professionals now find Clarksville a fashionably lowbrow/downscale place to live. Still, Clarksville clings stubbornly to its traditional identity, even though its streets have recently been paved. It is listed in the National Register of Historic Districts.

You see it all on this driving tour, along with some great views of Lake Austin. These roads wind around a lot, so keep your rubber-necking down to a level commensurate with the center stripe and un-wrinkled fenders.

Start at 6th and Congress, heading west on 6th towards Lake Austin. Before you finish the first block, you pass O. HENRY HALL (601 Colorado), Austin's first Federal Building, built in 1878. O. Henry's 1898 embezzlement trial was conducted here, hence the name. Abner Cook built it; the University of Texas System now uses it for offices, just as they use Austin's second Federal Building (220 W. 6th), now called CLAUDIA TAYLOR JOHNSON HALL. The latter was begun in 1912, finished in 1914, and designed to blend in harmoniously with its older brother.

Cross Lamar and turn left one block later on Baylor to reach the TREATY OAK (503 Baylor; see Picnic Spots) and the RAYMOND-MORLEY HOUSE (510 Baylor). John Raymond was one of those early land barons, and he built this place in 1877. Turn back onto W. 6th briefly, for you will turn right onto Blanco only a block later. But in that block of W. 6th, you pass the SMOOT HOUSE (1316 W. 6th). This stretch of 6th was once lined with fine old mansions like that of the Reverend Richmond K. Smoot. The clay for the bricks came from Barton Creek, and O. Henry married Athol Estes in the front parlor in 1887.

Once on Blanco, you begin to climb "Castle Hill." Some of west Austin's oldest homes are along this street and atop this hill. The HILL HOUSE (910 Blanco) has been occupied by the Hill family since the house was built in 1890. Austin's only remaining volunteer-built fire station still stands at 1000 Blanco. Constructed in 1907, it has recently been remodeled.

At 11th turn right, so that you may see the "castle" for which the hill is named. The TEXAS MILITARY INSTITUTE (1111 W. 11th) is Texas's oldest standing college building (1869) and was its first military school. Restored stone cottages at 11th and Blanco and at 1105 W. 12th are believed to have been TMI outbuildings. TMI eventually grew up and became Texas A&M.

Continuing north up the hill on Blanco, you come to W. 12th and the MARTIN-CABANISS HOUSE (1200 Windsor), one of the few examples of Steamboat Gothic architecture in town. It was built in 1887.

Turn left on W. 13th, then right on W. Lynn. After crossing Enfield, veer left onto Niles, passing first the Spanish Renaissance home of Roy and Ann Butler (2 Niles Road, built in 1930 for W. S. Drake), then WOODLAWN (6 Niles Road). Abner Cook built this grand Greek Revival house in 1853 for James Shaw. Governor Elisha Pease bought it in 1857. It remained in his family until 1957, when former governor Allan

Shivers bought it. Pease named his house Woodlawn after his Connecticut home. Several streets in the Enfield vicinity, like Hartford and Windsor, reflect Pease's home state in their names.

Turn right on Hartford, then left onto Windsor. Proceed west on Windsor to Sweetbrush. Turn right on Sweetbrush to catch a glimpse of SWEETBRUSH (2408 Sweetbrush). Abner Cook built this great house downtown for Colonel John Swisher in 1852. Dr. Zachary Scott bought what was left of it in 1925 for $300. They dismantled it in 1931 and rebuilt it brick by brick. Finish the loop you have started, and when you return to Windsor, continue straight across Windsor on what is now Rockmoor. Follow Rockmoor's convoluted path for several blocks, then turn right on Kennelwood. After making a hard ninety-degree turn to the right, Kennelwood becomes Scenic Drive, one of Austin's oldest roads. The Mormons built it in the early 1840s in order to travel back and forth from their gristmill on the Colorado River.

Of the many beautiful and expensive homes on Scenic Drive, one enjoys something of a celebrity status. The HART HOUSE (2006 Scenic) was the home of Robert Redford's grandmother. He summered here as a youth. It has, of course, a beautiful view of Austin.

Several blocks later, Scenic Drive crosses Taylor's Slough. This area was first developed by the Mormons, who built a mill on the falls of the Colorado nearby. Known in the past as Mt. Bonnell or Mormon or Taylor Springs, the Taylor Slough area once counted more than fifty separate freshwater springs, most of which have been inundated by Lake Austin. A plantation house, brick and lime factory, and cement factory were built here. Later it became a favored picnic and boating spot. Most all of this early development is gone, but the lime kiln still stands in Reed Park.

Scenic Drive eventually dead-ends into Pecos. Turn right on Pecos and continue to REED PARK (2600 Pecos), where you can see the lime kiln. From Reed Park, continue south on Pecos a few long blocks to Tanglewood. Turn right on Tanglewood, and shortly you will see the DONNAN HOUSE (2528 Tanglewood Trail). This elaborately decorated Victorian frame house originally stood at W. 11th and Lavaca. Attorney general John Hill and wife Bitsy moved the house out here, and restored and enlarged it to its present glory.

Finish the loop you have started, and when you come back to Pecos, continue straight across Pecos on what is now Greenlee. Stay on Greenlee to Hillview. This area and the acreage around Taylor's Slough were among the last pockets of west Austin's Hill Country to be developed.

Turn left on Hillview, which becomes Westover. Cross Exposition and MoPac before turning left on Jefferson. Turn right on W. 29th. You will turn right onto Wooldridge shortly; but before you do, go a few yards further on W. 29th to the BOHN HOUSE (1301 W. 29th). Chester Nagle designed this house, which overlooks Shoal Creek. It was built in 1938 and is Austin's best example of the Art Moderne style. Now you will have to backtrack a few yards on W. 29th to get back to Wooldridge. Go south on Wooldridge, following its wandering path to the intersection with Windsor.

Turn left on Windsor and continue south on Windsor, rather than veering off on W. 24th. Proceed on Windsor's rambling path, past ivy-covered houses from the 1920s. Turn left on W. 12th and descend Castle Hill to N. Lamar. The tour is now over, but there is one more attraction, the ENFIELD GROCERY (1201 N. Lamar). The building was built in 1914 and features gable carvings by Peter Mansbendel. It now houses the Tavern restaurant and bar.

★★

WEST AVENUE DRIVING TOUR

West Avenue began life in 1839 as just that—Austin's westernmost thoroughfare, civilization's last outpost west for the next 600 miles. West Avenue has long been a prestigious address; a string of mansions and elegant homes dating back to the 1850s attest to that. So does West's "Avenue" surname. City councilman Ed Bartholomew confirmed our suspicions in 1918, when he officially proclaimed West Avenue to be the prettiest street in Austin.

Although there are some condominium distractions, this rolling avenue, along with Rio Grande, retains the grace of old Austin almost as fully as does the Bremond Block, as well as providing an excellent representation of the progressions in building materials and styles in Austin over the years.

Begin at the corner of W. 6th and West Avenue, proceed north to Martin Luther King, turn right, then turn right on Rio Grande and continue to the tour's end at W. 6th and Rio Grande.

ROBINSON HOUSES
715, 717 West Ave.
1872

John H. Robinson, Sr., of the Bremond Robinsons, built these almost identical one-story Greek Revival limestone rubble houses for members of his family in 1872. Only a few years later, son-in-law Eugene Bremond conceived and began building the Bremond block for the two related-by-marriage families.

MONTGOMERY HOUSE
808 West Ave.
1886

This recently restored Renaissance Revival house overlooks Shoal Creek. Note the elaborate gilt Corinthian caps on the porch columns.

FISCHER HOUSE
1008 West Ave.
1882

Joseph Fischer was a stonemason, recently arrived from Prussia, when he and son Francis built this one-story brick house with Italianate details. They also helped build the granite Capitol.

GILBERT HOUSE
1402 West Ave.
1896

Local gambler Richard Coon commissioned this spacious building, built with handmade local brick and lumber imported from New Orleans. By 1900 laundry magnate Phillip Bosche had moved in; he was succeeded by Dr. Joe Gilbert and family. The original Victorian turret and wraparound gallery were removed in the 1920s in favor of the current Colonial/Greek Revival features.

D. H. CASWELL HOUSE
1404 West Ave.
1899

Daniel Caswell was a prominent cotton merchant and civic leader. A. O. Watson designed this sprawling, rusticated limestone home; its fat Richardsonesque tower has amused Austinites for years, reminding one local architectural historian of "a clown in his cap." Recently the house has been exquisitely restored and is available for parties and weddings.

W. T. CASWELL HOUSE
1502 West Ave.
1904–1905

William Caswell was Daniel's equally prominent son and helped forge the Austin Parks and Recreation System that we enjoy today. His Classic Revival mansion contrasts sharply with that of Dad's house across 15th. There were originally three Caswell homes located atop this commanding hill. The 15th Street extension wasted the middle house.

WESTHILL
1703 West Ave.
ca. 1855

Abner Cook designed this unique split-level Greek Revival house to conform to the sharply sloping hill. What you see from West Avenue is the back door, largely obscured by magnolias and shrubbery. The grand double-gallery entrance with its six Doric columns faces Rio Grande; visitors originally reached the house via a circular flagstone drive out front.

H. B. HANCOCK HOUSE
1717 West Ave.
ca. 1870

Hancock was a black businessman and saloon keeper and had this tidy Greek Revival cottage built on Robertson Hill, near the French Legation. It was moved here in 1979.

DENNY-HOLIDAY HOUSE
1803 West Ave.
1870

Charles Denny built a one-story limestone cottage here about 1870.

Mrs. N. L. Holiday bought it in 1898 and added the second story in 1906. The five fireplace mantels inside were carved by Peter Mansbendel. The exterior walls have long been stuccoed. What you see from West Avenue is actually the back of the house.

GOODALL WOOTEN HOUSE
1700 W. Martin Luther King
1899

This luxurious Classic Revival house was one of Austin's earliest repudiations of the flamboyant Victorian styles. Prominent local physician Goodall Wooten paid $19,000 for it. The impressive Ionic columns were carved by the same man who carved the columns for "Biltmore," the Vanderbilt family's house in North Carolina.

J. B. POPE HOUSE
1806 Rio Grande
1912

A. O. Watson demonstrated his ability to stay abreast of the times when he designed this four-story Classic Revival home for his sister and brother-in-law. The interior features many Peter Mansbendel carvings, added in 1924.

JACOB LARMOUR HOUSE
1711 Rio Grande
1875

Jacob Larmour came to Austin in 1871 as the town's first "official" architect. He had this cottage built in 1875. In 1879 he was named state architect. Through the end of the century he played a major role in the design of many of Austin's commercial and residential buildings. The cottage was relocated from 1909 Whitis in 1979.

GARDNER-RUGGLES HOUSE
1600 Rio Grande
ca. 1898

The Gardner-Ruggles is definitely Victorian, but a Victorian in transition, with both a Queen Anne turret and a shingled second-story and porch awning. The latter was no doubt in imitation of its trendy neighbor a few yards away on West Avenue, the E. M. House house (razed 1966).

NUMBERS-HAND HOUSE
1205 Rio Grande
ca. 1870

It's really easy to overlook this house altogether. Most onlookers would never guess it to be as old as it really is. Numerous additions and changes have been made over the years.

OLD AUSTIN HIGH SCHOOL
1212 Rio Grande
1915

This Classic Revival building, home of Austin High School for nearly fifty years, is now the main campus of Austin Community College.

PEASE ELEMENTARY SCHOOL
1106 Rio Grande
1876

Austin's oldest public school and the first in the state to be built with public funds. It stands considerably simplified from its original appearance, having once sported Second Empire styling, with a mansard roof and center tower.

SAMPSON HOUSE AND CARRIAGE
1003 Rio Grande
1875–1877

George W. Sampson, Captain CSA and Austin merchant, built this house out of limestone quarried at the site, for $8000. A cistern stored water for what was probably Austin's first complete indoor plumbing system. From Rio Grande you can see the original Italianate lines of the porte cochere. The front gallery with Corinthian columns, which faces 10th, was added in the 1920s.

BOSWELL HOUSE
801 Rio Grande
1905

Local businessman William A. Boswell had this three-story Georgian Revival house built for the grand sum of $1800.

JOSEPH SAYERS HOUSE
709 Rio Grande
Date unknown

Turn-of-the-century Texas Governor Joseph Sayers and his family lived in this rather plain two-story brick box, ornamented only by the flowery metal cornice.

ROBINSON-WAGNER HOUSE
706 Rio Grande
ca. 1860

One-story, handmade brick painted white, five-bay porch, Greek Revival, minimal detailing. Earliest known resident was Alfred H. Robinson.

ROBINSON-MACKEN HOUSE
702 Rio Grande
1887

This two-and-a-half-story house in the Second Empire style is one of the few of its type left in Austin, and its name reflects two of Austin's oldest and most respected families. Restored in early 1984.

★★
CONGRESS AVENUE WALKING TOUR

At nearly 150 years of age, Congress Avenue has recently been undergoing its greatest transformation ever. New skyscrapers have sprouted up and down its eleven principal blocks, and most of the remaining old buildings have been restored to their former glory. The Avenue, as it is often called, has been placed on the National Register of Historic Places. The recent Congress Avenue beautification project has achieved its intended effect—all of which makes Congress Avenue unique among Texas's great downtown streets. Congress Avenue is living proof of Austin's notable success in the field of downtown revitalization.

The Avenue's four newest giants represent a refreshing turn away from the snowdrift somnolent glass cubes of the 1970s, having prominently employed native stone or brick. One American Center and Capitol Center have taken an additional, daring step backward into the past by gainfully employing some purely decorative arches and gables. Thus they have proved that young upstarts *can* blend in harmoniously with the Capitol and its peers.

Hidden for decades by bland Moderne masks, the riotously detailed, restored facades of the Avenue's many remaining nineteenth- and twentieth-century buildings again invite a leisurely gaze. Buildings will continue to come and go on the Avenue, but the Capitol will always be king; local zoning laws see to that. There are so many sights to see—not to mention the traffic—that it is best to explore Congress Avenue by foot.

PEARL HOUSE
225 Congress at 3rd
ca. 1885

Hermann and Lena Schmidt were the first occupants of this two-story cast iron–fronted building. Their Pearl House was a hotel saloon and restaurant, conveniently located across 3rd (Cypress) from the railroad depot. Until the recent burst of restoration activity, Pearl House was one of the Avenue's most visible Victorian structures, still fully possessed of its original lines, down to the angled one-bay entrance.

SUTOR BUILDINGS
308–314 Congress
1876

Part of the Sutor Hotel complex, 1903–1968. Local brick, simple lines.

W. B. SMITH BUILDING
316 Congress
ca. 1889

W. B. Smith, local dry goods merchant, built this two-story limestone building with local brick six-bay facade sometime between 1884 and 1889. The structure is a good example of that period's commercial architecture, with the popular stepped, Alamoesque arched top. Smith died a few years later, and over the years the building has housed a variety of tenants, most notably the legendary Vulcan Gas Company, precursor to the Armadillo World Headquarters.

SWIFT AND COMPANY BUILDING
317 Congress
ca. 1905

Originally occupied by the meat-packing firm of the same name, this structure was made with local brick and minimal detailing. It was restored in 1982 in conjunction with the adjacent Day and McKean-Eilers Buildings.

DAY BUILDING
319 Congress
1886

This two-story brick building is saved from anonymity by its offset tower, which bears the name of the man who built it: J. M. "Doc" Day, one-time partner of Jesse Driskill. Early tenants were a grocer and a farm-implement dealer. The building housed a hardware store from 1914 to 1981.

MCKEAN AND EILERS BUILDING
321 Congress
1897

Hidden behind a flat, bland stucco facade until recently, the restored McKean and Eilers Building reflects a late Victorian commercial style first made popular in Chicago and New York. Texas grey granite, Burnet County red granite, Pecos sandstone, Austin brick, and copper cornice detailing were combined with lots of windows along simpler, Romanesque lines. The December 12, 1897, *Austin Statesman* described the just-finished building as "a palatial edifice of modern classic architecture . . . elegant, in a quiet dignified manner." McKean and Eilers was the only wholesale dry goods concern in Austin with a New York office.

KOPPEL BUILDING
322 Congress at 4th
1888

This two-story brick Gothic Revival building bears the name of Jacob and Sam Koppel, but it was built by William "The Microbe Killer" Radam. (See Noshes and Nebbishes.) Previous to 1982 restoration, a flophouse. Restoration tacked the long-departed corner towers and chimney finials back up on top.

327 CONGRESS AVENUE
327 Congress at 4th
1984

No one is ever going to mistake this five-story brick building for a contemporary of any of its immediate neighbors, but the clock tower and full-length colonnades show that it was designed to blend in comfortably with them.

SOUTHWESTERN TELEGRAPH AND TELEPHONE BUILDING
410 Congress
1886

Historian Frank Brown, author of *Frank Brown's Annals,* first owned this little building. Southwestern Telegraph and Telephone bought it and renovated it in 1898. Local architect A. O. Watson added the multi-material (granite, brick, limestone) Romanesque Revival facade. Compare its lines to those of the McKean and Eilers, built one year earlier.

JAMES H. ROBERTSON BUILDING
416 Congress
1893

Painstakingly—with a capital "P"—restored in 1983, the Robertson Building is the most richly textured building on Congress, and along with the Tips Building its most exuberant. With the completion of the Capitol in 1888, red granite became a very popular building material. Foreshadowing its upcoming neighbors the Southwestern T&T and McKean-Eilers Buildings, the Robertson structure made use of granite, as well as limestone and imported red brick. The third story shows off the Avenue's best example of bichrome brickwork, now largely vanished. Note how subdued styles had become just four years later.

SCARBROUGH BUILDING
512 Congress at 6th
1910

Along with its rival the Littlefield Building, the Scarbrough Building is more notable for its height than for its looks. The eight-story structure was Austin's first commercial skyscraper. Stylistic distinction came a few years later when the black Art Deco facade was added. E. M. Scarbrough came from a prosperous dry goods business in Rockdale and set up shop on this corner in the early 1890s. When built, this retail-office building had all the latest amenities, including a vacuum-cleaning plant with connections on each floor and a cooling system that circulated air that had been cooled by passing over refrigerated pipes. Until 1982 it served as spiritual home of the local department store empire that still bears Lem's name in the malls.

LITTLEFIELD BUILDING
601 Congress at 6th
1910, 1915

The year 1910 was a great one for architecture in Austin. The eight-story Littlefield Building followed hot on the heels of the Scarbrough Building as Austin's second skyscraper. Both were immense sources of public pride, and local papers devoted reams of copy to each move of the respective stonemasons and carpenters. (See also First, Biggest, Best—First Skyscraper.)

ONE AMERICAN CENTER
600 Congress at 6th
1984

New for 1984, One American Center represents a new breed in sky-scrapers, Austin style. Its three graduated towers sport a skin of Texas limestone with red Texas granite accents. Pillars, arches, and mansarded roofs give it classic lines designed to fit in with, rather than disrupt, the Avenue's vintage architecture. One American Center is every bit as significant for us as the Littlefield was for the Austin of 1910. Nevertheless, One American Center has met with more public disparagement than praise, because of its height and the fact that it replaced a much-loved Woolworth's store and luncheonette.

SAMPSON-HENDRICKS BUILDING
620–622 Congress at 7th
1859
Abner Cook built what is now the oldest remaining building on Congress for merchant Captain George W. Sampson. Its mild Italianate style broke new ground in an otherwise Greek Revival Austin. Excellent craftsmanship marks this three-story ashlar-and-rubble limestone building. It was restored and renovated in 1983 as part of the One American Center project.

EDWARD TIPS BUILDING
708 Congress
Early 1870s
The origins of this building are shrouded in mystery. Edward Tips started Tips Hardware in 1857. He died in 1872, and his brother Walter took over the business at this location. The current facade dates to 1877; once Walter was moved into his Venetian palace next door, he remodeled this two-story building to conform to it. Inside walls were opened up to link the buildings, and they operated together as such until the Tips Company moved out early in the next century.

WALTER TIPS BUILDING
710 Congress
1877
Austin eagerly welcomed the arrival of the iron horse in 1871, correctly anticipating the economic prosperity it would bring. The accumulating wealth began to show itself most conspicuously in a building boom that began about 1875. Walter Tips's Venetian palace of hardware was the most ambitious building of its type and era. Jasper Preston, who would later design the Driskill and supervise construction of the new Capitol, was given free reign in designing this $30,000 building. Preston did not resort to the use of mail-order cast-iron adornments until he reached the cornice. The first three stories are carved limestone, down to the elaborate column capitals and arch detailings. Franklin Savings, which makes a habit of restoring historic buildings for use of branch offices, did the honors on this Avenue showplace in 1980, and it now serves as the savings association's home office. Tips's business moved from here in 1905; in the meantime, he had established the Tips Foundry and Machine Company and Tips Engine Works. One of Tips's old steam engines now sits in the foyer.

PARAMOUNT THEATRE
713 Congress
1915

This Neoclassic theater looks older than it actually is, but its quiet lines stand in stark contrast to both the loud Victorian palace and castle across the Avenue and other moving picture palaces of its era. Sarah Bernhardt played here on her swan-song tour. It is now primarily a performing-arts theater. Perhaps the architects were saving their breath for the interior, which has been expertly restored and is alone worth the price of admission.

JOHN A. BARCLAY AGENCY
716 Congress
ca. 1870

Just two doors up from the Venetian palace is this Gothic castle built about 1870 for C. R. Johns and Company, Bankers and Land Agency. Having set up shop some ten years earlier on this spot, Johns and Company was Austin's first insurance agency. The fortress-like crenellations and towers were not idle whimsy; neither were the cathedral-like Gothic arched windows. Folks didn't trust banks or insurance peddlers much back then. The fortifications suggested permanence and impenetrability. Stylistically, it was a ground-breaking building for Austin, an attempt to bring the city into the civilized era, as C. R. Johns put it. One of the Avenue's most recent restorations, it was also one of the most difficult. Most of the original facade, including the fortifications, had been removed or covered with stucco; amidst a minor storm of controversy, restorers elected to duplicate the original facade using new limestone cut in Cedar Park.

OPENHEIMER BUILDING
105–109 W. 8th
1894

As nineteenth faded into twentieth century, Victorian tastes in architecture were simplifying. The Queen Anne style, imported from England, became popular. Its principal features were bay windows (oriels), lots of glass, and restrained classical ornamentation. The Openheimer Building, whose facade remained relatively intact and unchanged over the years, is a good example of the Queen Anne commercial style. It is about the only example left in Austin. Louis M. Openheimer was a prominent local businessman and major general in the Texas National Guard. John McDonald designed the building. (McDonald was mayor of Austin from 1889 to 1895 and was responsible for bringing the dam to Austin. The lake it created was named in his honor.) Renovated in 1980, the original jigsaw brackets support the three pressed sheet-metal bays, and each of the entry doors still sports original stained-glass panels. The steps west up the hill add a touch of romance.

JOHN C. BOAK BUILDING
801 Congress at 8th
Late 1880s
   Boak and partner W. H. Fiquet built this three-story brick and limestone building to house their furniture business. Like the earlier Pearl House and its peer the Koppel Building, the Boak Building sports an angled one-bay entrance once common to street corner commercial buildings.

LONG'S LIVERY STABLE AND OPERA HOUSE
901 Congress at 9th
1860s
   One of the oldest remaining buildings on Congress Avenue. In 1871 the Austin Opera House moved into the second story of this building, over M. M. Long's Livery Stable. It turned saloon in 1877.

MILLET OPERA HOUSE
110 E. 9th
1878
   C. F. Millet's limestone rubble Opera House was Austin's first proper one. Earlier it had camped out over City Hall and Long's Livery Stable. But even the Millet Opera House was makeshift, in a way. Millet had built here a few years earlier and had used the structure to house hardware and products from his planing mill. F. E. Ruffini and Jasper Preston were hired to enlarge and remodel it into a first-rate opera house in 1877. It was eagerly awaited, and the papers reported nearly every stone as it was laid into place. The legislature met here in between capitols. Double-front galleries in the Classic Revival style were added in 1911, changing its looks considerably.

905 CONGRESS AVENUE
905 Congress
Early 1870s, 1933
   Styles had changed considerably by 1933, but bankers were still not above invoking divine assistance in the facades of their institutions. The dress on this little gem may be Art Deco on the edge of Moderne instead of Victorian Gothic, but its classic temple inspiration shines clearly. It is made of hand-carved native limestone.
   The brick building behind the shell dates to the early 1870s, when the back part of it served as shop area for Long's Livery Stable. A couple of cleats still embedded in the mortar of the back wall were used by Long's mechanics; with some stout rope, they could lift carriages off the ground to work on them.

LARMOUR BUILDINGS
906–916 Congress
ca. 1876
   Local architect Jacob Larmour built nine buildings in a row here in the 900 block of Congress during the mid-1870s. Although each had its own distinct detailing—an arch here, some volutes there—they were

all of the same basic design, with carved limestone facades and cast-iron cornices. Six of them stand today, in various stages of restoration. The last three buildings on the block (918–922) are of the same period, but were not part of the Larmour series. None is particularly distinguished, but collectively they stand as an example of the way downtown Austin looked in its early boom years. Larmour was the only architect listed in the first city directory (1872–73), and along with two other architects, Larmour "was noted to have had a virtual monopoly on the design of most local and state buildings constructed in the 1800s," according to one historian.

CAPITOL CENTER
921 Congress at 10th
1984

The Avenue's other good example of how modern skyscrapers can be made to blend in tastefully with the Avenue's historic tradition. Native sunset-red granite, and wonder of wonders, pillars and a pediment!

WOOTEN BUILDING
107–109 E. 10th
1876

One of Austin's most entertaining buildings, containing a minilesson in Austin's early architectural styles. It started life as a single two-story rectangle with Gothic and Romanesque features. Thomas Wooten was both a prominent physician and University of Texas regent. He commissioned this building upon his arrival in Austin in 1876. In 1895, when sons Joe and Goodall were ready to join him in practice, he enlarged the building and added the Queen Anne bay with its party-hat dome. Shortly before World War I, caught up in the Renaissance Revival, the boys added the Corinthian columns, entablature, cornices, and balustrades.

THE OLD BAKERY
1006 Congress
1876

This long, lean-of-face building has been an Avenue landmark for some time, but even so it has faced several brushes with oblivion, the most recent in 1970. The Highway Department first planned to waste the bakery and everything else on the block in favor of a new headquarters building. Bowing to pressure, the department next proposed to incorporate the bakery into the new building. Legislators finally nixed the new HQ altogether, decreeing that the bakery be left alone and the rest of the vacant block be left as a park and visitor's parking area.

The Old Bakery was originally built for Charles Lundberg, a recently arrived Swedish emigrant. After becoming king of Austin's bakers here, he went on to organize the Austin National Bank. Gracefully proportioned, the building is limestone with a brick facade. Arches provide another rare example of the bichrome brickwork once so common in Austin. The dramatically poised eagle has been on duty since day one.

The north side of the building is a curious patchwork pattern of brick and limestone. In fact, the brick center section joined the bakery with a rear warehouse, which had previously been separated by chicken coops and washlines.

★★

HISTORIC WALKING TOUR

BREMOND BLOCK
Between W. 7th, Guadalupe, W. 8th, and San Antonio
Central West
W by car
When you are at the corner of San Antonio and high W. 7th, buried in the Bremond Block, you are in old Austin. This peaceful, shaded oasis in the heart of the city epitomizes the Austin of fifty, eighty, and one hundred years ago—a stately, tranquil city, with fine old homes and wide, cool lawns under big shady trees.

The John Bremond and John Robinson families, linked by three marriages, made this block entirely their own over a period of thirty years. Although other family homes were built nearby, this block remained the center of family activity. The alleys served as playgrounds for the children. The six houses on this block are a diverse yet harmonious collection of architectural styles. Nearby period homes contribute to the effect. A lushly planted limestone cliff still splits W. 7th into high and low for a block, between San Antonio and Guadalupe. The homes are all either offices or private residences.

You can drive the block, but to enjoy it to its fullest, park nearby and stroll it. Start at the corner of W. 8th and Guadalupe.

JOHN BREMOND/HALE HOUSTON HOUSE
706 Guadalupe
This little dogtrot cabin with subsequent Greek Revival embellishments is the oldest house on the block, dating to the 1850s. The brick sidewalk is original, as is the picket fence. John Bremond bought the place in 1863. He died in 1866, and son Eugene moved his family in.

WALTER BREMOND HOUSE
711 San Antonio
Eugene Bremond had the house built as a wedding present for his son Walter in 1887. Its elegant New Orleans style makes it a favorite of many. This is a relatively recent development; about thirty years ago, some of the exterior Victorian fixtures were removed, and a wrought-iron railing was added to the front balcony to emphasize the house's French qualities. There is a three-level cottage out back. The house was designed and built by prominent architect George Fiegel.

MCLAUGHLIN HOUSE
800 San Antonio, on the opposite corner from the Walter Bremond House
   This three-story limestone rubble and stuccoed brick home is one of the block's supporting players, built in 1876 for Dr. J. W. McLaughlin, Sr.

BELLEVUE (NORTH-EVANS CHATEAU)
708 San Antonio
   Harvey and Catherine North were prominent neighbors of the Bremonds and Robinsons, and they built several houses of their own across San Antonio from the block. The Norths moved to Austin from Connecticut about 1870. By 1874 they had built a French chateau out of Texas limestone. They called it Bellevue, and it was dramatically situated atop a hill, at the end of a cliff created by an old quarry. The neighbors called it North's Folly. In 1884 subsequent owners Major and Mrs. Ira Evans expanded the chateau into a Romanesque castle, with the help of San Antonio architect Alfred Giles.

BELLEVUE COTTAGE
706 San Antonio
   Harvey North built this brick cottage next door in 1879 as a home and music studio for daughter Athalia. She had been studying music in Europe and was sailing back to her new home when she caught pneumonia. She died in New York City, never having seen her Bellevue.

CATHERINE ROBINSON HOUSE
705 San Antonio
   Back on the Bremond Block, merchant banker Eugene Bremond built the first story of this limestone and brick house in 1872. In 1885 he added the second story, along with the Classic Revival double-front gallery. Catherine, Eugene's niece, was the house's longest tenant, having lived all but a few of her eighty-eight years here.

NORTH-HOWSON FLATS
700 San Antonio
   Before Harvey North's death in 1881, the family had also built this three-and-a-half–story apartment house. It was built into the steep cliff of the old quarry. The widowed Catherine North moved in after her husband's death and rented out the remaining apartments. Emilie Howson bought it in 1925. A large stone and brick cistern is at ground level.

EUGENE BREMOND HOUSE
404 W. 7th
   Eugene Bremond actually conceived the idea of a family-owned block. He built this one-story frame house (the only frame house on the block) for his second wife, Augusta Palm, in 1877. It has a New Orleans–style appearance, but as with the Walter Bremond House, some of the original Victorian features were removed, simplifying its looks. The home was owned continuously by the family until the mid-1970s.

PIERRE BREMOND HOUSE
407 W. 7th

This was the last house built by the Bremonds. Although grand and definitely Victorian, the tan brick residence is subdued in style when compared to its older brother next door. Eugene had this house built in 1898 as a wedding present for son Pierre and new daughter-in-law Nina Abadee. Pierre was a banker and auto buff.

JOHN BREMOND, JR., HOUSE
700 Guadalupe

Many Austinites cite this New Orleans–flavored Victorian eclectic mansion as their favorite. Authorities commonly cite it as the finest, most elegant, most outstanding example of its kind in Austin. It cost John, Jr., brother of Eugene, $40,000, but for his money Bremond got the region's most exquisite ornamental ironwork and Austin's first indoor toilet. This mansion is just plain fun to look at. It is exuberant in spirit, mirroring the mentality of the magnate who commissioned it. An elaborate mansard roof, wraparound double gallery, marble, tile, and a sweeping stairway add to the festive extravagance.

B. J. SMITH HOUSE
610 Guadalupe, across W. 7th from the John Bremond, Jr., House

This is probably the oldest house in the area, built in 1854 for the Reverend and Mrs. B. J. Smith. The one-story cottage is constructed of handmade brick atop a solid rock foundation. The original handmade hardware and doors are still in place. A five-bay gallery with Doric columns makes it a good example of early Texas Greek Revival.

Other nearby Robinson-Bremond family homes are the WEST-BREMOND COTTAGE (1872) at 609 Nueces, JOHN H. ROBINSON HOUSE (c. 1891) at 702 Rio Grande, and ALFRED H. ROBINSON HOUSE (c. 1857), 706 Rio Grande.

EMMA WEST FLATS (1905) at 511 W. 7th, MARTIN HOUSE (1902) at 600 W. 7th, OLD MAIN LIBRARY BUILDING/AUSTIN HISTORY CENTER (1933) at 410 W. 9th, and the HIRSCHFIELD MANSION and COTTAGE (1886, 1875) at 303–305 W. 9th are also worth seeing. One of the original MOONLIGHT TOWERS still stands in use at W. 9th and Guadalupe.

★★★

6TH STREET WALKING TOUR

Now, as 100 years ago, E. 6th Street—Old Pecan Street—is Austin's heartbeat; the street's steady procession of immaculately restored Victorian brick and native-stone buildings testify to that fact.

One hundred years ago, nearly all the city's important businesses had addresses on this main artery east to Houston and the rest of civilized Texas. Only after the completion of the new Capitol in 1888 did the Avenue eventually wrest the town's commercial crown from Pecan Street. Thus began a downward slide in fortune, and by April 27, 1895, William Sidney Porter was able to write, "East Pecan and the vicinity, once the center of business, where the mild-eyed granger traded eggs and butter for delusive red calico, and drank his old lemonade in peace, has now risen up and declared itself bold, bad, and hard to curry. Loafing, gambling, fighting, and drinking has invaded this Arcadian spot."

That trend finally bottomed out about 1970, by which time 6th Street had withered down to a string of shabby joints, pawnshops, and shine parlors. Junkers and bargain hunters visited Shanblum's, St. Vincent's, and the Junior League Thrift Shop by day, but knew better than to come window-shopping at night. The fact that, underneath the tawdry dress, E. 6th was a nearly unbroken string of essentially intact vintage commercial buildings did not particularly impress many Austinites of that era. We were still tearing these kinds of buildings down in the name of progress and parking garages.

The tide began to turn in 1968, when a local architect made an honest townhouse out of an aging (1881) saloon and bawdyparlor. It was an unheard-of act. Old Pecan Street Cafe followed in 1972, begetting Gordo's, the Raw Deal, Wylie's, Alana's, and you know the rest.

During the early years of this 6th Street renaissance, the street was esteemed for its blend of sheen and shabby. Now it is almost exclusively sheen and looking its best yet. Old Pecan Street is a Registered Historic District, and new buildings must conform in flavor and style to the originals. Austin's biggest businesses no longer line the seven blocks of Old Pecan Street, but it is definitely big business on the street today, especially on Friday and Saturday nights. Old Pecan Street has much to see and sample. The traffic is heavy, too, so it's really best to park somewhere and hoof it.

DRISKILL HOTEL
122 E. 6th at Brazos
1886

Jasper Preston designed it; Jesse Driskill spent $400,000 building it in 1886. Then, as now, majestic—or as close as commercial Austin comes to majestic. That's the Driskill Hotel. An attractive, endearing brick and limestone structure in the Richardson Romanesque style, it is not a particularly distinguished example of that style. That's Jesse and his boys Tabe and J. W. pulling sentinel duty up on top, gazing down over their limestone longhorns at the sidewalk rubberneckers below. Jesse's bust has hung on considerably longer than Jesse himself, who busted out of this life on May Day of 1890. The hotel passed through a number of different hands over the years, none of which ever pocketed much of a profit on their investment. Still, the Driskill continued as Austin's most prestigious hotel. The high-rise addition dates to 1930. Threatened by demolition in the 1960s, the Driskill was saved by the people of Austin. A series of owners has managed to restore the hotel to much of its former glory, and the current owners are continuing the process. (See Hotels.)

JACOBY BUILDING
200 E. 6th
1874

Austin contractor Ferdinand Dohme built this two-story, simply articulated squared limestone building for lease space. Dohme also built the Hirschfield Cottage and the original Main Building at Texas A&M. The Morley Brothers' drugstore was one of this building's early occupants. Recently restored.

HANNIG BUILDING
204 E. 6th
1871

First owner J. W. Hannig, cabinetmaker and undertaker (a common combination in those days), is most famous as the second husband of Susanna Dickinson, survivor of the Alamo. Jasper Preston added the third story and the elaborate smooth-cut and carved limestone High Italianate facade in 1876. Recently restored.

PADGITT AND WARMOUTH BUILDING
208 E. 6th
1885

This pair of wholesale/retail saddlemakers moved into this brick building the year it was built. They added the third story in 1889. J. H. Warmouth served on the Austin City Council. The elaborate cast-iron cornice with its fleur-de-lis cutouts and Star of David cap amounts to the grandest facade on 6th east of the Driskill. Recently restored.

Nearly all this side of the 200 block of E. 6th has been restored now, and with the exception of the old movie palace on the corner (now 6th Street Live), this is the most complete string of commercial buildings from the grand Victorian years left in Austin.

GROVE DRUG
209 E. 6th
1906–1907

Originally a two-story building. The Morley Brothers added the third story and cast-metal Queen Anne bayfront about 1906. This is the only facade of its type left on E. 6th and one of the few remaining in Austin. Passersby today generally overlook the rows of electric light bulbs that run up and down the bayfront. In 1906 their lavish display of electric power drew admirers from all over. Just as interesting inside as out. (See Shopping.)

PLATT-SIMPSON BUILDING
310 E. 6th
1871, 1901

Radcliffe Platt built the core of this building in 1871, and it served as a livery stable till 1890. In 1901 J. S. Simpson bought the building and enlarged it to accommodate his hardware store, adding the red brick facade and distinctive limestone-trimmed arched windows.

ST. CHARLES HOUSE
316 E. 6th
1871

Seba Bogart Brush built this skinny arrangement of Austin common brick; it housed one of Austin's earliest ice-cream saloons, as well as the prestigious St. Charles Hotel and Restaurant, Madame Saffroi, prop. One of the earliest 6th Street restorations.

SMITH BUILDING
325 E. 6th
1873

One of the grander efforts of that year, built for Robert H. Smith, dealer in hardware, groceries, and dry goods. Two-story Victorian commercial building, topped by a metal cornice with arched centerpiece.

COTTON EXCHANGE BUILDING
401 E. 6th
ca. 1875

Merchant Charles Wolf built this two-story brick-with-limestone-trim building, whose chief distinction is an alley facade as elaborate as the front.

DRISKILL, DAY, AND FORD BUILDING
403 E. 6th
1875

The hotel was not Jesse Driskill's first Old Pecan Street building. He constructed this twin to the Cotton Exchange in partnership with cow buddies J. M. "Doc" Day and James Ford. It originally housed a wholesale grocery outlet. Like other buildings on this side of the block, its rear entrance is equally elaborate, because the city market was across the alley.

The BUAAS BUILDING (1875) next door at 405 E. 6th has a limestone facade but is otherwise identical in style to 401 and 403. These buildings, and the rest on the south side of the block, are excellent examples of the prosperity carried into Austin by the railroad.

NALLE BUILDING
409–413 E. 6th
1875

Joseph Nalle served Austin as mayor and otherwise prominent citizen. The three units of this two-story brick building are united by a common facade and cornice. Nalle built it with materials from his lumberyard. It has a double front.

THAISON BUILDING
410 E. 6th
1881

This plain little two-story brick building first housed William Thaison's Saloon and Billiard Parlor, but it soon fell into use as a bawdyhouse. Restored in 1968, it was the first such project on E. 6th.

QUAST BUILDING
412 E. 6th
1872

One of the earliest stone buildings still standing on E. 6th, built as a residence by Julius Quast. His wife later operated it as a grocery store. Wrought ironwork and a roof garden set it apart from its neighbors.

PAGGI'S CARRIAGE SHOP
421 E. 6th
ca. 1875

Michael Paggi dealt in wagons and carriages, among other things. This limestone rubble with brick facade building housed his showroom and yard. Like his neighbors, Paggi didn't slight his back-door customers, giving them an equally attractive entrance.

BREMOND BUILDING
501 E. 6th
1873

Eugene Bremond built it; Thompson's Farm Implements first occupied it. The Bremond Building is another of the street's earlier, simpler commercial buildings. The most distinctive feature of this limestone rubble structure is its "Austin arch"—segmental arch—windows. Similar buildings from that period are next door (Hawkeye's) and across the street (Republic Oyster Bar).

E. H. CARRINGTON STORE
522 E. 6th
1872

E. H. Carrington was a former slave made good, a prosperous grocer and respected black community leader. He operated his store here from 1873 until 1907. His son-in-law Louis Lyons took over, operating the store through the 1920s. The second story served as Lyons Hall, a center for black social affairs.

OLD DEPOT HOTEL
504 E. 6th
1872

With the railroad station's arrival in Austin in 1871, depot hotels were not far behind. This limestone rubble building, adjacent to Market Square and only a block away from the original H&TC depot, operated first as the Railroad House, then under a succession of different proprietors and names. Hang a right on Red River, then right again on 5th a few feet.

CARL DAYWOOD BUILDING
600 Sabine at E. 6th
1982

A good example of the new ornamentalism in architecture, and designed to blend in with the street's Victorian structures. Native brick, two-story with a decorative brickwork cornice and pillar caps.

RANDERSON-LINDAHL BUILDING
701 E. 6th
1898
First a grocery store, later a meat market (yes, the two were beasts of a different flavor back them), now a hot-tub works, this building was initially one story. The second story was added about 1910. Features one of the few angled corner entrances on E. 6th.

★★★

MUSEUMS

ARCHER M. HUNTINGTON ART GALLERY
Art Building, University of Texas (E. 23rd and San Jacinto), and Harry Ransom Center (W. 21st and Guadalupe)
University/Central West
471-7324
Monday through Saturday 9–5, Sunday 1–5
Free
W call ahead
The singular is a little misleading, at least to those patrons who are accustomed to finding all their art under one roof. UT's Huntington Gallery actually consists of two exhibit halls on the university campus: the Art Building, which has a large lower gallery and smaller mezzanine gallery; and the first two floors of the Harry Ransom Center.

Generally, several exhibits are on view in each hall, and the exhibit schedule is one of the most diverse of any United States university. The Huntington Gallery's growing permanent collection is exhibited and stored in the Ransom Center. The permanent collection comprises Greek and Roman art, nineteenth- and twentieth-century American art (including the Michener and C. R. Smith Collections), and contemporary Latin American art, plus 4000 more paintings and drawings from all periods.

Displays from the permanent collection are supplemented by an assortment of temporary loan exhibits from art centers all over the world, including a long-term loan of medieval art from the Metropolitan Museum. Annual student-faculty exhibit at the Art Building gallery each spring. Guided tours are available by appointment.

ATRIUM GALLERY
Moody Hall, St. Edward's University, 3100 S. Congress
Southwest
444-7172 (campus information)
Monday through Friday 8–8, Saturday and Sunday 8–5
Free
Exhibits change on a regular basis. Past exhibits have ranged from contemporary fiber art to local artist Geneva Moore's brightly colored dyed paintings on silk.

BARKER TEXAS HISTORY CENTER
Sid Richardson Hall 2.109, Red River and Manor, adjacent to LBJ
Library
University/Central West
471-5961
Monday through Saturday 8–5
Free
W

Excellent archival library with rotating exhibits, mostly literary in nature—for example, the papers and letters of "Bigfoot" Wallace, books about him, his coat, and other personal effects. "John Lomax: Ballad Hunter" and "Women in Texas" are other recent exhibits. (See also Libraries.)

DOUGHERTY ARTS CENTER
1110 Barton Springs Rd., two blocks east of S. Lamar
Southwest
477-5824
Tuesday through Thursday 1–10, Friday, Saturday, and Sunday 1–4, closed Monday
Free
W

Once a National Guard Armory, now a 2000-square-foot exhibition space. Exhibits may include touring and/or local exhibitions by local and regional artists. Past shows have included a PARD Employee Art Show, a Fall Membership Show, Black Arts Alliance, Women and Their Work, and LUChA. The Center actually houses a number of other facilities. (See also Revelation, Performing Arts.)

ELISABET NEY MUSEUM
304 E. 44th at Ave. H
Northwest
458-2255
Tuesday through Friday 11–4:30, Saturday and Sunday 2–4:30
Free
W partial (first floor only; narrow doorways)

Built by Ney in 1892 (subsequent addition in 1902), this is one of only four intact nineteenth-century sculptor's studios in the United States. A National Historic Site, it houses the collection of Ney, who lived in Texas from 1873 to 1907. Following her death here, friends and admirers acquired the studio and founded the museum.

Connoisseurs of vintage Texas buildings will appreciate the building itself, as well as its contents. Ney named her studio Formosa, meaning "beautiful," after her former studio in Europe. Since the studio became a museum almost immediately after her death, Formosa has remained pretty much as it was during Ney's heyday—pegged rough cedar stair railings, cast-iron spiral staircase up to the loft, graceful pine flooring, cast-iron door fittings, masterful stonework. Small wonder that she loved the place. Many of her original belongings, including her rustic cedar cot, are still here. The track lighting is one of the few jarring additions. Most visitors leave wishing they lived here. The grounds are a pleasant place to escape bustling downtown Austin. And the city— shame, shame—was considering razing Formosa as recently as 1977, back when the museum's annual attendance was 2500. Now it's more like 35,000.

Freshly restored, the museum offers classes in sculpture and life drawing, as well as various audiovisual presentations on Ney and her work. Dozens of plaster models, marble busts, and bronze statues of European dignitaries and famous Texans make up the collection on display.

GEORGE WASHINGTON CARVER MUSEUM
1165 Angelina
Central East
472-4809
Tuesday and Wednesday 10–6, Thursday noon–8, Friday and Saturday noon–5
Free
W

This little brick veneer building opened up here during the Depression as the Austin Public Library's first branch. Since 1980, however, it has functioned as the George Washington Carver Museum, the first local black history museum in Texas. Exhibits present black history, art, and culture. Recent exhibits have ranged from "Martin Luther King, Jr., and the Civil Rights Movement" to "Blacks of Distinction in Travis County, 1839–1940" to "Afro-American Abstraction" and "Austin Quilts and Quilters."

FRENCH LEGATION
802 San Marcos at E. 7th
Central East
472-8180
Tuesday through Sunday 1–5
Adults $2, children under 10 50¢, high school students $1

Comte Alphones Dubois de Saligny, His Majesty's chargé d'affaires to the Republic of Texas from France, had this charming French Provincial cottage built in 1841, employing hand-sawn Bastrop pine and French fitments. Back then, this now-modest palace was regarded as the most pretentious in Austin, as befitted a man every bit as overblown as his bogus title. It originally commanded 21 1/3 acres on what was later known as Robertson Hill.

The indelicate manners of Austin's frequent red-skinned visitors disturbed the count's finely balanced composure, as did that comedy of manners more commonly known as the "Pig War," to the end that the legate actually spent little time here. (See History.)

The Daughters of the Republic of Texas operate the museum, which is nicely furnished with nineteenth-century antiques and some of the comte's original effects. The kitchen out back, with its inventory of pewter utensils and copper pots, is supposed to be the only authentic French creole kitchen in the United States. The grounds seem perfect for wedding receptions and such, and in fact they are available for that.

HARRY RANSOM HUMANITIES RESEARCH CENTER
W. 21st and Guadalupe
Central West
471-9111
Monday through Friday 8–5
Free
W

Like the Huntington Gallery, the name Harry Ransom Humanities Research *Center* is a bit misleading, at least when it comes to exhibit space. Although most of the collection is housed within the confines of the Harry Ransom Center, exhibits from that vast collection populate both the Ransom Center and the nearby Academic Center (on the West Mall, W. 23rd and Guadalupe, west of the Tower). (See also Libraries.)

HARRY RANSOM CENTER
Besides showing off the center's Gutenberg Bible and Huntington Gallery art, the Ransom Center maintains several more public exhibition rooms. The PHOTOGRAPHY COLLECTION on the sixth floor contains more than 5 million photographic prints and negatives and 3000 pieces of antique camera equipment. Four small exhibit areas display representative examples from the collection on a rotating basis. The collection includes a 20,000-volume reference library, the E. O. Goldbeck panoramic photography collection and the world's first photograph, taken by Joseph Niepce in 1826. The HOBLITZELLE THEATRE ARTS COLLECTION is located on the seventh floor and has gathered in such diverse items as Harry Houdini posters and correspondence; the stage, military, and industrial designs of Norman Bel Geddes; the Burl Ives collection of folk-music records; and the Stanley Marcus collection of Sicilian marionettes. Some of those marionettes, along with costumes, programs, Roman hair curlers, and other bits of theater paraphernalia through the ages, are sometimes on display. The adjoining WILLOUGHBY-BLAKE ROOM is filled with exquisite eighteenth- and nineteenth-century silver, crystal, china, and furniture.

ACADEMIC CENTER
The Academic Center's fourth floor contains a number of exhibits. The LEEDS GALLERY shows various rare books, photos, manuscripts, and arts, as well as Charles Umlauf's *The Three Graces* (on the inner patio). The ICONOGRAPHY COLLECTION contains sculpture, paintings, and artworks in every medium from the past four centuries. This means the artwork of Albrecht Dürer may hang next to that of e. e. cummings. The KNOPF LIBRARY contains a complete collection of all Knopf first editions and the Knopf personal library. Books from Edward Tinker's collection are on display in the TINKER ROOM, but it's his silver saddle that catches the eye. The J. FRANK DOBIE LIBRARY is the fulfillment of a personal dream of Dobie's. On display are volumes

from his library and works from his art collection, such as Frederic Remington's watercolor *A Mexican Longhorn* and a Thomas Hart Benton lithograph. His desk and a horn chair add additional flavor. The Dobie Library also contains the Frank Caldwell collection of Texas books and documents.

ESTHER HOBLITZELLE MEMORIAL PARLOR is furnished with Gibbons carvings, Chippendale furniture, and silk wallpaper from the Hoblitzelle family home in Dallas. The parlor is open by request. The creator of Perry Mason donated his professional effects to the university, including the contents of his study, which was originally located in his ranch house at Temecula, California. The ERLE STANLEY GARDNER STUDY was faithfully reconstructed here, and through the magic of recording tape he reminisces about his eventful life and elaborates on some of his favorite furnishings: guns, tribal masks, bows and arrows, and other manly paraphernalia. The CHINESE GARDEN AND WALKWAY, an outdoor porch, contains eighteenth-century Chinese artifacts. It is open every day, and smoking and eating are permitted. The view of the western hills and campus buildings is especially nice up here. Also on the fourth floor are the DAISY YOUNT SILVER COLLECTION and the JACK JOSEY HONORS ROOM.

LAGUNA GLORIA ART MUSEUM
3809 W. 35th at the end of Old Bull Creek Rd.
Central West
458-8191
Tuesday through Saturday 10–5, except Thursday until 9, Sunday 1–5
Guided gallery tours by appointment
Free

Set on Lake Austin, this twenty-eight-acre piece of peninsula at the foot of Mt. Bonnell has an impressive past. Stephen F. Austin was planning to soak his feet here on a permanent basis once he had finished founding Texas, until the Grim Reaper intervened. It took the savior of the Alamo to finally build the Mediterranean villa that now houses the art museum on the glorious lagoon. Clara Driscoll Sevier aroused public sentiment and convinced the legislature to preserve the Mission of the Cottonwoods rather than raze it. The villa was built in 1916 as a winter retreat for herself and her husband H. H. Sevier, founder and editor of the *Austin American*.

The museum features changing exhibitions of twentieth-century art; to be more specific, about half is new local and regional art and photography, and half nationally prominent artists. Recent exhibits have included fluorescent light sculptures; the panoramic photographs of E. O. Goldbeck, who is past ninety and still taking pictures; and the worlds of Buckminster Fuller. No cowboy art. Films, lectures, concerts, and a new art school complement the gallery. Allow enough time for a stroll through the naturally landscaped grounds, where palms, pecans, and cacti share space along the cobble paths. It's cool out here even during the heat of summer. (See also Annual Events—Fiesta.)

LORENZO DE ZAVALA STATE ARCHIVES AND LIBRARY
1201 Brazos, Capitol grounds
Central West
475-2445
Monday through Friday 8–5; genealogy section and lobby Monday through Saturday 8–5
Free
W

Genealogists and historians are the chief patrons here, burrowing through a vast collection of archival books and documents spanning the length and breadth of Texas history. But lobby visitors will also see an exhibit of historical maps and writings, including the Texas Declaration of Independence and the beleaguered Travis's eloquent plea for help from the Alamo. The Pease Room, named after early Governor Elisha M. Pease, contains furniture and artifacts from his terms in office and artifacts from the present Capitol building. A Texas-sized mural of Texas history by Peter Rogers dominates everything else.

LYNDON B. JOHNSON LIBRARY
2313 Red River near E. 23rd
Parking on Red River between Manor and E. 26th
University/Central West
482-5136
Open seven days 9–5
Tours for groups of 12 or more by appointment
Free
W

The LBJ Library's commanding location atop this high knoll overlooking the UT campus, and on equal footing with the Capitol, is not happpenstance. The spirit of the library and museum is best summed up in a 1971 cartoon on display here. Lyndon, portrayed as the consummate wheeler-dealer Texan, is hunkered down on a stool-sized version of the museum, begging the rhetorical question, "D'yuh all mind if I rest on muh laurels?"

Well, anyway, the exquisite array of ceremonial gifts given to Johnson during his sovereignty make for great window-shopping. The historical displays ("softened" here and there) tracing his career make for interesting reading, and political campaign paraphernalia fans will enjoy those particular displays. And don't miss the Oval Office replica several stories up. Oh, yes, four stories' worth of the presidential papers are the core of the temple, in matching imperial red boxes with gold seals. Traveling exhibitions, films, concerts, and lectures are usually interesting.

MUSEO DEL BARRIO/GALERIA TONANTZIN
1619 E. 1st
Central East
474-5770
Monday through Friday 9–5, Saturday and Sunday by appointment
Free
W
   Some of Austin's art galleries are in restaurants, others in bank foyers. El Museo del Barrio shares space with the Austin Tenants' Council, which is about as unlikely a combination as you will ever see, but which is nonetheless important: the ATC sign is the only identification on this little eastside commercial building.
   But this museo is worth the trouble of finding; the exhibits posted here are uniformly imaginative and interesting to see. Local, Texas, and Mexican artists and photographers of Hispanic extraction have been represented. Recent shows have included a retrospective of the late, great Emilio Amero and "Magia del Barrio: Manos que Crean Cultura," which was a collection of works by Barrio Elders. Another recent show, the "Barrio Art and Realities Exhibition," included a self-guided tour brochure to notably artistic barrio homes, yards, and gardens. A few of the tour guides may still be available.

NEILL-COCHRAN HOUSE
2310 San Gabriel at W. 23rd
Parking in rear, off W. 23rd
Central West
478-2335
Wednesday through Sunday 2–5
Hour-long guided tours at 2, 3, and 4
Adults $1, children under 6 free
   Abner Cook built this graceful Greek Revival manse for Washington Hill in 1855. Mr. Hill never really established proper residence here, and by 1856 he had leased it to the state, which put it to temporary use as the Blind Institute. In 1865 it served as a hospital for federal prisoners. The building is said to be haunted by some of its more ill-fated patients, who were buried on the grounds. During the 1880s the big house finally blossomed forth into a social center of state and community elite, under the successive ownerships of Colonel Andrew Neill and Judge T. B. Cochran. The Colonial Dames of America have owned the house since 1958. They have restored and furnished it with a variety of seventeenth- to nineteenth-century antiques that reflect the eclectic tastes of its Victorian owners. Almost all the doors, doorknobs, windows, outside shutters, and hinges are original. Experts have pronounced it "a perfect example of the Texas version of the Greek architectural revival in the South."

O. HENRY MUSEUM
409 E. 5th at Neches
Central West
472-1903

Tuesday through Saturday 11–4:30; Sunday 2–4:30
Free
"There are many historical and otherwise interesting places that you have revived in my recollection—the Alamo, where Davey Jones fell; Goliad, Sam Houston's surrender to Montezuma, and petrified boom found near Austin, five-cent cotton and the Siamese Democratic platform born in Dallas. I should so much like to see the gals in Galveston, and go to the wake in Waco."—President Grover Cleveland to intrepid *Rolling Stone* reporter, O. Henry's "A Snapshot at the President"
William Sydney "O. Henry" Porter is famous the world over for his impeccably written short stories. What is not generally known is that he was also editor of a short-lived Austin weekly, the *Rolling Stone*. His observations on life in Austin are often very much as telling now as they were in 1894. As local humorist, he remains unsurpassed.
All of which is an introduction to the tidy Victorian cottage in which he lived during his tenure as editor-in-chief and chief bottlewasher at the *Rolling Stone*. Some of his printing equipment stood on the back porch. The house is furnished with period pieces, some of which actually belonged to the Porters. Also on display are mementos from Porter's life, including a yellowing original issue of the *Rolling Stone*. Knock to enter; the door is sometimes locked to keep out the transients who live in the bushes outside. Home of the "O. Henry Pun-Off" each spring. (See Annual Events.) Adults' and children's writing classes, history programs offered several times yearly.

OLD LAND OFFICE BUILDING
DAUGHTERS OF THE CONFEDERACY MUSEUM
DAUGHTERS OF THE REPUBLIC OF TEXAS MUSEUM
112 E. 11th, Capitol grounds
Central West
472-2596 (DOC Museum)
477-1822 (DRT Museum)
Monday through Friday, 9–noon, 1–5
Free, donations accepted
This medieval castle dates back to 1857, its original purpose to house the deeds, patents, maps, and other records of the state's General Land Office. In 1917 the Land Office moved on to more spacious environs, and the legislature gave this most romantic of Capitol Hill buildings to the Daughters of the Republic of Texas and the Daughters of the Confederacy, who maintain museums, offices, and research facilities within.
The TEXAS CONFEDERATE MUSEUM (first floor) houses a collection of state and Confederate exhibits, along with numerous portraits of war heroes. Amid all the period clothing, weapons, and other contemporary tools of living and dying, you'll see a surgeon's saw with a handle articulated out of a human thigh bone, and a unique three-way portrait of that trinity of Confederate heroes: Davis, Lee, and Jackson.
The DAUGHTERS OF THE REPUBLIC OF TEXAS MUSEUM (second floor) contains a similar collection of relics from the colonial, Republic,

and statehood eras. Of special interest is the drafting desk used by Will Porter during his four-year stint as a draftsman here. Resting on the sprawling desk is a copy of the *Rolling Stone*, which even today makes interesting reading. The museum also has a gift shop.

TEXAS MEMORIAL MUSEUM
2400 Trinity
Central West
471-1604
Monday through Friday 9–5, Saturday and Sunday 1–5
Free
W call ahead

Paul Cret, the man of the Tower, served as supervising architect on this chunk of institutional Art Moderne, which is nicely foiled by Phimister Proctor's group of wild-eyed bronze mustangs. One of the grander flourishes of the 1936 centennial celebration, the Texas Memorial Museum now sits in the shadow of a university and state that have since far outgrown it. It's still a fun place to visit.

A thirty-foot-long fossil mosasaur, gleaming minerals from the Barron Collection, and weaponry that spans four centuries are just a few examples of the permanent exhibits to be seen on the museum's four floors. In addition to the many other permanent exhibits in geology and paleontology, natural history, and anthropology, there are special temporary exhibits.

Natural history exhibits concentrate on the plants and animals of Texas. The museum gift shop sells high-quality imports, museum replicas, books, art objects, and cards.

★★

CHILDREN'S ACTIVITIES

Children enjoy many of the attractions listed elsewhere in this book, such as the State Capitol, Barton Springs, Mayfield Park, Austin Nature Center Annex, Texas Memorial Museum, People's Renaissance Market, Wild Basin Wilderness Preserve, Northcross Mall's ice-skating rink, and a number of special events and classes, like Zilker Park's spring kite-flying contest and YuleFest, the Capitol 10,000, Laguna Gloria's Fiesta and art classes, Zachary Scott Theatre Center's acting classes and children's plays, Hyde Park Showplace's children's theater, Easter Eggstravaganza and Children's Days at Symphony Square, the Austin Public Library system's monthly kids' programs, and the PARD's abundance of community center classes and activities.

A good source of activities for children is *The Parent's Guide to Austin*. (See For Your Information—Books.) Besides information on child-care centers and schools, social services, and adoption, and help for parents of adolescents in trouble, the book provides page upon page of camps, sports, clubs, art, music, and dance. It is available at most local bookstores.

Other favorite kids' spots within a thirty-minute drive of Austin are Wonder World and Aquarena Springs in San Marcos and Inner Space Caverns in Georgetown.

JOURDAN-BACHMAN PIONEER FARM
11418 Sprinkle Cut-Off Rd.
837-1215
Open by reservation only
The Pioneer Farm purports to portray farm life in Central Texas as it was a century ago. Twelve reconstructed farm buildings, crop fields, pastureland, and an Indian midden are contained within this seventy-acre tract on Walnut Creek northeast of Austin. Programs and classes such as beekeeping, sausage stuffing, quiltmaking, hayrides, and rock masonry are designed to give participants a real understanding of pioneer life.

The Pioneer Farm is continuing to acquire more period buildings, equipment, and furnishings in order to further this delightful historical deception. Midway between the old Sprinkle and Dessau communities, the farm was originally part of a 2000-acre cotton plantation established in 1852.

Summer camp for kids and family events throughout the year are on the annual calendar of events out here, but remember that the farm is otherwise open to visitors by reservation only.

KIDDIE ACRES
12713 Burnet near Parmer, four miles north of US Hwy. 183
Northwest
Tuesday through Sunday noon–9, except closes earlier October through April
Admission
A small-scale, clean amusement park ideal for younger children. Includes pony and train rides. Concessions available.

STEAM LOCOMOTIVE NO. 786
E. 4th at Trinity
Central West
Open at all times
Free
W but not locomotive
This 1916 steam engine and tender was supposedly the last steam locomotive to puff in Austin. Southern Pacific Railroad donated the eighty-foot behemoth to the city in 1956. It is now a permanent monument favored by children of all ages. Concrete steps make it easy for kids to climb aboard and explore and pretend to their hearts' content. Now that the Capitol is closed at night, this is about the only fun and free place to hang out at four in the morning.

TOWN LAKE
Tom Miller Dam (Redbud Tr.) to Longhorn Dam (Pleasant Valley Rd.)
Central
Free

This is the closest place in town for kids to try their luck at fishing, and many do. (See Outdoors.)

ZILKER EAGLE
Zilker Park, 2100 Barton Springs Rd.
Southwest
478-8167
Closed Monday
Admission

Currently Austin's only light-rail system, and its most popular form of public transportation. The train usually runs fuller than any city bus and is a lot more fun. Tour Zilker Park in comfort and leave the driving to them. The runners may be passing you, but not the weekend cars on nearby River Road.

★★
POINTS OF INTEREST

Points of Interest includes places to see or visit that aren't easily pigeonholed or adequately covered in other sections such as Historic Places, Museums, and Outdoors. Some of these points transcend such limiting categories, such as the Capitol and 6th Street. And since without the Capitol Austin would probably be a little fishing village on the Colorado called Waterloo, we shall start with it. The other Points of Interest follow in alphabetical order.

STATE CAPITOL COMPLEX
11th and Congress
Parking at the intersection's southeast corner and in the 1500 block of Congress north of the Capitol
Central West
475-3070
Capitol rotunda open seven days 7 a.m.–9 p.m.
Free
W+

As befits a state like ours, the Texas Capitol is the largest of state capitols, second in size only to the one in Washington, D. C., and the tallest, period—seven feet taller than even the nation's capitol. These impressive details aside, it is also one of the Fifty's most beautiful statehouses, a grand Renaissance Revival palace that nearly always outshines those mortals who inhabit it for the first 120 days of every odd year and special sessions in between.

Most everyone has heard the official yarn of the Capitol, how the state government swapped three million acres of the Great American

Desert to four bagmen from the Windy City, and how we got Elijah Meyer's Texas pink granite palace and they got the XIT Ranch and several counties to boot.

This place really is big—and beautiful. The exquisite wainscoting—oak, pine, cherry, cedar, walnut, ash, mahogany—goes on for seven miles. The carved oak and pine door and window frames wrap around 500 doors and 900 windows.

The beautiful, delicately pink granite came from Burnet County, 15,000 railroad cars worth. The cornerstone alone roughed out at 16,000 pounds. Covering three acres of ground with eight and a half acres of floor space, the Texas Capitol was said to have been the seventh-largest building in the world at the time of its birth. It was also either the eighth or ninth wonder of the world, depending on whether you were an Austinite, or just a Texan.

Laid on Independence Day (March 2, not July 4), 1885, that cornerstone contains an Austin city directory, city statistics, Texas newspapers, money of the Republic of Texas and the Confederacy, two roasting ears, an olive leaf from Mt. Zion, a buttonhole bouquet, and a 25¢ meal ticket.

Dedication Day—May 16, 1888—was perhaps the grandest day Austin has ever known. It capped more than a week's worth of balls, parades, sham battles, and other generalized entertainment. But most telling about the dedication's stature was the price paid for its beer concession: a cool $5150. Extrapolate that out into 1980s simoleans.

Like any great building, the Capitol has acquired a past, partly tragic. One of the most romantic tragedies concerns the worker who is forever trapped between the Capitol's high walls; he fell to his death while laying the last brick (or something like that, depending on who's telling the story), and his body was not retrievable. Well, it ain't so, Joe. The guy in question died when a section of the second-story floor gave way as a load of limestone was being carried up.

State comptroller R. M. Love was talking with a former employee one day in 1903 in a first-floor corridor, when the ex pulled out a gun and mortally wounded Love. A Love assistant grabbed the gun and shot the killer dead on the spot.

Copies of the Texas Declaration of Independence and Ordinance of Secession decorate the walls of the rotunda and halls, along with paintings and statues of Texas heroes, governors, and otherwise public men and women.

Several exhibits are scattered throughout the building, the most interesting of which displays photos and artifacts from the Capitol's construction and early days. There is also a composite antique capitol office with authentic furnishings. Free guided tours begin at the Visitors' Desk in the south foyer, take about half an hour, and are available between 8:15 and 4:30 each day. An excellent free pamphlet, *Texas Capitol Guide*, is available at the Visitors' Desk. It guides you through the Capitol grounds and complex as well, with a map, photos, and commentary.

Just east of the Capitol is the Archives Library (see Museums), with exhibits on major events in Texas history. On the southeast corner of the grounds is the Old Land Office. (See Museums.) Across the street at 1006 Congress and on the site of the old temporary capitol is the Old Bakery and Emporium. (See Museums.)

ANDERSON MILL
RM Rd. 2769 near Anderson Mill Rd., 4 1/2 miles west of RM Rd. 620

Thomas Anderson first came to these hills that delineate the Colorado River and Cypress Creek west of Austin in the 1850s. By 1863 he had built a gristmill on Cypress Creek, near its juncture with the Colorado. That year the Confederates converted it into a gunpowder mill. Later on, it powered a cotton gin. The original mill and most of the community of the same name that surrounded it were obliterated by the rising waters of Lake Travis during the late 1930s. Part of the mill was reconstructed at its present site during the 1960s and is maintained by the local garden club. The water that turns the big wheel is purely decorative these days, but who's going to quarrel with that? Continue the scenic drive you have started in coming out here by continuing west on Ranch Road 2769 to its dead end at Volente. Then proceed north (right) on Lime Creek Road. (Your only other choice is to drive straight into the lake.) Lime Creek Road twists and turns up and along the Lime Creek arm of Lake Travis eight or ten miles before finally running into RM Rd. 1431 one mile west of Cedar Park. Turn right on Ranch Road 1431, then right on US Hwy. 183 to return to Austin.

BALCONES ESCARPMENT

Whose fault is it, anyway?

It's all Balcones' fault, mostly.

Without the Balcones Fault Austin would have no Mt. Bonnell or Barton Springs—for starters—and without all of those, Austin would probably still just be Waterloo and we would be toasting Hill Country sunsets in Abilene or College Station or some other nonsensical place.

A lot of little faults share Balcones' blame, actually. The Balcones Fault is more properly known as the Balcones Escarpment, a geologic fault zone that bisects Texas in a bowed line from Del Rio to the Red River. It is visible for only a comparatively few miles, however, east from Del Rio and northeast from San Antonio to Austin. From northwestern Bexar County the fault line runs through Comal, Hays, and Travis Counties, crossing the Colorado just above old Austin, about where Tom Miller Dam is.

The Handbook of Texas describes the escarpment like this:

Several miles wide, the escarpment, which appears from the plains below as a range of wooded hills, separates the Edwards Plateau in the west from the Coastal Plains. The Balcones zone was formed under conditions of strain during the Tertiary time when there was a down-warping near the Gulf coast and a moderate uplift inland. Water-bearing formations passing beneath the plateau to the plains are broken across by the Balcones fault group, and much water is forced to the surface by artesian pressure. Barton Springs, San Marcos Springs, and Comal Springs are examples of such artesian wells or springs."

Okay. So where exactly can I see this fault? And who was Balcones? About the best—and only—place to see the fault line proper is inside Wonder Cave in San Marcos. This dry-formed cave was shaped during those early turbulent days, and only a few critically placed keystones keep the cave from closing up again.

Take a glass-bottom boat cruise of the San Marcos (Aquarena) Springs to see the fault once removed. Guides will point out dozens of individual little springs bubbling up through the sands twenty and thirty feet below.

Drive the stretch of IH 35 between New Braunfels and Austin, glance west once or twice, and you should be able to figure out who—or what—Balcones was. "The hills look like balconies," the first Spanish *conquistadores* remarked among themselves, and so they were christened. But like so many other early Spanish names, "Los Balcones" did not slip into the subsequent Anglo lexicon. The gringos just called them "the hills" or "the mountains"—depending on whether they were honest or land salesmen—and didn't think too much more about it.

Pioneer geologist Robert Thomas Hill was the first human being to figure out exactly what had transpired underground, and it was shortly thereafter, in 1887, that Hill revived the romantic slumbering Spanish name "Balcones" by way of qualifying the type of geologic zone he had identified.

Besides Barton Springs, another good place to see the fault at work is at Seiders Springs in central west Austin. (See Picnicking.)

BRIDGES

Today we take our bridges—especially over Town Lake—for granted. But can you imagine trying to ford the lake in your car? Or having to take a ferry across? Can you imagine the traffic jams?

Travelers through Austin had no other choice until 1869, when a pontoon bridge was built at the foot of Brazos. This low-slung floating bridge did just that a year later, when a fall flood washed through.

After this brief, heady taste of luxury and dry feet, Austin went bridgeless for another six years. In 1876 an $80,000 wooden toll bridge opened, located where the present Congress Avenue bridge is. It lasted only a little longer than the first one. Colonel W. B. Blocker was driving a herd of longhorns over it one day in 1882 when the leaders began milling on the first span. The concentration of weight was too great, and the bridge gave way. The entire herd fell fifty feet into the river, and all but a few drowned. The bridge was rigged back up, but nobody trusted it anymore. They cheered its iron replacement in 1884 but didn't really trust it, either. As the bridge underwent its load tests, most spectators declined to stand on it, preferring to watch from a safe distance. Less than ten years later, a local paper wrote that the bridge built to last an eternity was in fact "worn and weakened until the danger of a repetition of the disaster of 1882 is not only present but apparent."

Traffic limped cautiously along until 1909, however, when the bridge was closed and eventually torn down. Part of it ended up at Moore's Crossing on Onion Creek in southeast Travis County, where it still stands. Meanwhile, Austin was waiting for the present Congress Avenue bridge to be built. Everyone—pedestrian, cyclist, horseman, wagoneer, autoist—spent the intervening year crossing the river at an "improved ford" at the mouth of Shoal Creek.

The new, four-lane Congress Avenue Viaduct was finished in mid-1910, the subject of public rejoicing and several color penny postcards. Typical was this comment in "People's Forum" of the *Austin Statesman*, March 5, 1910, by Frederick Cushman of south Austin: "Soon the bridge will be completed, which, it is hoped will stand for all time as a monument to the public spirit, progressiveness and generosity of the taxpayers of Travis County of this day and generation." Found to be dangerously weak during the mid-1970s, the venerable viaduct was rebuilt and widened rather than demolished, and its timeless Beaux Arts lines survived intact.

Subsequent tamers of the Colorado—the S. 1st and Lamar spans in particular—hold their respective charms, but none matches the romantic lines of the original crossing.

GOVERNOR'S MANSION
Colorado and W. 11th
Central West
475-2121
Guided tours Monday, Wednesday, and Friday every 20 minutes
from 10 to 11:40
Reservations required for groups of 15 or more
Free
W rear entrance

It's something of a miracle that our 130-year-old Governor's Mansion stands at all. But it does—proudly so—and it looks as if the recently renovated and restored veteran of thirty-six different duty elected tenants will serve the state through at least as many more administrations.

Abner Cook built this stately Greek Revival residence according to the plans of Richard Payne, using locally fired bricks and Bastrop pine. He had $17,000 with which to work. There was no money left over for furnishings. The first inhabitants, Governor Elisha Pease and family, brought their own when they moved in during the summer of 1856.

This was the first governor's mansion; previous steerers of the tiller of state had been left to shift for themselves. When Governor Pease moved to Austin to assume office in 1853, he rented rooms in the home of Mrs. Thomas William "Pegleg" Ward at 8th and Lavaca. The only previous office residence had been built during the days of the republic, and the roughly built two-story "President's House" at 7th and San Jacinto served us only briefly before it began to fall apart.

More history has been made in this one official house of state than in any other residence in Texas. Here in 1861 Governor Sam Houston decided not to support the Confederacy; and shortly thereafter, the Mansion acquired its first permanent boarder, its first ghost. A nephew of war Governor Pendleton Murrah committed suicide in an upstairs bedroom, the unhappiest end to an unhappy love affair. Murrah's own administration was only slightly more cheerful. He quarreled constantly with the Confederate military authorities and fled to Mexico with the Confederacy's fall, where he died soon after, shrouded in mystery and obscurity.

But the state survived, and so has its mansion, in a condition more nearly like the original than any of the three older houses in the United States still in use as governors' residences. This good luck is not the result of any great historical foresight, but through the cumulative frugality of forty-odd legislatures, who were too cheap to keep it fixed up and too cheap to tear it down and build something better.

The most recent restoration project, designed to return the house to its original simple elegance yet provide the modern conveniences needed for comfortable living and official entertaining, cost more than $2 million, money for which came out of both state and private pockets. The house was essentially rebuilt from the ground up, and a number of museum-quality nineteenth-century American and Texas furnishings and works of art were added to complement the Mansion's existing collection of historic furnishings, among them the writing desk of Stephen F. Austin. Tours include the six public rooms of the first floor and the grounds. There is a free, informative brochure about the Mansion available there or at the Visitors' Desk in the Capitol foyer.

GROVE DRUG
209 E. 6th
Central West
478-1663
W

It is a delicious irony that the closest thing in Austin to an old-time Texas drug store is smack-dab in the heart of upscale 6th Street. Grove Drug has been such since the grave days of the Depression. Before that, it was Morley Drug. Admire its two-story sheet-copper Queen Anne bay front, unique now in downtown Austin.

Inside you can get your prescription filled or pick up Granny's catnip tea and some Dr. LeGear's Poultry Inhalant for your ailing chickens. Maybe you'll finally spring for those Burdizzo's (all real Texas ranchers have a set and pronounce them "bedeezers") and learn how to use them.

Then you can take breakfast or lunch at the lunch counter (real revolving stools and the cheapest waffles in town). Grove doesn't sell bullets, but you can still keep that favorite Hopalong Cassidy six-shooter loaded, 100 Jackson-brand caps for a nickel.

OAKWOOD CEMETERY
E. 16th and Navasota
Central East
478-7152
Open seven days sunrise–sunset
City cemetery since the 1840s, Oakwood Cemetery is probably the most overlooked historic point of interest in Austin. Not all of Texas's notable fallen inhabit the State Cemetery; Governor Hogg and Miss Ima, Bad Ben Thompson, and other less-well-known but colorful characters such as Bristletop Johnson and the Lone Palm Tree rest here.

Now some people have a prejudice against the concept of cemetery as place of beauty; the fact of the matter is, Oakwood Cemetery is more comely and comfortable a resort than most parks. Majestic cedars, live oaks, pecans, and pines supply lots of summer shade, and the bluebonnets here are always the first and often the best of the spring in Austin. One of the most peaceful and quiet spots in Austin (no double meaning intended).

PILOT KNOB
Take U.S. Hwy. 183 south from Austin. Pilot Knob is 1 mile west of Hwy. 183, just south of the junction with FM Rd. 812, about 6 miles south of Austin
Pilot Knob is the only exposed submarine volcano in Texas, formed about eighty million years ago when Texas was under water. Lava shot up through the cracks of the Balcones Fault here, hardened, and rose high above the shallow sea. Reef organisms were attracted to its irregular surfaces, and the reefs they formed were not unlike the coral reefs of the South Pacific. The sea receded, and the volcano began to weather away to its current state, the vent rising 710 feet above sea level, 180 feet above the surrounding valley. Rim diameter is 1.5 miles. Both Pilot Knob and the several smaller knobs are principally basalt. A lot of cotton was grown in the surrounding valleys, for they are rich in volcanic ash.

Indians and early settlers used it as a landmark. Travelers on the Pinta and Chisholm Trails knew that the Colorado River was just a few hours north, and that a good place to cross was a shallow ford about where the Montopolis Bridge is now.

Central Texans have also long regarded Pilot Knob as a treasure mountain, believing that riches had once been buried here, or more down to earth, believed they could find diamonds here. (The great diamond mines of South Africa and Arkansas dig into similar geologic formations.)

In 1919 Professor J. A. Udden announced that the entire dome of the knob was composed of nephelite basalt, also known as "traprock," and that this was the toughest rock to be found in Texas. Promoter Arvid Franke of San Antonio promptly announced his high hopes of leveling this knob of noble rock for road surfacing material. He said he would build the crusher if the International and Great Northern Railroad would extend their tracks six and a half miles in his direction. The railroad declined, and so the knob sits here, still covered with scrubby oaks and mesquite, getting a little smaller each century.

ST. DAVID'S EPISCOPAL CHURCH
E. 7th and San Jacinto
Central West
472-1196
Call Monday through Friday 9–4, and the office will arrange for a guided tour

The body of St. David's Church dates to 1854, its current whimsical gothic castle facade to 1870. The congregation wanted to build a new sanctuary; failing to collect enough money, they chose instead to remodel what they already had. The minister's plan won. It should be easy to see from whence some of his inspiration came; the old 1856 Land Office, with its classic, popular Rundbogenstil lines is only a few blocks away and was easily seen by the rector.

The limestone rubble walls are covered over by a pinkish articulated stucco skin. The bell in the tower dates to 1853. Some of the stained glass windows are genuine Tiffany. The interior is spacious, colorful, and very Victorian. This is the second-oldest protestant church in Texas and is sometimes called the "Gamblers' Church"; legend has it that some of the money to build the original church came from the pockets of gamblers. Like many other congregations, this one split over the issue of slavery but reunited in time to get the church remodeled.

SANTA RITA NO. 1
Trinity at Martin Luther King
Central West
Open 24 hours
Free
W

Many pass by, few stop. Yet everyone has seen this quaint shrine to the vicissitudes of crude, which stands on a tiny island on the southernmost edge of UT Austin's main fief, along Martin Luther King Boulevard. If UT ever had a patron saint, Santa Rita is it, and Santa Rita No. 1 is her holiest of icons.

In its infinite mercy, the Texas Legislature had, during the latter half of the nineteenth century, endowed its university two million acres of land out on the edge of the Great American Desert with which to support herself. Now let's see; how much does two million times a nickel equal? That's about what West Texas ranchers paid for grazing rights.

Then in 1916, after poking around "out there," UT professor John A. Udden got the harebrained idea that oil just might be lurking somewhere beneath the university's share of the desert floor. No one paid much attention to the perceptive professor, except for recent UT graduate Rupert Ricker, who had grown up on a ranch out in that patch of West Texas. Now he was back at the ranch, scheming for a way to make it pay. Livestock alone was no longer enough. He grasped at Udden's straw of hope, and during 1919 leased 431,360 acres from the university at ten cents per. He had thirty days to raise the requisite forty-three thou and change. He failed, and sold all his rights to Frank T. Pickrell and Haymen Knapp of El Paso for $500.

They organized a company, raised the necessary money, hired a driller, and managed to spud in just before midnight on the last day of grace. The well produced water.

Work on the real derrick commenced in June 1921. Pickrell christened it Santa Rita, as he sprinkled rose petals over the rig. The name came from a consortium of Catholic investors from New York; their priest admonished them to invoke the name of Santa Rita, the saint of the impossible. He evidently didn't believe Udden's reports, either.

Drilling began in August 1921. It was early morning May 28, 1923, when the well finally blew in, from a depth of 3055 feet. And that, folks, was only the beginning. Oil royalties have flowed into the Permanent University Fund ever since, to the tune of $1.75 billion by the end of 1982. (UT gets two-thirds, A&M one-third.) Short of being born, Santa Rita has been the greatest thing that ever happened to UT-Austin.

This rig stayed on location for nineteen years, intermittently pumping oil. For all its ground-breaking precedence, Santa Rita No. 1 was never much of a producer—AAA league at best. It was dismantled and shipped to Austin in 1949 so that it might be suitably enshrined for posterity. The rig stayed in storage for another eighteen years, while a placement debate sputtered along. Finally, on Thanksgiving Day 1958, in a brief halftime ceremony during the annual Longhorn-Aggie clash, the university memorialized the rig. And Santa Rita No. 1 has sat here ever since, set in motion for state occasions, while its tape-recorded story plays on and on for the occasional visitor.

SYMPHONY SQUARE
Red River at 11th
Central West

No, the four limestone buildings that constitute Symphony Square were not built this way originally. Three of them were moved stone by stone from nearby locations, which just goes to show you the lengths that some Austinites will go to save a nice old building.

The Jeremiah Hamilton home is the sole original edifice here, and it is the square's keystone. Hamilton was the former slave of Reconstruction governor A. J. Hamilton. A carpenter by trade, he was a representative in the 1870 House and a delegate to the state Republican convention in 1873. Sometime during that period, he built this distinctive limestone two-story triangular house, wedged into a triangular plot formed by Waller Creek and 11th and Red River Streets. It is one of only three triangular houses left in the state.

Over the years it housed a grocery store, a saloon, a barbershop, and a music club. The Symphony Society saved it from the jaws of urban renewal, along with the old Wilson Mercantile–New Orleans Club (ca. 1870), the Hardeman House (1887), and Doyle House (1880).

The Mercantile has housed an antique and crafts shop in the past. Currently it serves as a refreshment hall for Symphony Square functions. The sidewalk in front of it is probably the oldest in Austin, and it too was moved stone by numbered stone from its original location. The Hardeman House has been restored as the Hearth restaurant. These three buildings frame the creekside amphitheater, and this is as close as the Waller Creek Trail gets to looking like the River Walk in San Antonio. The Doyle House, located across 11th from the Hamilton House, is a center for symphony youth programs. The Hamilton House serves as symphony business and ticket office.

WATERLOO COMPOUND
600 E. 3rd at Red River
Central West
476-2590

The land and buildings that make up the Waterloo Compound remained in the founding family for more than a hundred years. H. F. Hofheintz bought the land and built a little Sunday house on it in the early 1850s. About 1855 he added the two-story limestone building with the outside stairs. It was a grocery store then, and it is now an antique store.

Hofheintz's daughter and son-in-law added a saloon and domino parlor in the 1880s. Neighbor William Sydney Porter regularly patronized the conveniently located oasis. Two houses were built for the families. The saloon was closed by Prohibition, but Hofheintz's grandson Herman Reisseg operated the grocery store until the end of 1952. This makes the compound's buildings the oldest extant cluster of commercial buildings in Austin. The present owners, who acquired the property in 1966, have restored all the buildings. The old grocery-turned-antique store, though, remains the stellar attraction, if not for what's outside, then certainly for all the neat antiquities within: American, Texas, and European furnishings, interiors, china, period clothes, and antique lighting fixtures.

PARKS & LAKES

PARKS

You have to stray far, far from the heart of Texas to find a city park system as large and innovative and enjoyable as Austin's. Austin was one of the first cities in the state to adopt a city plan, back in the late 1920s. Those first city planners were determined that Austin's natural beauty would be preserved forever and that visitor and Austinite alike be allowed to enjoy that beauty to its fullest. The current result is that the City of Austin Parks System is more than 8500 acres and still growing, divided into approximately 130 parks, greenbelts, and centers. Some are vest-pocket historical sites; others offer a wide range of amenities, from camping and fishing and swimming to tennis lessons and arts and crafts classes. Many are linear parks that carry the city's impressive hike-and-bike trail network.

The Austin Parks and Recreation Department (PARD) sponsors athletic leagues year-round; its programming and facilities are among the best in the country. It also has strong adaptive (handicapped) and senior citizens' programs. The Jourdan-Bachman Pioneer Farm is a good example of the department's innovative programming. Perhaps not quite as innovative but extremely popular are its summer entertainment offerings, which include live music, movies, and theater productions all summer at parks across the city. The best way to keep track of all these special summer events is to read the calendars and listings in the *Austin American-Statesman, Texas Monthly, Third Coast,* and the *Austin Chronicle.*

Twice a year PARD mails a brochure (actually a twenty-four-page tabloid catalog) citywide, announcing its programs, leagues, services, special events, and hours for the fall and spring. You can pick up copies at the main office.

PARKS AND RECREATION DEPARTMENT
Main office, 1500 W. Riverside
Southwest
477-6511
Monday through Friday
W

MAJOR PARKS

JOURDAN-BACHMAN PIONEER FARM
See Children's Activities.

LAKE AUSTIN METROPOLITAN PARK (CITY PARK)
City Park Rd. off FM Rd. 2222
About 15 miles from Austin
346-1831
Open at all times
Day use fee of about $2 during spring and summer; overnight use about $3–5
W variable

One of Austin's oldest and biggest parks, City Park offers a wide range of picnicking, boating, fishing, camping, and swimming activities. Boat ramps and canoe rentals are available. The park's three miles of winding Lake Austin shoreline include both sheer cliffs and bathing beaches. Much of the acreage has been left as it was when the park was established, and 1000-foot elevations offer good views of Austin.

LAKE W. E. LONG METROPOLITAN PARK
Decker Lane; take Martin Luther King (FM Rd. 969) east from Austin and follow signs
About 8 miles east of Austin
926-9067
Open every day 6–dusk
Fee of about $2 per car; $1 pedestrians and bicyclists
W variable

Picnicking, boating, fishing, and swimming on or beside this manmade lake. Roads around the perimeter of the park are a scenic and popular circuit for runners and bicyclists.

MAYFIELD PARK
3505 W. 35th (Old Bull Creek Rd.)
Central West
453-7236
Open seven days 8–5 (gates closed Saturday and Sunday)
Free
Children especially enjoy the peacocks and tame deer that reside in this twenty-two-acre nature sanctuary, which is tucked away in far west Austin, next door to Laguna Gloria on that glorious lagoon of Lake Austin commonly called Taylor's Slough. Several short nature trails wind through the dense vegetation.

MT. BONNELL
Crest of Mt. Bonnell Rd., about 1 mile past the west end of W. 35th
Central West
Open seven days
Curfew at 10 p.m.
Mt. Bonnell is one of Austin's oldest tourist attractions, having first been officially sighted as such in the 1850s. At 785 feet, it is the highest point within the city limits of Austin (Mt. Larson across the lake in West Lake Hills is actually taller at 920 feet). Day or night this is the acme of Austin viewpoints.

As befits a landmark of its stature, Mt. Bonnell is cloaked with mystery, romance, treasure, and tragedy, alone and in various combinations. Even the stories behind the crag's name are laced with romance and tragedy. Most will cite George Bonnell as the peak's namesake.

Texas was created for men like George W. Bonnell. In 1836 he was sitting in New York awaiting further definition in life, when he caught wind of the Glorious War for Independence and Open Shops down Galleria way. Bonnell recruited a company of buddies to go along, so's he wouldn't have to fight with strangers. Soon he was a philosopher and commissioner of Indian affairs. By 1836 he was an Indian fighter, by 1840 an author and newspaper publisher. He turned mercenary in time for the ill-fated Santa Fe Expedition, and got out of the Santa Fe juzgado just in time to ride with the Mier Expedition down to the Big River. There he was captured and shot by the Mexicans on Boxing Day 1842 while trying to recover his troops' horses.

But unabashed sentimentalists speak of Golden Nell, who was married atop this high peak. The Indians waited till after the kiss to attack, and to avoid torture, she and hubby jumped out into the void together. Thus the name Beau + Nell, subsequently bowdlerized to the colloquial "Bonnell."

Beau and Nell were not the first ill-timed lovers to avail themselves of the mountain's obvious charms. A beautiful Spanish señorita named Antoinette (they're always beautiful, aren't they?) leapt to her death on the rocks below to avoid capture by the Comanches, who had slain her paramour as he had fought to protect her.

Or take the lovely Indian princess, who had been promised by Poppa to the tribe's bravest warrior. While he was out splitting heads and hairs, she fell in love with a handsome young man from Waterloo. Each day they would meet by the river. One night, Mad Max told his little maid-to-be that he had spied on her and the honky, and that Poppa Chief would hear of the illicit tryst. Terror-stricken, she ran up the ninety-nine steps and dove down onto the river boulders below.

With the redskins' demise, love on the mountain was not nearly so dear a proposition but was increasingly popular. A young man knew he was marked when a young girl started dragging him up to Mt. Bonnell on any and every pretext, because everybody in Austin knew that when a young lady and man climbed to the summit together, they would fall in love. If they climbed up a second time, they would get engaged. The third trip was inevitably fatal.

And the treasure? Strontium. This rare mineral used in making flares was mined from the mountain during World War I.

By 1924 the view of Lake Austin from the north side of Mt. Bonnell was gracing the menu cards in dining cars of the Missouri-Kansas-Texas Line's crack "Texas Special" passenger train. It is probably the most enduring postcard view in Austin.

TOWN LAKE PARK
Colorado River, dam to dam
Central
Open at all times
W most areas

Town Lake Park and Zilker Park are the twin crown jewels of the Austin park system and also its most heavily used. Thousands of Austinites use the eight-and-a-half-mile Walk and Bikeway daily. Hundreds of others fish from favorite spots along the banks. Picnics, concerts, and Fourth of July fireworks go off here. Sailing and canoeing are permitted, but no motorboats. And no swimming; the undercurrents are too dangerous. And finally there is spring at Town Lake. More than 3000 trees and shrubs have been planted along the length of the park, many of them endangered Texas species. Come spring they are in radiant bloom: the redbuds, peaches, cherries, plums, and so on, for miles and miles. The cherry blossoms of Tokyo and Washington got nothing on a Town Lake spring. You can thank Lady Bird Johnson and the National Recreation Trails System for it all. Ball fields and playgrounds. Public boat launches.

Longhorn Shores, Pleasant Valley Rd. between Longhorn Dam and Lakeshore Dr.
Travis Park, S. IH 35 turnaround, near Town Lake Holiday Inn
Waller Beach, Brazos at Willow
Austin High School, Stephen F. Austin Dr.

ZILKER PARK
2100 Barton Springs Rd., between Robert E. Lee and Loop 1 (MoPac)
Southwest
477-6511

Open every day 6 a.m.–10 p.m.
Free
W

Four-hundred-acre Zilker Park is of course best known as the home of Barton Springs, Texas's most venerated swimming hole. It has been a spot favored by mankind for thousands of years. It has been a city park since 1917, when Colonel A. J. Zilker donated the initial acreage to the city with the stipulation that Austin endow its public school system with an industrial education program fund. Picnic tables, playgrounds, ball fields, and group shelters are scattered throughout the park. A miniature train runs through, and you can rent canoes and rowboats. You can also fish, hike, bike, and run.

Barton Springs is the fourth-largest natural spring in Texas and named for the white settler who originally homesteaded the area in 1837: William "Uncle Billy" Barton. The spring's extraordinarily clean, limestone-filtered water stays a constant 69 degrees. Always a popular Austin swimming hole, the spring at one time powered sawmills and flour mills. Although the water was as wonderful as ever, the trappings have been altered over the years; the rocky banks were grassed over and the pool enlarged to its present 1000-by-125-foot size in the late 1920s.

The Hillside Theater is host to many musical and theatrical productions. Zilker Park also hosts the spring kite-flying contest and YuleFest. (See also Zilker Gardens.)

ZILKER GARDENS/AUSTIN AREA GARDEN CENTER
2200 Barton Springs Rd.
Southwest
477-7341
Open seven days until sunset
Free

Zilker Gardens: an oasis? Well, maybe in Las Vegas, but not here in Austin, unless you consider the acres outside the Garden Center to be wasteland. Still, "oasis" has a good emotive feel when it comes to describing these twenty-two luxuriously planted acres that overlook Zilker's vast playing fields. Any number of trails lead you through the grounds, through the Oriental Garden, Rose Garden, Water Garden, Garden for the Blind. The Zilker Gardens are well maintained, but like the rest of Austin are still informal and unstuffy. In the fall, fruit from the native persimmon trees stain the cobbled limestone sidewalks with purple blotches. The rock-and-bamboo shelter overlooking the Oriental Garden offers a panoramic view of downtown Austin. On rainy grey days up here, when the fog rolls in to obscure the great buildings and everything else save the dark outlines of the hills of west Austin, you can catch a glimpse of the untamed beauty to which Austin and Lamar and Jake Harrell and Uncle Billy succumbed.

Blended into the Garden Center's natural beauty are bits and pieces of Austin's civilized past: a Swedish log cabin from Govalle, authentically furnished; the 120-year-old Esperanza Schoolhouse from northwest Travis County; the Queen Anne cupola from the gay nineties Bickler School; a granite and brick window arch from the grand old Butler Mansion; an iron footbridge used on Congress Avenue a century and more ago.

The Garden Center grounds are a popular wedding spot, as you can imagine. On weekdays you can practically be by yourself here.

DISTRICT PARKS

Austin has eight district parks, several of which are not fully developed. Developed district parks have pools, picnic areas, sports fields, playgrounds, and trails.

BARTHOLOMEW ● 5200 Berkman ● Northeast ● 928-0014
GARRISON ● 6001 Manchaca at Stassney ● Southwest ● 442-4048
GIVENS ● 3800 E. 12th ● Central East ● 926-2339
NORTHWEST ● Ardath at Ellise ● Northwest ● 453-0194
PEASE ● 1600 Parkway ● Central West
ROSEWOOD ● 2300 Rosewood ● Central East ● 472-6838

HIKE AND BIKE TRAILS

Barton Springs. City Park. Recreation centers. Community education. The Austin Parks and Recreation Department has some pretty popular parks and programs, but reigning over them all as the day-in, day-out favorite of Austinites is the Austin Trail System, more popularly known as the Hike and Bike Trails. Walkers, runners, and cyclists by the tens of thousands are on these twenty-plus miles of trails at all hours of the day and night. All are a part of or are easily accessible from the city's parks and greenbelts. Not all the trails are fully developed yet, but all are generally well maintained. Some of the trails damaged by the Memorial Day floods of 1981 may not be fully repaired yet but are generally navigable.

Because assaults do happen on some of these trails, it makes good sense to run with a partner during and after the twilight hours.

We begin with the major trails.

TOWN LAKE HIKE AND BIKE TRAIL

This eight-and-a-half-mile trail along the north and south shores of Town Lake is the longest and most heavily used of the city's twelve trails. It is not a complete loop, however. On the south, the Town Lake Trail starts at the Congress Avenue bridge and runs west past Auditorium Shores into Zilker Park before it crosses Town Lake on an award-winning pedestrian bridge under MoPac. The trail then turns back east from Deep Eddy past Lamar and Shoal Beaches, past Fiesta Gardens, till it reaches Longhorn Dam. The trail crosses back over the river to the south bank via the dam, and runs another mile or so along Longhorn Shores before ending across the lake from Fiesta Gardens.

SHOAL CREEK HIKE AND BIKE TRAIL

Three miles long, the Shoal Creek trail runs from Town Lake up to W. 38th, following Shoal Creek and Lamar Boulevard. It passes Austin

Recreation Center, Pease Park, Caswell Tennis Center, and the Senior Activity Center before ending at pretty, tranquil Seiders Spring Park. Shoal Creek was the most heavily damaged trail from the 1981 flooding and is the second most popular trail.

WALLER CREEK WALKWAY

The Waller Creek Walkway has been designed to resemble more nearly the San Antonio River Walk than a nature preserve, running as it does through a heavily urban area. It traces the original eastern boundary of Austin for slightly more than a mile, from Town Lake to Martin Luther King and the University of Texas campus. It intersects Old Pecan Street and continues north through Symphony Square, Waterloo Park, and the new Centennial Park. Plans call for the walkway ultimately to function as a shopping and dining promenade. These plans are some years away from fruition, and lately the stretch between 6th and Town Lake has become a wino hangout. Joggers should avoid the tunnels here, unless their noses are stopped up.

JOHNSON CREEK HIKE AND BIKE TRAIL

The Johnson Creek trail runs about a mile, from Enfield to Town Lake. It parallels MoPac, anchored at the north end by Westenfield Park.

BOGGY CREEK HIKE AND BIKE TRAIL

This mile-long trail runs along Boggy Creek from Rosewood Park to Zaragosa Park.

BLUNN CREEK HIKE AND BIKE TRAIL

Less than a mile long, Blunn Creek trail runs along Blunn Creek from Stacy Pool in Big Stacy Park (800 E. Live Oak at Alameda) to Little Stacy Park.

MINOR TRAILS

The six minor trails are less than a mile in length and are contained within individual parks. BARTON CREEK HIKE AND BIKE TRAIL follows Barton Creek along the greenbelt from Barton Springs Road south. BUTTERMILK BRANCH HIKE AND BIKE TRAIL follows Buttermilk Branch Creek from Blessing to Bennett within the greenbelt. The following district parks have trails: BARTHOLOMEW PARK, GARRISON PARK, GIVENS PARK, and NORTHWEST PARK.

LAKE TRAVIS PUBLIC PARKS

ARKANSAS BEND
Sylvester Ford Rd., off FM Rd. 1431
473-9222
Open at all times
Free
W variable
This park consists of 195 acres, with camping, a picnic area, rest-

rooms, a boat launch, and scenic peninsulas jutting into Lake Travis. Fourteen-day camping limit.

CYPRESS CREEK
Anderson Mill Rd. at FM Rd. 2769
About 15 miles west of Austin
473-9222
Open at all times
Free
W variable

Vest-pocket fifteen-acre park located where Cypress Creek flows into Lake Travis. Picnic area, swimming, boat launch, restroom, primitive camping. Fourteen-day limit.

MANSFIELD DAM
FM Rd. 620 at Mansfield Dam
11 miles west of Austin
473-9333, 266-2600
Open at all times
Free
W variable

Forty-two acres on a rocky point just west of the dam. Thirty-six primitive campsites, picnic area, swimming, boat launch. Fourteen-day camping limit. Good swimming cove and sailing make it popular.

PACE BEND (PALEFACE PARK)
FM Rd. 2322, 4.6 miles east of Texas Hwy. 71
About 30 miles east of Austin
473-9333, 264-1482
Open at all times
Day use fee of about $2 per car; overnight fee of about $2
W variable

More than 1500 acres located in the Pace Bend of Lake Travis, "Paleface" is one of the most popular area parks among young people. Picnic and primitive camping areas (150 sites), restrooms, swimming, boat launch. Its popularity has left it with a checkered reputation; recently instituted admission fees are designed to control the crowds better.

SANDY CREEK PARK
Lime Creek Rd., 3.5 miles north of Volente, just past the green water tank
264-1482
Open at all times
Free
W variable

Twenty-five-acre park on the Sandy Creek branch of Lake Travis. Boat ramp, swimming, primitive camping, picnicking, restrooms. Water access is mostly from a bank of sharp broken rocks, so it's a good idea to wear sneakers. There is a dab of sandy beach next to the boat ramp. Often less crowded than other Lake Travis parks. Fourteen-day camping limit.

MCKINNEY FALLS STATE PARK
Scenic Loop Rd.; take US Hwy. 183 south to FM Rd. 812, and turn right on Scenic Loop Rd.
243-1643
Open seven days
$2 per vehicle per day; camping fee $4 per day
W variable
   This state park on the southeast edge of town is usually filled on weekends and all summer, but not with Austinites, who generally forsake the place. Perhaps it is because of what they have done to the water and falls for which the park is named. This stretch of Onion Creek with its two sets of scenic falls has long been popular with fishers and swimmers, but due to intermittent nonpoint-source (read you, me, and the world in general) pollution, the creek and falls have been permanently closed to swimming. The creek, with its cypress and cedar sentinels, still makes for a scenic stroll, and the remains of the old Thomas McKinney house (for whom the falls were named) still stand, near the confluence of Williamson and Onion Creeks. One of the trails also takes you through an ancient Indian campground, one of the oldest yet discovered in Central Texas. Restrooms, picnic sites, several trails, group shelters, primitive and trailer camping sites with hookups, but no swimming pool.

OTHER PARKS

WILD BASIN WILDERNESS PRESERVE
4 miles west on Loop 360, .75 miles north of Bee Caves Rd.
Southwest
476-4113
   Consisting of nearly two hundred acres along and around Bee Creek, this is a sanctuary and wilderness preserve for native plants and animals, and for research and environmental education. It offers programs for elementary schools and weekend tours for the general public. Specialized tours each Saturday identify plants, trees, native grasses, wildflowers, wildlife. Call for details. No restrooms or drinking fountains.

★★
PICNICKING

   Although picnicking will never be an Olympic sport, Austin does boast a number of world-class picnic spots. And given our mild climate, we can enjoy them year-round. Practically every one of Austin's more than one hundred parks has picnic facilities; the following are the crème de la crème.

STATE CAPITOL GROUNDS
   Lots of pecan and oak shade and carpet grass make the statehouse grounds a comfortable lunching spot even during the dog days of sum-

mer. The south mall offers a great view down Congress to the river and
beyond. Be sure to bring a little extra for the brazen squirrels.

MT. BONNELL
3800 Mt. Bonnell Rd.
Central West
The view of Austin and the western hills is always great up here, but
Mt. Bonnell peaks as a picnic spot during spring and fall, when the
sun's warmth is a blessing, not a hindrance, and the hills of Austin are
plastered with patches of red and orange and yellow and blue.

PEASE PARK
1600 Parkway, along Shoal Creek between W. 24th and W. 12th
Central West
Pease Park is popular with area office employees, who often take a
stroll along the Shoal Creek Hike and Bike Trail with their lunches.
They are hardly doing anything new. Former Governor Elisha M. Pease
donated the original twenty-three acres to the city in 1875. Left largely
undeveloped until 1913, it was nonetheless highly favored for picnics
and outings. George Armstrong Custer and his cavalry camped here
after the Civil War; O. Henry and a friend looked for buried treasure;
and prospectors dug for oil on the banks of Shoal Creek and gave up
after striking coal at fourteen feet.

SEIDERS SPRINGS
W. 34th through W. 37th, on Shoal Creek
Central West
W
Seiders Springs (Seiders Oaks, if you prefer), at the north end of the
Shoal Creek Hike and Bike Trail, is popular with nearby hospital and
medical-center employees. Gideon White, daughter Louisa, and son-
in-law Ed Seiders built a log cabin here in 1839, located in a grove of live
oaks, near springs that bubbled out of the limestone creek bank. In 1842
White was ambushed by Indians, scalped, and killed. By 1853, the
Austin-to-Burnet highway passed by Seiders, crossing Shoal Creek at
34th Street.
Shoal Creek was a perennial stream then, full of fish. Robert E. Lee
camped here, as did Custer after him. Seiders eventually turned the
springs into a little resort, carving bathtubs out of the rock into which
the spring waters flowed. The tubs are still there, and the springs still
trickle into them most of the year. Shoal Creek runs mostly dry these
days, but patrons of the historic vale still enjoy the shade of Seiders'
venerable oaks.

TOWN LAKE PARK
Colorado River, dam to dam
Town Lake Park has mile upon mile of picnic possibilities. The stretch
of north bank west of Congress is particularly nice in the early spring,
when the redbuds, peppermint peaches, and other trees and shrubs
are in full bloom.

TREATY OAK
503 Baylor
Central West

What better place to picnic than in the shade of the most perfect specimen of a tree in North America? The Treaty Oak was once the center of a group of trees known as the Council Oaks, whereunder Stephen F. Austin supposedly first entreated the Indians. The Treaty Oak was already 400 years old. Although it now stands alone, it has grown only more graceful with age and has been part of the Austin parks system since 1937. If you don't feel like packing your own, pick out your lunch at the nearby Sweetish Hill Deli.

WATERLOO PARK
1300 Red River, E. 11th to E. 15th, along Waller Creek
Central West
W

Favorite weekday lunching spot of nearby state and Brackenridge Hospital employees. Quiet, shaded, and courtesy of urban renewal. Northern anchor of the Waller Creek Walkway.

WOOLDRIDGE SQUARE
W. 9th and Guadalupe
Central West
W

Named for early twentieth-century mayor Alexander Wooldridge, this block of park was laid out as one of four public squares on the original 1839 plat of Austin. The block was left undeveloped, and the natural amphitheater it contains became a favored dumping ground. But in a burst of civic pride orchestrated by newly elected Mayor Wooldridge, the square was cleaned up and dedicated as a park in June 1909. The Greek Revival gazebo cost all of $550 and has been the site of countless concerts, weddings, and at least one murder since.

ZILKER PARK
2100 Barton Springs Rd.
Southwest
W

Zilker Park offers a number of picnic possibilities, but a good spot is the Polo Picnic Area, located in the southwest section of the park, south of Barton Springs Road and west of the pool.

THE HIGHLAND LAKES

The bright, sparkling Highland Lakes play such a large recreational role in our lives these days that we tend to forget the first noble purpose of these seven pools, which was to control the Colorado River's destructive flooding capacities. Control in turn begat electric power, drinking and irrigation water, and fun.

The Highland Lakes take seven giant steps up the Colorado, climbing 646 feet over 150 continually scenic miles. Together the lakes offer 56,000 surface acres of clean blue water for your recreational pleasure, more than 700 miles of shoreline, and 1 trillion, 780 billion gallons of water. These statistics make the Highland Lakes the greatest concentration of freshwater lakes in Texas. The fishing is good in every lake—black, white, and striped bass; cats, crappie, perch—and there have been some whoppers. You can sail, scuba, snorkel, ski, and windsurf.

Every dam but Longhorn is operated by the Lower Colorado River Authority, a state agency charged with the control, storage, preservation, and distribution of the waters of the Colorado. Longhorn Dam is operated by the City of Austin in cooperation with the LCRA.

For more information, write the Highland Lakes Tourist Association at P. O. Box 1967, Austin 78767, or call 478-9383.

From Austin, the lakes are as follows.

TOWN LAKE
416 surface acres
5 miles long
Formed by Longhorn Dam (1960), 54 ft. high, 512 ft. wide. Pleasant Valley Rd. at E. 1st
Flood control only

Town Lake is the youngest of the Highland Lakes, but it was one that Austinites had wanted since the dawn of the century. Back then, damers were talking about an eight-foot wooden dam, to be located about a half mile downstream from the Congress Avenue bridge. With such a structure, they figured, Austin could offer fishing, swimming, and boating year-round, not to mention the shoreside amusement park and the hundred guest cottages—all this conveniently in view of the hot and dusty passengers on the International and Great Northern trains as they crossed the high bridge that still spans the Colorado downtown. Well, the dam is concrete, and we don't have swimming or an amusement park; but Auditorium Shores and the Town Lake Walk are pretty nice, aren't they? (See also Town Lake Park and Sailing and Boating.)

LAKE AUSTIN
1830 surface acres
20.25 miles long
Formed by Tom Miller Dam (1940), 100 ft. high, 1590 ft. wide. Lake Austin Blvd., just north of Redbud Tr.

In a sense, Lake Austin is the oldest of the Highland Lakes, and the oldest major artificial lake in Texas.

Completion of the million-dollar dam in May 1893 ushered in a grand new era for Austin. The dam endowed Austin with both cheap, abundant power and an attractive lake. Mules didn't pull the streetcars anymore, and Lake McDonald made Austin the crewing capital of Texas, if not the world. On Sundays, Austinites jammed into the sleek new streetcars and glided out to their dam, just to gaze upon the 65-foot-high, 1100-foot-wide obstruction that created their 21-mile lake. Steamboats plied the lake's sinewy course, treating rubberneckers to the "Palisades of the Colorado," where the river is chuted through mile after mile of sheer high limestone cliffs. At the time, the dam was supposedly the largest dam across a major river in the world.

Austinites generally held their dam and lake in higher esteem than the elected dignitaries they were doomed in perpetuity by law to play host to. Austin's economic lions abandoned their east Austin estates for lakeside chateaus. But there was trouble in Paradise. Silt from upstream was accumulating behind the dam. It was the only major obstruction in the Colorado River, and the storage capacity of its reservoir was relatively small. Doomsayers warned of the possible dire consequences, and indeed on April 7, 1900, the worst happened. Heavy rain throughout the Colorado's watershed above Austin sent a sizable wall of water rolling downriver. And as it squeezed through the Palisades, its destructive forces were enhanced. Already strained by the force of the accumulated silt, half the dam gave way. Many people drowned, and much of lower Austin was flooded. The electricity was gone.

A million-dollar reconstruction job commenced in 1912 and continued through mid-1915, when it halted. The city wouldn't pay up; the design was unsafe and the workmanship shoddy. What there was of the dam failed again that year. Work didn't commence again until 1938, when the LCRA began to rehabilitate the old Austin dam as part of its master plan to tame the Colorado. Finished in 1940, it was later named in honor of one-time mayor Tom Miller. Huge chunks of granite from the original dam still lay scattered like pebbles below the present one.

Lake Austin provides its namesake's drinking water, which has made it a battleground in recent years between developers and environmentalists. Boating and swimming are as popular now as they were on Lake McDonald. (See also Lake Austin Metropolitan Park and Sailing and Boating.)

LAKE TRAVIS
18,930 surface acres
64 miles long
Formed by Mansfield Dam (1941), 266 ft. high, 7098 ft. wide. FM Rd. 620 3 miles west of FM Rd. 2222

Lake Travis is the largest and longest lake in the Highland chain, and the most important in controlling the Colorado's floods. Most of the other lakes have fixed levels; Travis has gone as low as 614 feet above sea level and as high as 707 feet. The spillway tops out at 714. A normal level of 681 feet at the spillway provides an ample reservoir against floods.

At its completion in 1941, Mansfield Dam (named for Congressman J. J. Mansfield of Columbus) was the fifth-largest masonry structure in the world. It had originally been called the Marshall Ford Dam, in reference to its location at an old low-water crossing called Marshall's Ford.

Lake Travis is the most popular of the Highland Lakes, if you go by numbers of users; and it is now beginning to become the center of a developers-vs.-ecologists controversy as Austin grows closer. Fishing,

boating, scuba-diving and sailing are its current most popular uses. By
the turn of the century it may be supplying Austin's drinking water, as
well. Numerous private campgrounds, resorts, and boat launches. (See
also Lake Travis Public Parks and Sailing and Boating.)

LAKE MARBLE FALLS
780 surface acres
5.75 miles long
**Formed by Max Starcke Dam (1951), 100 ft. high, 860 ft. long. About
1 mile east of US Hwy. 281**
Lake Marble Falls is the smallest of the Highland Lakes. Its creation
meant the disappearance of the lake's namesake, the marble falls on the
Colorado River, located where Highway 281 crosses the Colorado.
Nearby Marble Falls City Park offers camping, boating, fishing, swimming, and skiing access to the lake. Good fishing. Several private campground and boat-launch facilities.

LAKE LYNDON B. JOHNSON
6375 surface acres
21 miles long
**Formed by Alvin Wirtz Dam (1950), 118 ft. high, 5491 ft. wide. Two
miles south of FM Rd. 1431 between Marble Falls and Sherwood
Shores**
Limestone cliffs give way to granite along the course of this medium-
sized lake. Fishermen love Lake LBJ. There are many caves and coves.
Skiers love the total absence of obstructions and the stretches protected
from high winds. Many private campgrounds and boat-launch facilities.

INKS LAKE
803 surface acres
4 miles long
**Formed by Roy Inks Dam (1938), 96.5 ft. high, 1548 ft. wide. About
five miles south of Texas Hwy. 29 off Park Rd. 4**
Inks Lake may be the shortest of the Highland Lakes, but it has the
largest and most complete campground on the lakes (down to the nine-
hole golf course): 1200-acre Inks Lake State Park. Phone 1-793-2223. The
rough-and-tumble granite country that Inks Lake traverses makes it
uniquely scenic among the Highland Lakes. Park Road 4 is one of the
most scenic in the Hill Country. Some private campgrounds and boat-
launch facilities.

LAKE BUCHANAN
23,060 surface acres
31 miles long
**Formed by Buchanan Dam (1937), 146 ft. high, 10,988 ft. wide. Texas
Hwy. 29 and FM Rd. 690**
Lake Buchanan (pronounced "Buck-Cannon") is the largest of the
Highland Lakes. "Now hold on," you say. "Didn't you just call Lake
Travis the largest lake?" Well, yes, we did, and we're right both times.
Lake Buchanan covers the largest surface area; Lake Travis has the

greatest capacity. Lake Buchanan is so wide that you may think you're out to sea in its middle. Travis and Buchanan are the two most popular Highland Lakes. It is lined with fishing camps and retirement cottages, and filled with boaters and fishers and skiers.

Adam Johnson picked out the site for this great dam in the 1850s. Construction on it actually commenced in 1931, and it impounded the first of the permanent Highland Lakes. Originally called the Hamilton Dam and Reservoir, it was named upon completion in honor of the late and great Texas Congressman James Buchanan. In 1938 it was the largest dam of its type in the world.

The LCRA and Burnet County operate several parks on the lake.

BLACK ROCK PARK, Texas Hwy. 261, 4 miles north of Texas Hwy. 29, primitive camping, ramp, no charge.

SHAW ISLAND, 4.2 miles off Texas Hwy. 261, primitive camping, no charge.

BURNET COUNTY PARK, FM Rd. 2341, picnic area, ramp, no charge.

There are many more private campgrounds, resorts, and cottages for rent.

SPORTS

Austinites love to watch their football, basketball, and baseball heroes in action as dearly as any other nominal aggregate of American citizenry. The seasonal hordes at Memorial Stadium, Disch-Falk Field, and the Erwin Center testify deafeningly to that fact. But when it comes to sports, Austinites are doers as well as watchers, probably more so than in any other Texas city. Austin's trails, courts, and various brands of playing field are filled around the calendar. This segment encompasses both spectator and participatory sports. It is not a complete list of the sports in Austin, but it includes all the favorites.

PARKS AND RECREATION DEPARTMENT
1500 Riverside near S. Lamar
Southwest
477-6511, ext. 2737 or 2738
Fees vary

Approximately 30,000 Austinites participate in the various recreational sports of the Athletics Division of PARD. The lineup includes classes and leagues for youth and adults. The department sponsors leagues in basketball, flag football, softball, soccer, and volleyball. Classes stretch out even further, into badminton, boxing, gymnastics, racquetball, self-defense, tennis, and weight training. In addition, the

Adaptive Programs section provides a variety of sports activities for persons with handicapping conditions.

PARD sports activities play at all the city's Community Recreation Centers, as well as at many other locations. If you haven't figured it out yet, Austin's PARD ranks among the top such departments in the country, offering Austinites some of the best athletic programs and facilities to be found in *any* American city. The city also maintains many swimming pools, tennis courts, and several golf courses. For more details on these sports, see the separate headings below.

The department's free seasonal brochures give complete listings for all city-sponsored leagues and classes.

YOUNG MEN'S CHRISTIAN ASSOCIATION
1100 W. 1st near Lamar
Central West
476-6705
Monday through Friday 6 a.m.–9 p.m., Saturday 8–5
W

The YMCA offers a wide variety of lessons, leagues, and programs for all ages, male and female, singles and families at its three locations. Activities vary at each location. Town Lake facilities include the latest in Nautilus equipment, whirlpool, dry sauna and wet steam rooms, an indoor track, and gymnasium equipment. Family programs include Trail Blazers and Indian Guides.

YOUNG WOMEN'S CHRISTIAN ASSOCIATION
W. 18th and Guadalupe
Central West
478-9873
Open every day except Labor Day weekend, Thanksgiving weekend, last week in December

Swimming lessons, tai chi chuan, ki-aikido, yoga, dance classes (belly, rhumba, country and western, waltz), workshops like CPR, wreathmaking, and defensive driving. Men and boys are welcome as associate members. Current membership is required for participation in activities, classes, and use of the YWCA facilities. Nonmembers may audit any class for a fee of $2 on a one-time basis.

ARCHERY

ARCHERY UNLIMITED
749 E. Ben White
Southeast
443-8345
   Indoor range.

ARCHERY WORLD
7601-E N. Lamar
Northwest
454-4593
   Indoor range.

BASEBALL

UNIVERSITY OF TEXAS LONGHORNS
Disch-Falk Field, E. Martin Luther King at Comal, near IH 35
Central East
471-7437
General admission $2, students $1
February through May
   The Longhorn baseball team is kind of like the Dallas Cowboys, in
that each team perennially makes the postseason playoffs. But the
'Horns have managed to do the 'Pokes two better over the years when
it comes to winning world championships, all of which keeps the fans
happy. And even during the years the Longhorns spend without the
College World Series title, they usually manage at least to rack up the
best won-lost record in the Southwest Conference.

BASKETBALL

MUNICIPAL LEAGUES
   Winter and spring leagues are conducted by PARD. Call 477-6511,
ext. 2737 or 2738.

UNIVERSITY OF TEXAS LONGHORNS (WOMEN)
Erwin Center, 1701 Red River near IH 35
Central West
471-7437
Admission
November through March
   Like most of the other Longhorn teams, the women's basketball team
is always among the best in the country.

UNIVERSITY OF TEXAS LONGHORNS (MEN)
Erwin Center, 1701 Red River near IH 35
Central West
471-7437
Admission
November through March
   For many years, basketball was sort of a stepchild at UT and in the
rest of the Southwest Conference, and the SWC was sort of a stepchild
in national roundball circles. Then along came Elvin Hayes and the rest
of the University of Houston Cougars, and the 'Horns, Frogs, et al. rose
up to take the challenge. The Longhorns have had their ups and downs

ever since, but at least they have this neat pillbox hat of a pavilion to play in.

BICYCLING

Austin has long been a cyclists' paradise: good weather and roads are matched by varied terrain; flat-to-gently-rolling prairies lie to the east, the twisty and sharply steep escarpment to the west. The United States Olympic cyclists have been conducting spring training in Austin since the early 1970s. A number of local cycling organizations exist around town, and Austin is one of the few cities of any size in the state to have a full-time cycling coordinator in the city government.

AUSTIN BICYCLE CLUB
478-9719
Primarily (though not exclusively) a racing club. Maintains several different local training race series during the year for those who like their competition informal.

AUSTIN CYCLING ASSOCIATION
P. O. Box 5993, Austin 78763
451-3175
A touring/cyclocommuter club. Sponsors several century rides each year and coordinates a number of weekly informal rides for all levels of riders throughout the year.

UT CYCLING CLUB
471-3116 (UT Division of Recreational Sports)
447-1614 (Robert Boyd, president)
Racing and touring club for UT-Austin students.

BOWLING

Countless commercial bowling alleys, with still more leagues, abound in Austin. For more specific information, call the Austin Bowling Association at 452-1440, or Austin Women's Bowling Association at 892-0705.

BOXING

Several of the PARD Recreation Centers have boxing programs, and there are several amateur tournaments during the year. Call 477-6511, ext. 2737 or 2738. (See also Calendar of Events.)

CANOEING AND TUBING

You are perfectly free to canoe on any of the lakes in and around Austin, but it does get boring. Whitewater enthusiasts have to go at least as far as San Marcos, where they can dip into the river of the same name. Diehards go the few extra miles down to New Braunfels, where they pick up the Guadalupe below Canyon Dam. Local television weathercasters usually give the dam's release rate each day on the evening news.

FISHING

Local Zeke Waltons have no shortage of holes in which to sink their lines. Many go no further than downtown and Town Lake. Those smitten with wanderlust may choose between Lake Austin, Lake Long, McKinney Falls State Park (Onion Creek), Lake Travis, the Pedernales River, and the rest of the Highland Lakes. Various species of bass, catfish, perch, and crappie abound throughout, if you are in the right place at the right time with the right bait. You need to obtain a Texas fishing license, available at most sporting goods stores at a nominal price.

FOOTBALL

MUNICIPAL LEAGUES
PARD has flag-football leagues ranging from peewee to adult. Call 477-6511, ext. 2737 or 2738.

UNIVERSITY OF TEXAS LONGHORNS
Memorial Stadium, University of Texas, 23rd and San Jacinto
University/Central West
471-7437
General admission about $10
September through December
Is it really necessary to say anything about the Longhorns? Let the consistently capacity home-game crowds do the talking. Collegiate amateur football is a big industry in Austin, just in terms of the numbers of postgame margaritas and enchiladas consumed. What makes the provender more palatable is the fact that it usually follows an orange-and-white success down in the scotchgarded pits d'combat. What need has Austin for a pro (or semipro) team when it has the Longhorns?

GOLF

The City of Austin operates four golf courses. Each offers a full range of professional services. Fees range from $3 to $7. Each course closes one Monday per month; call ahead to confirm.

HANCOCK
811 E. 41st
Central West
453-0276
Short, nine-hole course.

JIMMY CLAY
5500 Nuckols Crossing near Teri
Southeast
477-1938
Long, open eighteen-hole course.

LIONS MUNICIPAL
2910 Enfield near Exposition
Central West
477-6963
Short, tight, heavily wooded eighteen-hole course.

MORRIS WILLIAMS
4300 Manor, across from the airport
Central East
926-1298
Hilly, medium length, partially wooded eighteen-hole course.

GYMNASTICS

Check YMCA, YWCA, and PARD schedules for gymnastics classes and competitions.

HIKING AND WALKING

Walkers as well as runners enjoy Austin's nationally acclaimed Hike and Bike Trails system. (See Outdoors.) The Colorado River Walkers sponsor several Volksmarches/Walkfests during the year. (See Organizations.)

HORSEBACK RIDING

"Greater" Austin has a number of privately owned stables and riding academies, most of which offer services such as boarding, breaking, rentals, riding instruction, training, and trail rides.

HORSE RACING

The only horse racing in or around town is at Manor Downs, fifteen minutes east of Austin and just north of Manor, off US Hwy. 290. Call the track at 272-4042 or 272-5581 for the latest race schedules and other information.

ICE SPORTS

NORTHCROSS MALL
The only action in town for blades. Figure-skating lessons and a hockey league duel it out here in one of Austin's biggest shopping malls.

RACQUETBALL AND HANDBALL

There are several first-rate commercial clubs in town.

ROCK CLIMBING

The Hill Country offers plenty of opportunities to do so. Central Texas Mountaineers offers rock-climbing classes for all levels for a nominal fee (around $30). Call 478-7216.

ROLLER SKATING

There are several commecial roller rinks scattered about Austin.

RUNNING

Austin was one of the first cities in Texas to embrace the sport on a commoners' level. There are plenty of 5K-and-up races year-round if you have the competitive urge. Check the sports listings in the *American-Statesman's* Saturday "Time Out" supplement. The biggie is the *American-Statesman's* Capitol 10,000, held in mid-March. (See Calendar of Events.) For more information, call the Austin Runners' Club at 444-9104. The club also maintains Runners' Hotline, which gives details of upcoming races and results (837-5433).

SAILING AND BOATING

Skiing and pleasure boating are good on all of the Highland Lakes, except Town Lake, where motorboats are prohibited. Lake Travis is excellent for sailing. Boat ramps are found in most public parks, marinas, and campgrounds. The following local lakes have public ramps not otherwise mentioned in the Parks listings.

LAKE AUSTIN
Walsh Boat Landing, Lake Austin Blvd. near Enfield
Quinlan County Park, about 5 miles off FM Rd. 620, downstream from Mansfield Dam
Fritz Hughes Park, off FM Rd. 620, just below low-water crossing and Mansfield Dam

LAKE TRAVIS
Lake Oak Park, about 5 miles north of Spicewood (take FM Rd. 191, then County Rd.), about 40 miles west of Austin

TOWN LAKE SAILAWAY
1800 S. Lakeshore near Town Creek Dr.
Southeast
442-8872
Canoes, catamarans, small sloops, and windsurfers. Sailing lessons given on vessels it rents.

ZILKER PARK BOAT RENTALS
Zilker Park, below Barton Springs Pool
Southwest
478-3852
Canoe and aquacycles (pedal-powered paddleboats) for use on Town Lake, for rent by the hour. Driver's license required as deposit.

SAILING CLUBS
For information on local sailing clubs, call the Austin Yacht Club at 266-1336, or the Lake Travis Cruising Association and ask for Gary Schmidt at 346-2828 or 345-6677.

SOCCER

MUNICIPAL
There are more local soccer leagues than you can shake a stick at. City leagues play in the autumn, winter, and spring. For more information, call PARD at 477-6511, ext. 2737 or 2738.

INDOOR SOCCER LEAGUES
476-6705
The Town Lake YMCA has a fall indoor soccer season, adult, co-rec.

YOUTH SOCCER LEAGUES
476-6705
The YMCA sponsors citywide soccer leagues for boys and girls aged six to seventeen.

SOFTBALL

MUNICIPAL LEAGUES
Along with soccer, softball is the king of team sports in Austin. Thousands of Austinites play in the spring, summer, and fall leagues that are sponsored by PARD. Call 477-6511, ext. 2737 or 2738.

SWIMMING

The City of Austin operates more than two dozen municipal neighborhood swimming pools. Some pools open in late April, most in late
May. Most close in late August and early September. Fee of about $1.25
adults and 50¢ children to use Barton Springs and the seven municipal
pools. The city also operates designated swimming areas at City Park
and Decker Lake.

BARTON SPRINGS
Zilker Park, 2100 Barton Springs Rd. between Robert E. Lee and
Loop 1 (MoPac)
Southwest
476-9044
   Open year-round, fee charged March–October. (See also Zilker Park.)

DEEP EDDY POOL
401 Deep Eddy at Lake Austin Blvd.
Central West
472-8546
   Longtime favored Austin bathing resort. Like Barton Springs, the
water is brisk, coming from an artesian well. Fee charged.

STACY POOL
800 E. Live Oak at East Side Dr.
Southwest
   Warm, spring-fed pool, open year-round. Free.

TENNIS

The City of Austin has more than one hundred courts at more than
twenty-five locations throughout the city. Most are free courts in neighborhood parks. The five following tennis centers require reservations
and a fee of about $1.25 per person. Lessons are available for groups
and individuals of all ages and abilities.

AUSTIN HIGH SCHOOL
1715 W. 1st, just east of Loop 1 (MoPac)
Central West
477-7802
Pro Shop

AUSTIN RECREATION
1213 Shoal Creek Blvd. at W. 12th
Central West
476-5662

CASWELL
W. 24th and Lamar
Central West
478-6268
Pro Shop

PHARR
4201 Brookview, Wilshire near Airport Blvd.
Northeast
473-8799
Pro Shop

SOUTH AUSTIN
1000 Cumberland at S. 5th
Southwest
442-1466
Pro Shop

TRAP AND SKEET

The Capitol City Trap and Skeet Club on Lake Long is open to the public from noon till dark Wednesdays through Sundays. The club has four skeet fields and two trap fields. Call 272-8456 for more information.

VOLLEYBALL

PARD has a volleyball league; call 477-6511, ext. 2737 or 2738.

PERFORMING ARTS

GENERAL

If you were to judge Austin solely on the strength and vitality of its performing arts, you would probably think the city much larger than it really is. Certainly the strong performing arts programs at UT and St. Edward's have something to do with it. But the performers are only half the story. You need audiences. Austin, more than any other city in Texas, is populated by "educated" (as opposed to merely "professional") folks, whose tastes in dance, theater, and music are equally well developed.

Not everybody in Austin goes to plays, the opera, and the ballet, but obviously there are enough patrons and performers to make for a rich and exciting lively arts scene.

Listed below is a good sample of the performing arts in Austin. Even if you're living on a budget, there is plenty of free entertainment in town. (For informal live music, see Clubs and Bars.) Sometimes no phone number or address is listed for small arts groups, because they lack permanent offices. Austin's colleges, universities, and public schools sponsor many concerts and performances; ditto the shopping malls—so many that an entire book of these listings alone could be compiled.

The best means of keeping track of activities is to check the entertainment section of the *American-Statesman* and the calendars of events in *Texas Monthly*, *Third Coast*, the *Austin Chronicle*, and *Austin* magazine.

BLACK ARTS ALLIANCE
2330 Guadalupe
Central West
477-9660
This is an umbrella organization that sponsors and participates in activities that address the unique needs of black artists. The alliance also offers technical and creative assistance to emerging visual, performing, and literary artists. The alliance sponsors a variety of black cultural experiences, such as plays, indoor and outdoor concerts, art exhibitions, and artists' workshops.

DOUGHERTY ARTS CENTER
1110 Barton Springs Rd., two blocks east of S. Lamar
Southwest
477-5824, 477-5826
W
The Dougherty Art Center functions as a municipal arts center, serving as administrative headquarters for PARD's cultural arts staff and as home base for the annual Zilker Hillside Summer Musical, spring and summer concerts, and YuleFest. Dougherty also serves as a performing arts center, most notably for the Dougherty Readers Theater. This group of local actors meets on the second and fourth Mondays of each month at Dougherty and again on the last Sunday of each month to present publicly staged readings of plays and other literary works.

The center's auditorium and open classrooms are available for rehearsal and high-quality presentation of performing arts events by non-profit performing arts organizations. For more information on availability and reservation applications, contact the Dougherty building supervisor. For more information on performing arts programs, call the Dougherty office at the number listed above.

PARAMOUNT THEATRE FOR THE PERFORMING ARTS
713 Congress near 7th
Central West
472-5411
W+
This grand, pre–World War I vaudeville and movie theater has been lovingly and lushly restored. Classic movies are shown, in festival form, but the Paramount really shines as a center for performances by local and national touring artists, ranging from plays and operas to dance (ballet and modern), concerts (pop, jazz, ethnic, classical), and stand-up comedians. (See also Live Theater.)

After 6 p.m., the box office phone (471-1444) plays a recorded list of music, drama, and arts events. (See also Revelation—Backstage Tours.)

SYMPHONY SQUARE
E. 11th at Red River
Central West
476-6064
Home of the Austin Symphony, the square's 500-seat open-air amphitheater on the banks of Waller Creek is a favorite location for a variety of performances during the spring, summer, and fall months. One particular Austin favorite is the summer "Catch a Rising Star" series. (See also Calendar of Events.)

WOMEN AND THEIR WORK
2330 Guadalupe
Central West
477-1064
Women and Their Work is a multidisciplinary arts organization that presents innovative art activities that bridge sexual, ethnic, age, and cultural barriers. Women and Their Work presents visual arts, experimental and performance art, fine crafts, music, and photography, as well as symposia on art and artists. Women and Their Work participates in more than thirty arts events annually statewide.

★★★
DANCE

AUSTIN DANCE UMBRELLA
P. O. Box 1352, Austin 78767; 1704 S. Congress
444-8698
Austin Dance Umbrella is a nonprofit service organization that helps individual dancers and dance companies obtain city, state, and federal arts funding; it also offers technical, promotional, and other forms of assistance, as well as general referral on Austin dance to the general public. In addition, the Dance Umbrella puts on dance events of its own at various times during the year. While this is not exactly an all-inclusive citywide "guild," quite a few local companies, studios, and individuals belong, and it is as good a place as any to go for more information on the state of dance in Austin.

BALLET AUSTIN
3002 Guadalupe
Central West
476-9051
Admission
Ballet Austin (formerly Austin Civic Ballet) was Austin's first professional ballet company, under the direction of Eugene Slavin and Alexandra Nadal. It is a classical, precise company, although it does try to present both classical and contemporary works during its fall-to-spring

season. The *Nutcracker Suite* is an annual event, presented each December. Ballet Austin performs at the UT Performing Arts Center. The
studio is located in a renovated firehouse just north of the UT campus.

AUSTIN BALLET THEATER
1501 W. 5th
Central West
478-9957
Admission
  Austin Ballet Theater is Austin's other established ballet company. Its
repertoire tends to be more dramatic than that of Ballet Austin's (as the
name implies), but it does perform some classical ballets. *Romeo and
Juliet* is an example. Stanley Hall is artistic director. ABT performs at the
Paramount Theatre.

**BALLET FOLKLÓRICO AZTLAN DE TEJAS/ACADEMY OF
MEXICAN DANCE AND FOLKLORE**
3601 South Congress
South
441-4101
  The Ballet Folklórico is the first professional dance company of its
kind in Austin. Its repertoire consists of dances from thirteen regions of
Mexico and features authentic traditional costumes. The Academy of
Mexican Dance and Folklore is the official school of the Ballet Folklórico
and offers classes for children and adults at beginners', intermediate,
and advanced levels.

★★★

LIVE THEATER

AUSTIN CIVIC THEATRE/ZACHARY SCOTT THEATRE CENTER
1421 W. Riverside at S. Lamar
Southwest
476-0541
Admission
W
  For more than fifty years, the Austin Civic Theatre, which operates
out of the Zachary Scott Theatre Center, has been treating those Austinites afflicted by the acting bug by giving them a chance to perform in
a theater company. This is about as professional as amateur theater
gets. Winter, spring, summer, and fall, something is always playing.
Past productions such as Edward Albee's *Seascape*, Woody Allen's *Play It
Again, Sam*, Dickens's *A Christmas Carol*, and Gilbert and Sullivan's *The
Gondoliers* typify the theater's diverse offerings. The theater also pro-
duces a youth season, aimed at youngsters and families. Recent performances have included *The Hound of the Baskervilles*, *Just So Stories*, *The
Boy Who Talked To Whales*, and *Jack and the Beanstalk*. Adult and youth
theater classes are also offered. (See Revelation.)

with the Austin Symphony and serves as a backup chorus for UT Opera, in addition to its own October-through-June season. General auditions are held during August and September. Call Morris Beachey at 471-4687 for an audition.

AUSTIN COMMUNITY ORCHESTRA
UT's Bates Recital Hall, Zilker Hillside Theater, various other locations
926-4687, 926-5323
This community orchestra performs five or six times a year. Indoor performances are in UT's Bates Recital Hall. At approximately fifty-five members, it is a small symphony orchestra, but complete. It performs a broad spectrum of symphonic literature but doesn't tackle the broad, romantic works of Mahler, Wagner, or Bruckner, because they require too many musicians. Instead, it opts for smaller pieces like Mozart's *Concerto for Flute and Harp*. The orchestra has performed several times with Austin Ballet Theater and the Austin Civic Chorus.

AUSTIN SYMPHONIC BAND
Various locations
836-2497, 926-6999
This symphonic wind ensemble is loosely affiliated with the Austin Community Orchestra. It performs every two or three months at places like UT's Bates Hall and Zilker Park. During the fall, winter, and spring the band performs mostly symphonic orchestral transcriptions. During its summer outdoor performances the band stretches out into marches, film scores, and Broadway show songs. They rehearse every Tuesday evening at Pearce Junior High, and anyone who is of high-school age or older is welcome.

AUSTIN SYMPHONY
1101 Red River (Symphony Square)
Central West
476-6064
While the Austin Symphony is a regional orchestra, it is a very good regional group, comparing favorably with the bigger boys in Dallas, Houston, and San Antonio. Much of this is due to the University of Texas music department, which fills out the ranks quite nicely.

Many folks feel that conductor Sung Kwak has begun to tap the orchestra's full potential during the last couple of years, and this positive effort is nicely complemented by the symphony's new performing home, UT's Performing Arts Center. The symphony performs here monthly October through May. During June, July, and August the symphony sponsors three evening concert series in the Symphony Square outdoor amphitheater. (See Points of Interest—Symphony Square and Calendar of Events.)

REVELATION

Although other Texas cities offer a few educational opportunities not available in Austin, on the whole Austin is the greenest of intellectual and educational oases in Texas and the South. The primary watering hole is of course the University of Texas at Austin, chief of the University of Texas System's thirteen branch campuses and five medical centers. But the University of Texas is not the only game in town. Austin Community College, with 20,000 students, is bigger than most colleges and universities in the country. St. Edward's University and Concordia College offer a more personal brand of higher education. Together, they work to make Austin the greatest all-around learning and research center in the South. About the only things missing are agricultural and medical schools.

In addition to these more formal brands of education and personal enrichment, there exist literally hundreds of less structured continuing education classes, offered not only by local colleges and universities, but by dozens of local businesses and community organizations.

IVORY TOWERS

AUSTIN COMMUNITY COLLEGE
205 E. 5th (administrative offices)

River between Manor and E. 26th)
Central West and East
471-3434
W

It is impossible to speak of Austin without bringing up the Capitol or the University of Texas at Austin. UT-Austin is not just the 321-acre Main Campus, the 445-acre Brackenridge Tract, and the 393-acre Balcones Research Center. And it's more than the 400 professors and teaching assistants, 12,000 assorted other staff, and 48,000 students. Even Memorial Stadium, the Ransom Center, the Tokamak, and Jester Center tell only part of the UT story.

The most impressive figures come in dollars. A recent study (made by UT's Bureau of Business Research, naturally) reveals that the University of Texas at Austin directly or indirectly generates $1.9 billion in the area economy and accounts for 16 percent of our area's earnings. It is not coincidence that Austin's ongoing condominium boom commenced in the West Campus neighborhood.

At approximately $500 million a year (construction and nonconstruction), UT-Austin's budget is only a hundred million or so behind the budget of the city that hosts it. And we'll leave the Permanent University Fund out of it altogether, for now, at least. (See Points of Interest—Santa Rita No. 1.)

Like a city, a university needs to expand to stay healthy, and UT-Austin has, most notably in east Austin where land is still cheap and otherwise available. The result will be a total economic restructuring of the 100-odd blocks bounded by IH 35, E. 38th, Airport Boulevard, and Martin Luther King Boulevard, even though UT will actually occupy maybe a quarter of that area.

Yes, UT is Memorial Stadium, the Tower, the Gutenberg Bible, and all the wealth they represent; but it is also a good university—maybe not one of the first class, yet, but the best in the Southwest and one of the fifty best in North America. A number of schools and degree programs rank in the top ten nationally: the Graduate School, the LBJ School of Public Affairs, and the business school's Department of Accounting among them. And determinedly, the university rolls on, towards that "first-class" status, despite differing opinions among the regents, faculty, and students on how to get there.

UT-Austin and the still-blossoming Microelectronics and Computer Technology Corporation are not synonymous, but they seem destined for the coziest relationship this side of Romulus and Remus, as Austin becomes our national center of command in the Computer Wars. On the flip side, UT-Austin is one of the world's leading preservers of data from the past. In Anthony Hobson's *Great Libraries*, UT-Austin's is among the thirty-two cited in North America and Western Europe, and one of only five in the United States.

UT-Austin is so big that few of its degree-winners come away with an accurate conception of just how encompassing their alma mater is, much less with the satisfaction that they have experienced all the uni-

versity has to offer. Take the centennial celebration's Showcase on October 2, 1983, which presented well over a hundred shows, demonstrations, and exhibits, all on one grand and glorious Saturday, making it
literally impossible even to sample all of them.

And so it is with the visitor to the university's sprawling main campus. A guide to UT-Austin alone could run to as many pages as this
guide to the entire city. But even the university hasn't come up with
anything like that yet. It has published a number of free maps, brochures, guides, and tours of the university complex, which visitors will
find to be of interest.

Ample free visitor parking is available on the lot adjacent to the Arno
Nowotny Visitors' Center and Erwin Center, and at the lot adjacent to
Sid Richardson Hall (Red River and Manor), near the LBJ Library. Parking meters and several commercial parking lots and garages are located
around the periphery of the campus.

Visitors may use the Central Campus (CC) shuttle bus for transportation around the campus. The CC shuttle runs at regular intervals,
which vary from five minutes in the morning to twenty-five minutes in
the evening, on all official class days, exam days, and registration days
(basically, no weekends or holidays). All other shuttle bus routes are
restricted to student use. Most visitors confine themselves to the
LBJ Library, Memorial Stadium, or the Erwin Center, and the "Forty
Acres"—the original core campus located atop College Hill.

Aestheticians decry the current architectural game plan (or lack of
one), which seems to boil down to "How fast can we get it built?" 'Twas
not always so, even as recently as thirty years ago, as anyone who has
strolled the Forty Acres knows. It was 1930 before the university really
began to step outside its original perfect square, and we were well
into "I Like Ike" before the staked claims finally began to fill out with
buildings.

None of the university's original buildings still stand. The Gothic
towers and ivy-covered brick walls of Old Main gave way in the early
1930s to the present Tower. The oldest building still extant on the Forty
Acres is the anonymous Student Services Building on Inner Campus
Drive, which dates to the turn of the century. Just a couple of years
later, Cass Gilbert began to draw up the first comprehensive architectural plan for the university campus.

He began with the Library Building (now Battle Hall) in 1911. It set
the theme for the next half-century of UT construction, that of a modi-
fied Spanish Renaissance, using native limestone, brick, red tile, and
terra cotta detailings. Many regard Battle Hall as the prettiest building
on campus. Cass followed it with nearby Sutton Hall in 1914, in the
same updated indigenous style. And that is as far as Gilbert's ambitious plan got. Farmer Jim Ferguson was governor by then, and he
begrudged the university every penny it got.

When the boom of the 1930s commenced, architect Paul Cret was at
the helm. Although his grandiose, centerpiece Tower drew hisses and
catcalls from many native leagues, sections, and quarters, the rest of

BIRDING HOTLINE
451-3308
The Travis County Audubon Society provides this birding and environmentalist twenty-four-hour hotline with current taped information on birding, field trips, outdoor and environmentalist news, and more.

COMMUNITY EDUCATION PROGRAM
Austin Independent School District Community Education Office
1604 Pennsylvania
476-7212
The Community Education Program is a joint program of the City of Austin and the Austin Independent School District. Through the program, AISD school buildings across the city stay open afternoons and evenings year-round, offering hundreds of classes and activities for everyone from toddlers to senior citizens.

Take the C classes. Want to learn calligraphy? How to clown? CPR? How to survive your child's adolescence? Computer programming? Coping with stress? How to bake a cake? There are approximately 690 more altogether, offered at fourteen different community schools. Many local agencies, museums, and businesses cosponsor or assist with classes.

Registration for classes is in early January, May, and September each year, and classes generally run for six weeks. Holiday minisession in December. Fees vary.

COMMUNITY RECREATION CENTERS
The Parks and Recreation Department's twelve Community Recreation Centers sponsor extensive programs of athletics, education, performing and visual arts, and special-interest subjects like wine tasting and Chinese cooking. Clubs and community organizations meet regularly at all the centers, and each offers a variety of special events, such as holiday parties, sports tournaments and events, and workshops. Programs are designed to offer something of interest to everyone, from toddlers to centenarians. Registration for most of the programs takes place in early January and early September each year.

Varying fees are charged. Call each center for more information on programs offered. Each center has playscapes, picnic areas, ball fields and courts, gyms, and swimming and wading pools.

ALAMO RECREATION CENTER
2100 Alamo at E. 22nd
Central East
474-2806

AUSTIN RECREATION CENTER
1213 Shoal Creek near Lamar
Central West
476-5662
City's oldest recreation center. Lighted tennis courts and impressive array of classes and sports programs.

DOTTIE JORDAN RECREATION CENTER
2803 Loyola
Northeast
926-3491
Senior citizens' tours, end-of-summer trip to Six Flags Over Texas.

GIVENS RECREATION CENTER
3811 E. 12th
Central East
928-1982
Austin's largest recreation center. Municipal swimming pool. League and tournament play in several sports.

HANCOCK RECREATION CENTER
811 E. 41st
Central West
454-5151
Located in the middle of Hancock Golf Course. Specialty courses like fencing, judo, Chinese cooking, wine tasting, photography. The Hancock Recreation Center will be closed through mid-1985 for renovation. For information on exact reopening date, call 477-6511, ext. 2746. The adjacent golf course will remain open.

METZ RECREATION CENTER
2407 Canterbury
Central East
478-8716

MONTOPOLIS RECREATION CENTER
1200 Montopolis
Southeast
385-5931
Special events include Olympic Powerlift Meet in October, Silver Gloves Boxing Tournament in December.

NORTHWEST RECREATION CENTER
2913 Northland
Northwest
458-4107
Field trips to events like Texas Renaissance Festival and Huntsville Prison Rodeo. Wide range of classes, from juggling to tortilla making.

PAN-AMERICAN RECREATION CENTER
2100 E. 3rd at Canadian
Central East
476-9193
Hillside theater with colorful mural depicting Mexican-American past, present, and future. Pan-Am hosts the best men's fast-pitch softball tournament in Austin, and also the local Golden Gloves boxing competition.

special events. Classes range in subject from Chinese cooking to time management; special events include "Breakfast with Santa" during the holidays, and various fashion and cosmetics shows.

LA BONNE CUISINE SCHOOL
P. O. Box 5681, Austin 78763
263-2034

Local kitchen legend Ann Clark teaches the fine art of French cooking in her comfortable Hill Country home, in between catering jobs and teaching assignments across the country. One-day classes of varying lengths cover basic skills such as buying and preparing fresh fish, steam cooking, regional specialties, and special menus for holidays and other special occasions.

Small classes, hands-on participation. Fee approximately $10 per hour.

LAGUNA GLORIA ART SCHOOL
3809 W. 35th at the end of Old Bull Creek Rd.
458-8196

Located in a new chic and energy-efficient building, the Laguna Gloria Art School offers more than two hundred classes throughout the year, divided into fall, spring, and summer sessions. Traditional subjects like design, drawing, ceramics, and painting, along with more nuevo wavo offerings like bookbinding, collage, and calligraphy. Co-op program with Austin Community College gives college credit for some courses.

Adult and children's classes, including the Art After School program.

LONDON FABRICS
2438 Anderson
Northwest
458-2214

Evening classes, generally eight weeks long; subjects like beginning and intermediate sewing for adults, tailoring, holiday and evening wear.

O. HENRY HOME MUSEUM
409 E. 5th at Neches
Central West
472-1903

One of the former residences of one-time Austinite and all-time short-story great O. Henry, this museum also offers a variety of literary programs, including creative writing classes for adults and children. Other special events include the annual Victorian Christmas open house in early December, and the annual Pun-Off in May.

UNIVERSITY OF TEXAS DIVISION OF CONTINUING EDUCATION
Joe C. Thompson Convention Center, E. Campus Dr. at E. 26th,
north of the LBJ Library
University/Central West
471-4652

The university's Division of Continuing Education coordinates and directs continuing education programs across the UT campus. In addition to the services it offers within the university, the division offers to citizens of Austin and Texas a variety of workshops, seminars, and ongoing classes in the areas of personal and professional skill development, engineering, fine arts, personal enrichment, and computers. To request a schedule, write:

The University of Texas at Austin
Division of Continuing Education
Thompson Conference Center
P. O. Box 7879
Austin 78712

The division also offers in-house training for businesses and associations.

UNIVERSITY OF TEXAS STUDENT UNION
471-5651

One hundred twenty how-to and specialty workshops, most ongoing, from ballroom dancing to bike repair. Registration in early January and early September. Call for brochure. Open to non-UT students. Most classes have wheelchair access.

OUTDOOR NATURE PROGRAMS

AUSTIN NATURE CENTER ANNEX
401 Deep Eddy
Central West
472-4523

The Nature Center Annex houses most of the Parks and Recreation Department's Outdoor Nature Programs. It offers youth (ages eighteen months to thirteen years), young adult (thirteen to eighteen), adult, and family classes and activities. Lots of field trips, like bug and wildflower hikes, Ottine Swamp trip, Lost Maples camping trip, and Wind River backpacking trip. Adults can learn uptown beekeeping and wildlife rehabilitation as well as "environmental eating."

JOURDAN-BACHMAN PIONEER FARM
11418 Sprinkle Cut-Off Rd.
837-1215

The Pioneer Farm offers a variety of educational programs, such as masonry, soap making, and sausage stuffing. (See also Parks.)

VANISHING TEXAS RIVER CRUISE
RM Rd. 2341, 16.5 miles northwest of Burnet
1-756-6986

Cruise Lake Buchanan and the lower Colorado River aboard a comfortable air-conditioned river cruiser, through a wilderness of towering cliffs, wild game, perennial springs, and waterfalls. Bring your camera,

that you can find anything at a flea market has been expanded here, leaping from a realm of just trash and treasures into a world where you can buy fresh zucchinis and bass boats as well.

BARTON CREEK SQUARE
2901 Capitol of Texas Hwy. (Loop 360) at MoPac
Southwest
327-7040
W

Lots of folks are expecting big things from Austin during the next twenty years. Barton Creek Square is proof of this. It is the largest shopping mall in the Southwest, with space for 200 merchants. Dillard's, Foleys, J. C. Penney, Sears, Montgomery Ward, and Scarbrough's are the major tenants. Full range of specialty shops, eateries, and two cafeterias. Tasteful Hill Country motif.

Until recently, most of Austin's shopping went on north of the Colorado River, with Highland Mall as the magnet. Barton Creek Square is now the keystone of a great South Austin shopping expansion.

CAPITAL PLAZA
5300 N. IH 35
Northeast
W

Capital Plaza is Austin's oldest shopping mall. The thirty merchants include Montgomery Ward, Beall's, Oshman's, and Shalimar, Austin's only Indian restaurant. (See Restaurants.)

HANCOCK CENTER
1000 E. 41st at IH 35 South
Northwest
459-6515
W

A classic early 1960s shopping mall, Hancock Center was hailed by progressive Austinites. Passed up since by such fourth- and fifth-generation hotshots as Highland Mall and Barton Creek Square, Hancock has eased into a comfortable middle age. Location on IH 35 near Airport Boulevard makes it very convenient. Major merchants are Sears, Beall's, Dillard's, HEB Grocery, and Wyatt's Cafeteria. Specialty shops and a genuine barbershop complete the thirty-vendor lineup.

HIGHLAND MALL
6001 Airport Blvd. between Austin Mall Blvd. and Middle Fiskville Rd.
Northwest
454-9656
W

Dowager queen of the Austin's regional shopping malls. Joske's, Foley's, J. C. Penney, and Scarbrough's are anchor stores. The other 150 merchants include countless specialty shops (from Storehouse to Le Must de Cartier), food kiosks, a full-line cafeteria, and hobby, gift, and book shops. Nearby movie-theater complex.

JEFFERSON SQUARE
W. 38th at Jefferson
Central West
One of those elite little "get-togethers" of boutiques, shops, and a restaurant. The Galleria restaurant (452-5510) is a dependable, longtime Austin favorite for continental cuisine. Anderson and Co. (453-1533) is equally favored for its stock of coffees, teas, spices, and condiments from around the world.

NORTHCROSS MALL
2525 W. Anderson Lane
Northwest
451-7466
W
Austin's only ice rink is a popular attraction. Beall's and Frost Brothers headline the list of the mall's more than sixty merchants. In-house theater with six screens. Nearby are the Village, Shoal Creek Plaza, and Creekside Square shopping centers.

PECAN SQUARE
W. 6th at Blanco
Central West
477-0734
The creation of Pecan Square during the mid-1970s was a groundbreaking project in Austin development. Rather than tearing down the old gas station and early twentieth-century cottages, the developers fixed them up and incorporated them into a shopping environment that gravitated to the pleasant tree-shaded patio of the square's star-in-residence, Sweetish Hill Bakery and Restaurant. Costars include a coffee store, an imported clothing shop, a print gallery, and one of Austin's best bookstores (and the only one open at eight Sunday morning).

Pecan Square is almost single-handedly responsible for the current popularity of vintage bungalows in Austin.

PEOPLE'S RENAISSANCE MARKET
W. 23rd and Guadalupe
Central West
W often congested
Most everyone calls it the Drag Vendors' Market, in honor of days long past when hippie craftsmen peddled their wares on the Drag in front of the Co-op. They've been on the reservation for nearly a decade now, but the name persists. And the mentality of many of the vendors, though more businesslike now, is still much the same as it was in the old days.

This first block of W. 23rd is closed off to traffic year-round, and open year-round to local artisans who set up makeshift stands and sell their own wares. Most bring the tools of their art along, and you may have to interrupt them at work to make your purchase. On football Saturdays

and antiques and Art Deco accessories and furnishings and you know the rest.

CHARLES LEWIS COMPANY
2301 Hancock
Northwest
454-5406
W

Why drive all the way down to the border *mercados* to shop for your Mexican dresses, crafts, and souvenirs when all you have to do is drive out to Hancock and Charles Lewis's shop? For those of us who are into Mesoamerican decor (and the number seems to be growing at a healthy clip), Lewis probably has anything in that line of interior embellishment that you've ever wanted and a lot more than you've ever dreamed of, both antique and contemporary. Try finding *retablos* for sale in Laredo, and then try getting them across the border these days.

DOLLY'S ODDMENTS
308–309 Parson St., Manor
Take U.S. Hwy. 290 east from Austin, turn right on Loop 212 to Parson St. and downtown Manor
272-4778

Dolly's is as good a reason as any and better than most to drive out to Manor, which is about as close as small town gets to Austin these days. If you're lucky, they'll be roasting coffee beans across the street from Dolly's shop, which is located in the old J. F. Nagle Building, next door to the old Red-and-White Store. Some of it is pure junque and some of it is purebred, but most of Dolly's inventory is somewhere in between. Dolly herself is a good conversationalist, and if you happen to notice the slightest resemblance to Kate Hepburn, don't say we didn't tell you so.

EAGLE'S NEST
1202 San Antonio
Central West
453-2012
W

Quite a few in Austin cite this shop as a favored place to browse and shop. The clientele generally reflects the owner's packrat/magpie tendencies. *Eclectic* is barely adequate to describe the inventory, which includes furnishings, furniture, art, sculptures, jewelry, clothing—for starts—manifested in Art Nouveau, Deco, American Indian modes— for starts. One thing, though: whether it's crystal or a tribal mask, it will be tasteful.

MARIA'S ANTIQUES
Village Shopping Center, 2700 W. Anderson near Burnet Rd.
Northwest
454-5492
W

Devotees of Art Nouveau and Art Deco will enjoy browsing through
Maria's Teutonic selection of mostly furniture, with a scattering of
lamps, paintings, little nightstand sculptures, and the like. Art Nouveau and Art Deco furniture, with their veneers and inlays, don't often
weather the passage of time well. Most of her inventory is a cut above
in this respect, but don't hesitate to inspect a piece thoroughly for flaws
before buying.

MORGAN'S
1101 W. 34th near Lamar
Central West
454-5225
W
    Ring the bell for admittance. This isn't Wall Street's House of Morgan,
or Helen's Club de Morgan, but rather Austin's most exquisite salon
d'collectibles. Art Nouveau, Deco, and Moderne furniture, furnishings,
and accessories are complemented by local art, jewelry, and clothing. Bill Montgomery, Thelma Kohls, Rodeane Landeaux, and others.
Beauty aids and a hair salon, too. Want a genuine Tiffany dragonfly
lamp? It's yours for only $19,500.

OLD 1898 STORE
Main St. in Buda
476-1088
Saturday and Sunday 10–6; occasionally other days
W
    "Prepare yourself for sensory overload," we were cautioned by de-
parting shoppers. We did. The first time you step into the 1898 Store
you will probably be overcome by its organizational chaos, its termi-
nally eclectic inventory. But don't let that stop you, not till you've found
that button hooker you've always wanted. And it was intermingled
with the old churchkeys, naturally.

PARKWAY ANTIQUE GALLERY
4400 Medical Parkway
Northwest
458-4781
    Austin antique shops don't get much tonier than Parkway Gallery.
Eighteenth- and nineteenth-century natural history and sporting prints,
particularly Audubon's *Birds of America*, are this shop's strong suit; but
the furniture, Oriental rugs, Chinese porcelain, silver, and duck decoys
are equally highbrow.

THREE GEESE ANTIQUES
1412 W. 9th
Central West
478-1465
    Have a cup of coffee; nose around; sit down and chat a bit with June
and Pat. Not the biggest or classiest antique shop in town, but one

GROK BOOKS
503-B W. 17th
Central West
476-0116
Austin's headquarters for metaphysics, philosophy, and other "alternative" subject-matter books.

HALF-PRICE BOOKS
3110 Guadalupe
Central West
474-5209
6103 Burnet Rd.
Northwest
454-3664
1914 E. Riverside
Southeast
443-3138
A favorite place for Austin bookhounds. Warehouse atmosphere. Best place in town to look for that elusive issue of your fave magazine, no matter how obscure. Lots of publishers' closeouts and paperbacks, some collectors' items. Prices generally cheap, and stock changes constantly. The record selection—rock especially—is nothing to write home about. Most of the dogs in town seem to find their way here. The 50¢ bargain bin contains occasional treasures.

THE NATURE STORE
401 Deep Eddy
Central West
472-4523
This commercial adjunct to the Austin Nature Center offers a variety of nature-oriented items in a relaxed, uncrowded atmosphere. The book section has recently been expanded and offers many field guides and children's books. Educational games and jewelry depicting native wildlife are also prominent in the scheme of things here.

PAPERBACKS PLUS
2900 Rio Grande
Central West
474-5488
The paperbacks are mostly used; some are new. The plus is everything else: used records, magazines, hardback books, and avant garde prose and poetry, local and not. The atmosphere and help are laid-back and friendly, and the shop is a magnet for local poets and proseurs.

ROBINSON'S BOOKS
1010 W. 38th
Central West
458-1247

A good general bookstore, convenient to Seton Hospital and the rest of the Central Austin mediplex.

TOAD HALL CHILDREN'S BOOKS
3918 Far West
Northwest
345-8637
Austin's most complete children's literature store.

UNIVERSITY CO-OP
2246 Guadalupe
Central West
476-7211
This is of course the great-granddaddy of Austin bookstores, serving UT students and the rest of Austin for nearly a hundred years. Much of the Co-op's annual multimillion-dollar book business is accomplished down in the basement, in Textbooks. But the General Books department upstairs is well-shopped, too, enough to be the largest general bookstore in Central Texas. There is usually always some sort of sale or bargain to be found here, and they will special order. If your interests or needs tend towards the arcane, you can always shop downstairs; you needn't be a UT student to buy textbooks.

WATSON AND COMPANY
406 Blanco
Central West
472-4190
Watson and Company deserves special mention for its 8 a.m. Sunday opening, which gives all the hungry souls waiting for Sweetish Hill's brunch some spiritual sustenance. But more than this, the bungalow-turned-bookstore has volumes crammed into every conceivable nook and cranny, yet still manages to look neat and composed and homier than most. You'll find books on the shelf here that you'd have to special order elsewhere. The well-rounded inventory includes a good children's section. Phone orders, book mailing, free gift wrapping, and a rental library are among the special services.

★★
KID STUFF

OVER THE RAINBOW
2739 Exposition; 3830 N. Lamar; 2438 W. Anderson Lane
477-2954; 458-6107; 452-1964
If you'd rather visit a toy shop than a toy warehouse, you'll like Over the Rainbow. These stores have a wide selection of toys, books, and other kid stuff, ranging from the esoteric to the banal, while avoiding the excesses of both. Good selection of "educating"—as opposed to "educational"—toys.

wine, to the point of establishing Dan's Wine Museum, which is an impressive collection of nineteenth- and twentieth-century wines from France, Germany, Italy, Greece, and California. Some are for sale. Bring a sweater if you're cold-blooded; the museum is kept at a constant 62 degrees for the wines' sake.

EL PORVENIR
2217 Santa Rita
Central East
477-0393
W

Grocery, *yerberia*, *panaderia* shoehorned into a small cinderblock building that stands in what is otherwise a residential neighborhood. The colorful mural that decorates the exterior is by D. Ruiz, the same D. Ruiz who took on the Texas Prison System and won. Best *yerberia* in town, and the *pan dulce* isn't bad, either. As few else do in Austin these days, this store serves as an informal neighborhood center.

GREEN & WHITE GROCERY
1201 E. 7th
Central East
472-0675
Open every day

The Green & White Grocery is just as its name implies. Step inside the Rainbo Bread screen doors into an old-time grocery store with a little bit of everything. Except for the PacMan game in the corner, it looks about like it did in 1946.

Good supply of yerba-like *canahuala*, *chichi nola*, and *pin guica*. Fresh *chorizo*, tripe, dried *chilis anchos*, and *chilis cascabels* are available in bulk.

Made-here tamales, refritos, menudo, flour tortillas, and white cheese are sold, along with a great supply of lucky candles, white magic books, tarot cards, and *aguas espiritual*.

HIGGINBOTTOM'S
3010 W. Anderson
Northwest
458-4111

The praise this shop draws from chocoholics is as rich as the chocolates themselves. And we are talking dollars (more than $30 per pound) as well as calories (who cares?). Cacao concoctions of the Swiss persuasion are the rage now; Higginbottom's stocks Moreau Chocolat of La Chaux-de-Fonds, truffles, chocolate bars, chocolate-dipped fresh fruits, and goodness knows what else; eyes and tummies soon begin to reel.

MARBRIDGE FARMS GREENHOUSE
FM Rd. 1626 and Bliss Spillar Rd.
Far Southwest
282-5504

There are lots of greenhouses not nearly so far out as Marbridge, but it's worth the trip out here, for good bargains on a great selection of carefully grown healthy fruit, vegetable, and decorative plants and shrubs. The Marbridge Ranch is a residential institution for retarded men, many of whom are employed by this perennial bloomer. Marbridge is some distance out, and very crowded on nice spring weekends; but this is where knowledgeable Austinites go. Open every day.

MELANIE'S INVESTMENT FASHIONS
809 Rio Grande
Central West
474-0148
W

Melanie is not kidding. These are big-league threads: designer (New York, London, Paris, the Far East), mostly exclusive, and meant to stay part of your wardrobe for many years. Evening wear, working wear, leisure wear. The elaborately beaded, sequined, and embroidered gowns, dresses, blouses, and sweaters testify that the New Ornamentalism has spread to the highest dollars of women's fashion.

MICHAEL'S
9632 N. Lamar; 5734 Manchaca
Northwest; Southwest
835-2413; 448-2633
W

A regular arts and crafts supermarket: Victorian dollhouse kits, dollhouse furniture, bins of picture frames, a framing department, yarn, crochet, decoupage, embroidery and painting supplies, dried flowers, balsawood everything; in short, if it has anything to do with arts and crafts, it's probably here.

NATURAL COMFORT BEDDING
4409 Medical Parkway
Northwest
459-7963

The *futon* (traditional Japanese mattress) is the newest alternative bedding rage to hit Austin. Versatile, easy to store, provides firm support for bad backs. Natural Comfort manufactures custom *futon*s and covers out of 100 percent cotton and sells all-cotton sheets in white and designer patterns, as well as *zabuton*s, oak bed frames and couches, *tatami*s, and window shades.

NEXT-TO-NEW SHOP
1712 Lavaca
Central West
472-9004

As at Lucky Attal's, you never know what you're going to find here, since all merchandise is donated or consigned. The Ladies' Auxiliary of St. David's Episcopal Church runs the shop. They're the ladies in the blue aprons.

You'll find fine gold jewelry and silver in one section, carnival glass in another, and plastic kitchenware, junque, and funky polyester clothing in back. "Antiques"—that word is sometimes used loosely here—are often overpriced, but there are bargains to be found, if you know what you are looking for. The selection of women's clothing is generally more interesting than the men's. Some patrons are in here almost daily, it seems, because the good stuff goes almost as fast as it is put out on the floor.

The shop is closed for about a month in August to give the good ladies a chance to vacation.

NOODLES
5416 Park Crest Square
Central North
441-9966

A former Basil's pasta chef has struck out on her own with this outpost in east Austin, much to the delight of fans of the three-minute egg and two-minute pasta. Fettuccine fans need boil the object of their appetites only sixty seconds; that's how fresh these various forms of semolina, wheat flour, whole eggs, and occasional herbs are. The herb variety is not to be missed.

For those who don't care to do it all from scratch, you can buy sauces, filled pastas, and ready-to-heat entrées.

OAT WILLIE'S
1610 San Antonio at W. 17th
Central West .
476-4193

Somebody is bound to make a shrine out of this head shop someday. Austin was, after all, the mecca of Texas hippiedom; and if the Armadillo World Headquarters was its great mosque, then Oat Willie's was the bazaar to which the faithful first flocked to anoint themselves. Oat Willie ran for president; his hose nose and feet-firmly-planted-in-the-oats stance has adorned countless T-shirts and matchbook covers. "Onward: Through the Fog" has taken up permanent residence in the Austin lexicon.

The bongs and exotic pipes are mostly gone from the shelves, but heads are still basically heads, so you'll still find the Wonder Warthog comix, Armadillo T-shirts, prisms, and the E-Z Wides that you (or your kids) demanded in the late 1960s and early 1970s. A line of casual wear has been added, but all in all, Oat Willie's is about the closest thing to a time warp that you'll encounter in Austin these days.

OLD BAKERY AND EMPORIUM
1006 Congress
Central West
477-5961
W

This city-sponsored emporium features quilts, wooden objects, and lots of other gifts to suit all sorts of budgets. Everything has been hand-

crafted by senior citizens from Austin and nearby communities. The
confectionary is well known for its home-baked cookies, cakes, and
bread. Sandwiches and snacks have been added. A hospitality desk up
front provides brochures and information on local spots of interest.
(See also Congress Avenue Walking Tour.)

RAINBOW WORKS
413 E. 6th
Central West
474-4511
W
    This gallery of a card shop is the place in town to shop for cards—
from tasteful to tasteless. Also beaded "Austin" belts, stickers, and
transfers for big and little kids, stationery, calendars, crystal, and Braun
products.
    And no smoking. The smoke would take the edge off the high-tech
black-glass chrome decor.

WHOLE EARTH PROVISION COMPANY
2410 San Antonio; other locations
Central West
478-1577
    Back when this store opened, in the dawn of the 1970s, the similarity
in name with that of the catalog was not coincidence. While the catalog
is now a collector's item, the little store it inspired has grown healthily
with the rest of Austin. You will find hippies, grandmas, Junior Leag-
uers, and Greeks all shopping under the same roof, for toys, clothes,
shoes, camping and hiking equipment, maps, books, canoes, and ka-
yaks. Some of the stuff—clothing in particular—may be a little on the
chic side these days; but it's all basically still in the spirit of the original
catalog, which shows you how far chic has come in ten years.

★★★
GALLERIES

COUNTRY STORE GALLERY
1304 Lavaca near W. 13th
Central West
474-6222
W call ahead
    The doyen of Austin galleries, and a must for those unfamiliar with
cowboy art. The decorating scheme is certainly in tune with the name.
All the clichés in Western art will be found here: longhorn statuettes
and paintings, cowboys and Indians in various media, wildlife and
bluebonnets. Yet amongst all the country-store clutter you'll find original works signed by the likes of Charles Russell, Frederic Remington,

and Bastrop's own Porfirio Salinas. They hide the Rembrandts and Picassos in the walk-in vault—honest Injun!

EL TALLER
723 E. 6th
Central West
473-8693
W
This spacious Santa Fe–styled gallery features works by the owner and sometime-Austinite Amado Pena, as well as work by Liese Jean Scott. Subject matter is Native American, colorful and expressionistic. Mostly serigraphs and monotypes, along with tiles, etchings, drawings, and posters. Floor space is defined by some artful inlaid wood furniture by Richwood Designs. Zapotec weavings from Oaxaca.

GARNER AND SMITH ART GALLERY
509 W. 12th
Central West
474-1518
This small, genteel gallery can claim what is probably the best graphics inventory in Austin, with works by Leonard Baskin, Joseph Albus, Willem de Kooning, Salvador Dali, Marc Chagall, Joan Miró, George Segal, and others. Good collection of art books, too.

GALERIE RAVEL
1210 W. 5th
Central West
474-2628
This gallery specializes in major American and Latin American artists. If you've never been here before, you may miss it; this stretch of E. 5th is about the last place you'd expect to find one of Austin's oldest and most tasteful galleries.

GALLERY AT SHOAL CREEK
1500 W. 34th
Central West
454-6671
If you had to categorize this gallery, "Southwest impressionism" would be about as close as you could get. The gallery handles around thirty arists; Sandy Scott, Vladan Stiha, Carroll Collier, Jerry Ruthven, and Rod Boebel are among them. This is one of the most established galleries in town. It was originally a Western art gallery, and the place is still trying to buck that reputation. On a recent visit, we sighted nary a cowboy nor a bluebonnet nor a longhorn.
Paintings, sculpture, some antique furniture.

MATRIX GALLERY
912 W. 12th
Central West
479-0068
For its size, Austin has quite a sophisticated art scene. Matrix Gallery, which specializes in glass as art, is proof. Glass as art is enjoying an increasing acceptance, and it's always fun to visit this place and see what's new in the world of glass.

NATIVE AMERICAN IMAGES
2104 Nueces
Central West
472-3049
This west campus gallery was known until recently as Ni-Wo-Di-Hi Galleries; as you can guess, Native American art is the ticket here. Although a number of artists are represented, the mainstays are artists-in-residence Paladine Roye, Donald Vann, and Steve Forbis. The gallery also does a large business in lithograph and serigraph publishing. You'll enjoy strolling through this restored Victorian house.

PATRICK GALLERY
721 E. 6th
Central West
472-4741
W
Changing exhibitions of the gallery's stable of artists, like Stephen Daly, Vicki Teague-Cooper, Sarah Canright, and Peter Saul.

RUTH BORINSTEIN GALLERY
1701 West Ave.
Central West
472-6943
In the past couple of years, this toney gallery has assembled exhibits of works by Picasso, Dali, and R. C. Gorman. You can also choose from a good selection of turn-of-the-century prints by American masters, plus some Europeans.

SOHO GALLERY
1509-B Old W. 38th
Central West
467-2219
Shows works by established Austin artists like John Guerin, Betty Osborne, and Fran Larsen; paintings, pottery, sculpture, prints, mixed media.

WILLINGHEART GALLERY
615-A E. 6th
Central West
473-8926
Contemporary gallery focusing on clay, fiber, wood, metal, paper, and jewelry.

★★★

SPECIALTY/FINE CRAFTS

CLARKSVILLE POTTERY
1013 W. Lynn
Central West
478-9079
And you thought that pottery was just for eating and drinking and flowers. Shame on you for small thinking. At Austin's most comprehensive and innovative pottery, you'll find clocks, wind chimes, mirrors, egg separators, match holders, hummingbird feeders, and more. Tortilla warmers and Melitta-sized coffee makers are longtime Austin favorites. The new chip-and-dip bowl looks as good on the antique washstand in your bathroom or bedroom as it does on the coffee table. Stoneware and porcelain can be used in microwaves. Artistically pleasing objects, eminently functional, imaginative in design and glazing. Eighty percent of the inventory is made here in the studio; the rest is done by local potters.

ECLECTIC
12th and Lamar
Central West
477-1863
Ozone *n.* Fresh, pure air (*informal*).
Once you're off Lamar and inside, Eclectic hits you—well, like a shot of ozone: heady, overwhelming at first. There's just so much to look at, most of it vintage and contemporary folk arts and crafts, all of it tasteful: Pre-Columbian pottery and shards, African masks, battered tin *retablos*, rugs, jewelry, clothing, and toys from Africa, India, New Guinea, Peru, Bolivia, and Mexico.

FIRE ISLAND HOT GLASS STUDIO
1003 W. 34th, next to Renaissance Glass
Central West
451-6913
W
One of the neatest things about Fire Island is that you can stand around and watch how your purchases are made. Visitors are welcome

in this loosely furnished workshop as long as they stay behind the yellow line and don't ask questions of the people at work. Fire Island's goblets and perfume bottles are currently hot items in several Austin galleries. This is a conscientious place; they even make their own glass, using lime from Austin White Lime and other locally purchased ingredients. Only the sand is Yankee, from Illinois.

Fire Island closes in August to cool off—you know these Texas summers.

KALEIDOSCOPES BY PEACH
509 Hearn
Central West
478-3967

There are kaleidoscopes, and then there are kaleidoscopes by Peach. His run the gamut from the traditional models with freefalling glass fragments, buttons, and beads to "aquascopes," with different colored oils flowing in and out of each other, to the kaleidoscope of the 1980s, which responds electronically to sound and music. See it to believe it. Kaleidoscopes by Cary "Peach" Reynolds are sold at several locations around town as well as at his Hearn Street workshop.

RENAISSANCE GLASS COMPANY
1003 W. 34th near Lamar
Central West
451-3971

Renaissance Glass Company is one of the leaders of the current glass-as-art rebirth in Austin. You can buy ready-made stained glass, or buy all the materials to do it yourself. Renaissance also teaches classes and does repair and commission work. Classes last three to five weeks, on subjects like beginning and intermediate stained glass and etching. They will do custom stained glass, as well as etching, sandblasting, glass beveling, and engraving. Renaissance also sells blown glass by various craftspeople, including Fire Island next door.

WRIGHT STUDIO
1900 Barton Springs Rd.
Southwest
474-2200
W

Located just east of Barton Creek and the entrance to Zilker Park, this large rustic complex houses the studio and showroom of potters Bob and Debbie Wright, creators of both decorative and functional pottery and stoneware.

★★
PARTY HOUSES

THE ABBEY
801 Rio Grande

Central West
477-6685
W first floor
It cost William Boswell $1800 to build this three-story Georgian mansion in 1905, another example of the flight away from Victorian styles. The Abbey is available for weddings, receptions, soirées, parties, or just plain meetings. Catering is available, though most folks provide their own. Best to call a month in advance. Furnished according to the period.

THE BARR MANSION
10463 Sprinkle Rd.
Northeast
926-6907
The grandest and about the only example of the Victorian "Eastlake" residential style around Austin today in fact stands just outside the city limits, in the Sprinkle community. When William Braxton Barr built this elaborately iced wedding-cake mansion in 1898, Sprinkle was considerably busier and very much further up the Missouri-Kansas-Texas road from Austin. Nearly everyone who has passed by the place has fallen in love with the wraparound double gallery (on three sides) and gazebo. What a marvelous place to get married! The Barr Mansion is in fact available for weddings, receptions, and parties. Proprietors will cater, or you can arrange your own. Weddings should be booked four to six months in advance to assure date desired. Ask for Melanie MacAfee.

Sprinkle, incidentally, was named for Barr's father-in-law, the eminent Captain Erasmus Sprinkle.

ACCOMMODATIONS

We arrived in a norther, and were shown, at the hotel to which we had been recommended, into an exceedingly dirty room, in which two of us slept with another gentleman, who informed us that it was the best room in the house. The outside door, opening upon the ground, had no latch, and during the night it was blown open by the norther, and after we had made two ineffectual attempts to barricade it, was kept open till morning.

When finally we got to breakfast . . . we naturally began to talk of changing our quarters and trying another of the hotels. Then up spoke a dark, sad man at our side—"You can't do better than stay here; I have tried both the others, and I came here yesterday because the one I was at was *too dirty!*"

That was how professional traveler Frederick Law Olmsted's first encounter with Austin hostelry went, 'way back in 1854. He never publicly mentioned the name of his host or the establishment.

Young Austin soon outgrew this phase of delinquency, reaching full maturity in 1886, when Jesse opened his Driskill at the corner of Pecan and Brazos. That the city was proud of its palace-by-the-night is something of an understatement. One local newspaper was moved to suggest that the hotel be exempt from taxes for ten or fifteen years because of what the Driskill had done for Austin.

That tax break would have come in handy. In the end, the Driskills paid a heavy price for celebrity, selling the hotel just a couple of years later. A number of successive owners never made much off the hotel, either. Nonetheless, the Driskill remained Austin's showcase for years; and despite a short lapse several decades ago, it still stands as the dowager queen of Austin's gracious hotels.

For a city of its age and essentially southern roots, Austin is remarkably devoid of the stately downtown hotels and inns that one expects to find in the capitals and large cities of the Old South—hotels that one does find in other Texas cities like Dallas and San Antonio.

It's not that we have torn them down; Driskill aside, they were just plain never built. The Stephen F. Austin is the Driskill's only rival, built in the Roaring Twenties as part of the budding Chamber of Commerce's attempt to transform Austin into the resort capital of the South. So short of rooms was Austin that the chamber underwrote the construction of this recently remodeled sixteen-story tower.

A number of hotels and motels have since popped up, mostly of the chain variety and mostly along IH 35, the road of convenience. With a few exceptions, Austin's better hotels are either in the downtown area or clustered around the Highland Mall stretch of IH 35 in north Austin.

Many hotels and motels in Austin are members of national chains. We have listed very few of these establishments, because visitors are likely to be familiar with them already. Their absence in this guide does not mean that they are less acceptable here than elsewhere; but if you have stayed at the Holiday Inn in Springfield, Illinois, you probably know what you're going to encounter at most of the Holiday Inns in Austin.

Austin's recent growth and building explosion has included the hotel business, and for the first time in its life, Austin is overbuilt, at least when it comes to hotel or motel rooms. You can often find special rates just by asking for them.

But not always; in fact, it's usually a good idea to call ahead for reservations. When the Longhorns are playing at home, you may even have trouble finding a place to pitch your tent. Austin is a popular convention town, too. If you find yourself in a bind, call the Chamber of Commerce room locator service at 478-0098. The service is a lifesaver for secretaries who regularly make last-minute reservations for busy bosses.

The designation W+ indicates that some of the rooms have special facilities for the handicapped. Prices change from time to time, so instead of giving exact charges, we have used the following codes to indicate general rate categories for a double:

$: under $40
$$: $40 to $60
$$$: $60 to $80
$$$$: $80 to $100
$$$$$: over $100

CENTRAL

DRISKILL HOTEL
117 E. 7th at Brazos
Central West
474-5911
$$$–$$$$
W

Along with the Stephen F., the Driskill is Austin. After all, LBJ and Lady Bird always stayed here; they had their very own suite. (Brother Sam Houston Johnson hung his hat at the Alamo, though.) The grand lobby was once the biggest in Texas, and it is still one of the nicest. Ditto for the bar, dining room, and ballrooms. The dining room and bar draw a lot of drop-in trade, owing to the hotel's posture as the western anchor of Old Pecan Street. In the past, some rooms have been grander than others, but the newest owners have polished up the place inside and out. Rooms with eastern exposures offer an entertaining view of E. 6th. No pool.

HOLIDAY INN-TOWN LAKE
20 IH 35, west of the highway on the north bank of Town Lake
Central West
472-8211
$$
W+ one room

What was that we said in the introduction about all Holiday Inns looking alike? Well, not exactly. This inn offers all the expected Holiday Inn amenities in a distinctive lakeside tower, convenient to IH 35. Every one of the stone-walled, wedge-shaped rooms offers a panoramic view. Most guests opt for the west side, which gives you downtown, Town Lake, and Hill Country sunsets in one glance. The view from the rooftop lounge is the Hyatt's only rival. The pool is on the small side.

SHERATON-CREST INN
111 E. 1st on Town Lake
Central West
478-9611
$$–$$$
W+ some rooms

Hyatt notwithstanding, the twelve-story Sheraton-Crest holds down the most enviable spot in Austin: downtown, on the north shore of Town Lake. The Capitol is but a dozen blocks up Congress, UT just a dozen more. Recent remodeling has improved the Crest's indoor looks, and the housekeeping staff recently won a Sheraton gold medal for their work. For a good night view of lively downtown Austin (sorry, no Capitol!), go for a north exposure. For a good day view of Town Lake and the competition, ask for the southern side. Every room has a good view of one or the other. There is a large pool, and the Town Lake Hike and Bike Trail is seconds away.

The Governors Room restaurant (lakeside, decorated by portraits of the appropriate Texans) is popular for breakfast and lunch among downtown workers. Danceable music by good groups in the Gazebo Lounge draw considerable local crowds. And for all you groupies, most of the big-name touring acts hang their hats at the Crest. It draws considerable convention trade, too.

STEPHEN F. AUSTIN HOTEL
701 Congress at 7th
Central West
476-4361
$$$$
W

After an awkward year or two as the Bradford, this historic downtown hotel is once again the Stephen F. Austin. Its California owners also operate the fashionable Westwood and Sunset Marquis Hotels out L. A. way, and thus they have gone for the look of casual elegance, Austin style, which translates into a western "living-room" lobby, kind of like LBJ's or Charlie Three's, but sans the excesses of wall-mounted saddles and snarling trophy javelinas. The SFA was long the pride of Austin, and the new management has publicly vowed to make the Stephen F. our only five-star hotel, offering as standard services amenities that cost extra or are unavailable elsewhere. At any rate, this venerable sixteen-story tower is pretty cushy, down to the brass beds and the original Remington bronzes and woven horsehair chair cushions in the Remington Room (restaurant) next door. The recent refurbishing has cut down the number of rooms to 167; a few are still on the cozy side, but all have great views. No pool.

VILLA CAPRI MOTOR HOTEL
2400 IH 35 at 24th
Central West
476-6171
$$
W+ some rooms

No, the Villa Capri is not the newest addition to the University of Texas chain. It is a UT tradition, though, located as it is across the street from the LBJ Library's parking lot and just down the street from Memorial Stadium. It is also next to IH 35, so if you are a light sleeper, ask for a westside room. There are two pools, a restaurant, and a lounge. The entertainment center has a huge dance floor. If you want to eat somewhere else, you'll have to drive.

NORTH

HILTON INN
6000 Middle Fiskville Rd., between IH 35 and Highland Mall
Northwest
451-5757
$$$–$$$$
W

The Hilton has recently undergone an aggressive remodeling, designed to keep up with the Marriott and La Mansion across the street. For those who prefer the wide-open spaces and drive-up rooms, the Hilton can accommodate you. And for a few more bucks, you can stay on the VIP floor and enjoy the limited-access elevator. Highland Mall is an easy three-minute walk. Car and plane noises are not a problem in any room, but try for one with a western view on one of the upper floors. If you can ignore Highland Mall, you'll see why the early Spanish explorers named the still-green western hills "Los Balcones." Large swimming pool, 340 rooms.

LA MANSION HOTEL
6505 IH 35
Northeast
454-3737
$$$$
W+

La Mansion certainly looks like one from the outside, with a decidedly indigenous, Spanish flavor. That flavor comes largely from the central courtyard, which contains a swimming pool, fountain, garden, and cafe tables. Following the La Mansion tradition, the rooms in this brand-new hotel are larger than they need to be, and there is plenty of convention space. The in-hotel clubs and restaurants of La Mansions in other cities enjoy citywide reputations and trade, and the Austin outpost promises to do the same. Three hundred fifty rooms.

MARRIOTT HOTEL
6121 IH 35 at US Hwy. 290
Northeast
458-6161
$$$–$$$$
W+ some rooms

Like its immediate big neighbors, the Marriott is a convention-oriented hotel, convenient to IH 35, Highland Mall, and the airport. Marriott makes a big deal about quality and service, so everything is spotless and tasteful, and everybody is cheerful and polite. The recent multimillion-dollar renovation underscores that policy. Although located only yards from the freeway and only slightly further removed from flight paths, the whole hotel complex, down to the last room, is blessedly free from traffic noise. Not many other IH 35 lodgings can make that claim. The Marriott also has one of the most inviting outdoor swimming pools in town. Three hundred and one rooms.

★★
SOUTH

HYATT REGENCY HOTEL
208 Barton Springs Rd. at Riverside
Southwest
477-1234
$$$–$$$$
W+ four rooms
    Once you've stepped inside the Hyatt, it's easy to see why this place was an immediate hit in Austin. Owing to the open nineteen-story atrium lobby, the space is broadly open yet cozy at the same time. All the rooms open onto the atrium, which doesn't exactly make the "hall" outside your door a good spot for one of those lingering moments of passion but does make for good people watching.
    The manicured rows of ivy cascading down from each level and the creekside ficus trees make this atrium sort of a 1980s *minceur* version of the Hanging Gardens of Babylon. Yes, Texana, there is a creek; it flows a rocky course through the Branchwater Lounge downstairs, out into the courtyard, and over the falls before disappearing into Town Lake. There's just no other place like it in town—yet. The Foothills Lounge up on top provides what is simply the best bird's eye view in Austin, except for the UT Tower. Most guests request a lake view, but west and south aren't bad, either. The Foothills Lounge, adjoining the restaurant, and the La Vista Restaurant and Branchwater downstairs are popular with Austinites.

RAMADA GONDOLIER
1001 IH 35 at E. Riverside
Southeast
444-3611
$$
W call ahead
    This inn does not offer the high-rise views found at the nearby Sheraton Crest, Hyatt, and Holiday Inn, but the lakeside rooms offer good views of Town Lake, and balconies from which to catch the cooling breezes. In contrast to the scrupulously kept grounds elsewhere, the Ramada has allowed its patch of riverbank to grow over, retaining a bit of the Colorado's original sleepy, Old South look. Restaurant and pool.

WYNDHAM SOUTHPARK
4140 Governor's Row at IH 35
Southeast
448-2222
$$$$
W

The parameters of Austin are expanding rapidly. Few people would have forecast a luxury high-rise hotel out here in far southeast Austin ten years ago. Yet exactly this has happened. The Wyndham opened in the summer of 1983 to take the Hyatt head-on, and this patch of South Austin may someday rival the Highland Mall area and downtown as major convention centers. To spice up the deal, the Wyndham offers a complete athletic club for registered guests and an indoor/outdoor pool. It's still too early to make any lasting judgments, but the management is certainly trying.

A luxurious Art Deco–Art Moderne decor pervades the place, executed in lots of heavy wood, imported marble, leaded and beveled glass, brass, and paints, from the lobby (perfect for a romantic rendezvous), through the Sweetwater Lounge and Onion Creek Grille, up to any of the Wyndham's 318 rooms. Claustrophobics can lay their fears to rest in any of the larger-than-average rooms.

CLUBS

> Clubs come and go in Austin, as regular as sunrises and sunsets and television news anchors. This is great for the legions of Austin's clubbing aficionados, but not so good for the club owners, who first search desperately for the right gimmick to get you into their establishments, then do whatever else it takes to keep you coming back.

So we aficionados get to choose from the beer bars, boogie bars, conversation bars, fern bars, gay bars, pickup bars; the ballrooms, bistros, cabarets, cantinas, clubs, drinkeries, lounges, taprooms, taverns, watering holes, parlors, and pubs. The collective atmosphere is generally relaxed and low pressure; Austin really has nothing to compare to the $10 cover, two-drink minimum, slinky waitress professionalism of, say, Chicago's Park West. In most places, the music is free or less than the price of a movie ticket.

Out-of-towners often see Austin as a party town, and the extraordinarily large assortment of nightlife does nothing to detract from this popular image. Given this dynamic scene, it's hard to make any long-term recommendations with confidence. But you will always be able to select from a respectable range of live music every night of the week. Read the *Austin Chronicle* or *American-Statesman* or listen to either KLBJ radio (93.7 FM) or K-98 radio (98.3 FM) for up-to-date club and roadshow schedules.

The following list describes a good cross-section of the better places thriving at the time of this writing.

ANTONE'S
2915 Guadalupe
Central West
474-5314
Open seven days
Cover
W

Antone's is one of those clubs that just won't quit. Austin's most prominent home of the blues is in its third incarnation, mostly because Clifford Antone hás a mission: to give Austin a healthy case of the blues. Low ceilings, a small dance floor, and a faint ventilation make the place hot enough; the music makes it even hotter. Antone always gets good bands and most all the legends, too. The Fab T-birds cut their teeth at Antone's. Angela Strehli and Little Charlie are among the most regular performers.

For a club so close to UT, the audience is remarkably devoid of students.

THE BACK ROOM
2015 E. Riverside
Southeast
441-4677
Open seven days
No cover

Eleven years open and still rocking strong, live music every night and never a cover. Sure, Dan and Dave are out to pasture, and there's a bit of a dress code now, but that's the price of progress.

BROKEN SPOKE
3201 S. Lamar past Manchaca Rd.
Southwest
442-6189
Closed Sunday
Cover; no cr.
W

Most folks think of this place as a country-western dancehall, which it is; but the Spoke also does quite well as a restaurant. Owners claim they serve up the best chicken-fried steak in town, and few diners disagree. Real country dancehalls are getting hard to find these days in upscale Austin, but the Broken Spoke is one of them. On any given night you're likely to find ex-hippies and venturesome nuevo wavos two-stepping alongside diehard good ol' boys and girls. Alvin Crow and Marcia Ball are about as trendy as the Spoke gets, and its devotees love that.

CHEZ FRED
2912 Guadalupe; 9070 Research Blvd. at Burnet Rd.
Central West; Northwest
472-8007; 451-6494
Open seven days; breakfast, lunch, dinner, Sunday brunch
$–$$
    With good Franco-Tex grub at both locations, and live jazz to boot up north, it's easy to forget that Chez Fred started out as a humble *panaderia*—oops, *patissiere*—on the Drag. The baked goods haven't taken a back seat to these newcomers, though; the croissant with fresh strawberry butter is still a singular experience, in Austin at least. And you may have chicken marsala or chicken-fried steak or fried cackleberries with your croissant and jazz until 1 a.m. up north.

CONTINENTAL CLUB
1315 S. Congress
Southwest
443-7141
    This hole in the wall has a sporadic track record. When it's open, it's consistently one of the hottest live-music clubs in town, the place where other musicians go to wind down and sometimes to join in. More than one Erwin Center headliner has dropped by here after work for some fun. Beer and wine.

DONN'S DEPOT
1600 W. 5th
Central West
478-0336
Monday through Saturday
    Whenever the lounge lizard inside you starts to crawl out, the antidote is simple: go to Donn's Depot Piano Bar and Saloon. Donn claims it's the biggest such bar in Texas. Who are we to quarrel with him? Anyway, it's plenty big enough for us, and it's Austin's most enduring piano bar, hands down. The train station really did come from the tiny white-lime-plant town of McNeil, which was just north of Austin.

THE DOUBLE EAGLE
5337 US Hwy. 290 West
Southwest
892-2151
Cover varies
    If the Broken Spoke don't butter your bread, this popular country-and-western dance warehouse is just down the road apiece. National acts and popular local bands fill out the dance card.

FOOTHILLS LOUNGE
Hyatt Regency Hotel, 208 Barton Springs Rd.

Southwest
477-1234
Open seven days
No cover; MC, V
W

If Holden Caulfield came to Austin, he'd probably start his evening off with a few drinks at the Foothills. Faced with the seventeenth-story panorama of Austin at sunset, it's easy to overlook the comfortable Art Moderne wraparound chairs, the tinkling piano, and the beautiful cocktail waitresses. You can wear your ranch clothes here, but you may be the Lone Ranger.

GAMBRINUS
314 Congress
Central West
472-0112
Monday through Friday, lunch and dinner; Saturday dinner only
AE, MC, V

Gambrinus is a good alternative to the 6th Street stockyard scene. It doesn't usually have as many people, and as properly befits a cafe, it's a little more relaxed. The walls are covered with flags of the world and photos and blueprints of the other, original Gambrinus back in Belgium, the land of French fries and mayonnaise. Imported beer selection rivals Maggie Mae's. The Belgian-French food served here is simple, rich, and generally good.

GORDO'S RESTAURANT AND BILLIARDS
421 E. 6th at Neches
Central West
477-6886
Open seven days
No cover; MC, V

Considering the massive tables, limestone-rubble walls, and heavy, varnished woodwork, you might expect to see a frockcoated Ben Thompson engaged in a friendly shootout with young Will Porter, a white-jacketed barkeep overseeing the free lunch, brass spittoons conveniently placed, and not a woman in sight.

Well, the lunch isn't free anymore (neither is the dinner), but it's pretty good: some Tex-Mex specialties, chicken-fried steak, steamed veggies, and daily specials like homemade fish sticks. The barkeep doesn't wear a starched white jacket anymore, and some of the women shoot a mean game.

HOLE IN THE WALL
2538 Guadalupe
Central West
472-5599
Open seven days, lunch and dinner
No cover
W

Just as the name implies. Reality here comes on a bun, with fries on the side and a jalapeño on top, and it sure beats the heck out of DQ's chicken-fried equivalent. Some of Austin's most talented musicians have found themselves here over the last ten years. Despite—or perhaps because of—its old-shoes-and-frayed-cuffs atmosphere, the Hole in the Wall is a real crossroads of life in Austin. Music every night out front, game room in the back.

HUT'S DRIVE-IN
807 W. 6th near West Ave.
Central West
472-0693
Open seven days
Cover; MC, V
W

Hut's streamlined Art Moderne facade has been part of the Austin skyline since 1939. A change of ownership a few years ago saw Hut's awnings, burgers, and music updated. The bands are loud, the dance floor and any other room to move almost nonexistent, but that's because the rock-and-roll and rhythm-and-blues played here are among the best in town. Tex Thomas and Angela Strehli, among others, are regular players. If the Drive-In cramps your style, try Hut's Diner (418 E. 6th, 477-6304) in the heart of Old Pecan Street. It's six of one, half a dozen of the other.

LIBERTY LUNCH
405 W. 2nd
Central West
477-0461
Cover varies
W

Avowed home of reggae and third-world music in Austin. Local and international acts play, and Austinites swing and sway—under the stars or under the old Armadillo World Headquarters' resurrected roof. Perpetually threatened with oblivion by the big boys downtown, who have larger designs on the block, the Lunch has managed to hang on longer here than most of us expected.

MAGGIE MAE'S
323 E. 6th near Trinity
Central West
478-8541
Open seven days
No cover; MC, V

Set down amidst fern, oyster, and boogie bars, Maggie Mae's is a beer bar. Dozens and dozens of stouts, lagers, pilsners, ales, from around the world. Maggie doesn't offer Point, from Steven's Point, Wisconsin, but then neither does anybody else south of Chicago. Otherwise, a truly prodigious selection. Most of the patrons do the stock justice.

Music is mostly acoustic and traditional, whether Celtic, French, or American.

This place is not at all pretentious; such luxuries are impossible in a shotgun gallery like this, where three is nearly a crowd.

OASIS CANTINA DEL LAGO
6550 Comanche Trail off RM Rd. 620
Northwest
266-2441
Open seven days
No cover; AE, MC, V
W but not all areas

Situated as it is high above the sparkling blue waters of Lake Travis, the Oasis's biggest draw is the view. Forget the food; have a drink or two and enjoy the broad western sunset over the lake.

PARADISE
401 E. 6th
Central West
476-5667
Open seven days, lunch
No cover

Although you'll never hear it played here, the recent country-western hit "I'm goin' hunting tonight" could serve as the theme song for Paradise. Even when the rest of 6th Street is dead, Paradise is usually full, as both hunter and hunted eye each other. Typical patented tasteful fern-bar trappings, entertaining beer selection. Located in the 1875 Cotton Exchange Building. Hunting license not necessary.

RITZ THEATER
320 E. 6th
Central West
479-0054

This old movie palace has got to be the Lazarus of Old Pecan Street; it's been playing the role for years. Movie house, X-rated movie house, ex-movie house, the Ritz always opens back up after each failure as the Ritz. In the last ten years it has also been a rock-and-roll arena, as well as a legitimate and not-so-legitimate stage. Currently it is open most nights, showing classic movies, Esther's Follies (until they rebuild), and various music and theater acts. There doesn't seem to be much direction to the programming, but this may change. Who cares? Where else in town can you go these days and get a beer or wine cooler to go along with your Marx Brothers and fresh popcorn?

6TH STREET LIVE
222 E. 6th
Central West
477-3766

Monday through Saturday
W partial

Like its cousin up the street, the Ritz, the building currently hosting 6th Street Live started as a movie theater. Unlike the Ritz, 6th Street Live is a music club, with a few acts like PeeWee Herman thrown in. 6th Street Live books an eclectic (some call it curious) assortment of talent, ranging from high-dollar road acts to local bands to canned dance music with live deejays. While this is not exactly an intimate club, it doesn't hold a lot of people. Bar.

SOAP CREEK SALOON
1201 S. Congress
Southwest
443-1966
Open seven days
Cover
W

First it was the honky-tonk in the hills, west out Bee Caves Road, out of town and just the wrong side of a quarter-mile driveway and parking lot that was the equal of any mine field. Then it was the honky-tonk on top of the hill, 'way out in the 11 million block of North Lamar, in what had previously been the legendary Skyliner Club. Now it is the honky-tonk at the bottom of the hill, stuffed into a JoJo-esque ex–coffee shop just up from the river on S. Congress. Soap Creek Saloon is a recurrent phenomenon among Austin clubs. In a town where clubs come and go at the rate of several per month, Soap Creek has successfully survived three changes of venue.

This is not coincidence. Tenish years ago, when Willie was still singing at the 'Dillo and Hill on the Moon picnics, Soap Creek was on the definitive edge of the developing "Austin sound." Saloongoers knew they were going to have a good time out there. They had better; the drive was too much of a pain not to.

Soap Creek III may not be perched on the cutting edge of the Austin scene anymore—if there is such a leviathan sound in existence these days, Cardi's must surely be leading it—but it still serves up a danceable and fun lineup. Willie and Clifton Chenier may not play here anymore, but Sir Doug, Alvin, and Roky still do, along with newer bands like the Big Boys, Brave Combo, and the Lotions.

STEAMBOAT 1874
403 E. 6th
Central West
478-2912
Open seven days
Cover; charge varies

Like its namesake, Steamboat just keeps churning away down on 6th Street, past the ghosts of clubs past, ones that ran ashore along this fickle stream of humanity. Sometimes the music is canned; mostly it's live. Always it's loud and danceable. Bar.

WATERLOO ICE HOUSE
906 Congress
Central West
474-2461
Monday through Saturday, lunch and dinner
Cover; no cr.
W

Lunchery by day, musical club by night. At lunchtime, crowded with downtowners who eat good burgers, salads, and soups. Good beer selection and pop in a bottle. At night the music is acoustic and harmonious, as is the crowd. Bobby Bridger, Uncle Walt's Band, and Shiner Bock are all key descriptives here. Local art and photography adorn the limestone walls.

EATING OUT

Not much more than ten years ago, the Austin diner struggled to decide among French, Thousand Island, or Roquefort salad dressings before moving on to the main event with fried chicken, chicken-fried steak, or griddle-fried steak.

Little Buda, meanwhile, was playing perplexed host to hippie artisans and one of three Indonesian restaurants in the country at the time. The pork *sates* and *bhami goreng* were memorable. And Round Rock boasted of Sam Bass and the historic Hill Country continental Inn at Brushy Creek.

After a protracted pubescence, Austin restaurants started to blossom. By 1974 Andre's and Hunan were making dining out exciting. Gradually the gates were opened, and Austin was flooded with trendy restaurants and those that loudly professed not to be.

Austin currently has the highest number of restaurants per capita in Texas, except perhaps nearby Creedmoor, where two weekend barbeque purveyors do battle for the appetites of a total population of 250. Our generous supply of restaurants means that many bite the dust in a couple of months (even on bustling 6th Street), and those that survive often undergo radical changes. Their battles for survival provide the diner with vast gastronomic opportunities, most of which are going to be rewarding, since bad places just don't have the room to make it.

Granted, Austin's restaurants don't quite run the gamut of the U. N.'s member nations the way Houston's legions do, and some of the Austin gang's bills of fare are tending to read more and more eclecticly alike. But a three-squares-a-day restaurant critic would be hard pressed to stay bellied up to the ever-changing buffet of Austin restaurants and clubs and bistros.

Dining out in Austin in the 1980s is more than just supernachos, *migas*, and *fajitas*, with a chocolate croissant on Saturday morning. It is also *sushi* and *barfi* and bangers and Oriental barbeque and vegetarian chili and homemade beet pasta and things Nantua. For those of you whose tastes still run to such things, you can still find fried chicken, steaks (chicken fried or otherwise), burgers and onion rings and fries, biscuits and gravy, and iceberg lettuce here in Austin that are every bit as good as anything you'll put a fork to in Damon or Dabney or Diboll or Domino or Dime Box or Durango.

It's really hard to spend $100 a couple on dinner out in Austin, and pretension is in short supply. How haughty can you get when half your dining room is wearing running shorts and thongs?

★★★
RESTAURANTS

ABUELITA'S
W. 24th at San Antonio
University/Central West
473-2332
Monday through Saturday, lunch and dinner
$; MC, V
W

Good Mexican food has long been hard to find in the university area. Now one of Austin's better *restaurantes* sits practically in the Tower's backyard. Little Grandma's chow is a little more Mex than Tex, though it makes no attempt to delve into the interior, as does San Miguel. This is pretty simple *carne* and tortilla food, like you can find at, say, Cafe Ernesto in Nuevo Laredo. Beer and wine.

ALDO'S
2201 College Ave., Live Oak at S. Congress
Southwest
447-4100
Monday through Saturday, lunch and dinner
$–$$; cr.
W

Aldo's is not a great Northern Italian restaurant, but for the price it is a good Northern Italian restaurant. Pleasant decor, inside or out; the limestone rubble walls are as Austin as it gets, and the centuries-old live oak that shades the garden patio makes a most pleasant dining companion. Beer and wine.

AMAYA'S TACO VILLAGE
4821 E. 7th
Central East
385-7534
Open seven days; breakfast, lunch, and dinner
Sunday breakfast and lunch
$; MC, V
W

Just what is a "taco village," anyway? Amaya's looks more truthfully like a taco office building.The name is in fact doubly mysterious, because the Village serves up more than just tacos. *Fajitas, carne guisada, migas,* and *machacado con huevos* are also stellar. Purist devotees of the latter northern Mexico dish (eggs scrambled with shredded dried beef) may be offended by the topping of gringo *queso amarillo* (instead of white goat cheese), but that's life here north of the border. Most people like it; that is why this village on the far east end of town bustles like a big city during peak hours. Bar.

ANOTHER RAW DEAL; LEGENDARY RAW DEAL
1110 W. 6th; 700 E. 6th
Central West
473-0015; 477-4889
Open seven days, lunch and dinner
$–$$; MC, V
W E. 6th

Certain of the icon-coiners among us have offered up the collective Raw Deal as being somehow symbolic of Austin of the 1970s and 1980s: vintage contemporary Austin, a legend always in the making, a legend almost waiting for time to catch up with it. Both Deals are certainly popular among Austinites, and the decks of both are loaded with no-nonsense fare: steaks, chops, burgers, beans, home fries, longneck beers, and honest drinks. E. 6th has Jim Franklin's whimsical pork-chop-cum-jalapeño mural; perhaps that wuz what they wuz thinking of.

ARMEN'S CAFE
2222 Rio Grande
Central West
474-2068
Open seven days, lunch and dinner
$
W

Middle Eastern food is good for you, whether you're a vegetarian or on the Scarsdale Diet. The Mac-in-the-Box decor goes with the Lebanese-Armenian food about like oil with water, but nobody comes for the atmosphere.

Beef, lamb, and liver kabobs, chicken *felafel, dolmas, borak, hummus,* and such in various plate and sandwich combinations. Those who grew up with it know how to pronounce it. The rest of us struggle through the ordering as best we can. Beer and wine.

AUSTIN'S COURTYARD
1205 N. Lamar
Central West
476-7095
Monday through Saturday, dinner only; reservations recommended
$$–$$$
AE, MC, V
W

An extensive menu, which includes varying selections of wild game (elk cutlets, Scottish wood pigeon, buffalo sirloin), makes choosing your dinner very hard. And considering the quality of what you get, the prices seem almost a bargain. Bar. Leave the running shoes at home.

THE AVENUE
908 Congress
Central West
476-3949
Open seven days; lunch, dinner, and Sunday brunch
AE, DC, MC, V
W

Like its icehouse cousin next door, the Avenue leads a dual existence: popular downtown lunching spot by day, respite from the 6th Street zoo at night. The menu manages to satisfy a variety of tastes and appetites, with soups, sandwiches, salads, pasta, and more substantial entrées. Tasteful understated Victorianesque decor; clientele often more casual. Bar.

BASIL'S
900 W. 10th at Lamar
Central West
477-5576
Open seven days, dinner only
No reservations taken; parties of five or more call ahead
$$$; MC, V
W+

You probably won't encounter a line here at six o'clock Monday night, but you will most of the rest of the time. The food you encounter is definitely Italian, fresh, exciting, deftly prepared. But it just as surely bears the mark of Basil's innovative chefs, who work with nothing but the likes of fresh herbs and produce, homemade pastas and sausage.

You can get red sauce with your pasta, as well as *primavera* (with snow peas, broccoli, zucchini, asparagus) and *paglia e fieno* (with prosciutto, peas, and mushrooms in creamy sauce). Seafood and veal dishes figure prominently in the scheme of things, like redfish *angelica* (with crabmeat in cream sauce) and veal *triestino* (with spinach, prosciutto, garlic, and white wine sauce).

Tables are not much more than an elbow apart in this converted cottage, so it's not exactly the place for an intimate dinner, unless you plan to be friendly with an adjoining table. Still, the high-tech Victorian interior contributes positively to the dining experience. The food tends to be rich. Wine and beer.

BRICK OVEN RESTAURANT
1209 Rio Grande
Central West
477-7006
Open seven days, lunch and dinner
$; AE, MC, V
W

This place has a lot going for it: extremely rich pizza made with whole-milk mozzarella (when you pull the leftovers out of the fridge the next morning, they're bleeding butterfat), lasagna, stromboli, steaks, veal, chicken cooked in a giant 1890 wood-fired brick oven in the middle of the main dining room, and a great view of the Capitol. This particular location has been a black hole in the past for otherwise good restaurants. Brick Oven seems to be making it. Some say it's the best pizza in town; if you're a garlic lover, ask for the fresh garlic topping. Beer and wine.

CHEZ NOUS
510 Neches
Central West
473-2413
Tuesday through Saturday, lunch and dinner
$$–$$$
MC, V
W

This little French cafe is, in a word, *personable*. The proprietors and help are all French (or very good imitations thereof); ditto the homey, relatively uncomplicated food. Most of the menu changes daily, according to what looks best at the market. Dinner (with an entrée like salmon *meunière*) or a snack (say, a slice of homemade duck paté with a *salade lyonnaise*) are equally satisfying. The wine list has been thoughtfully selected, right down to the house wines, which are reasonable and available by the glass or bottle. Shiner Bock is the only domestic beer offered, if that tells you anything. Some of the gallic ambience looks like it came straight from the UT Co-op's poster department, but this picayune observation aside, Chez Nous is about the closest thing to a French cafe that you will find in Austin. Once you are inside, the hoi polloi of 6th Street seem an ocean away. Beer and wine.

CHINA PALACE
6605 Airport
Northwest
451-7104
Open seven days, lunch and dinner
$$

King, or at least crown prince, of Chinese food in Austin. Many swear that it's their favorite, and the menu is just about the longest in town, with separate sections devoted to squid, cuttlefish, and sea cucumber. Hot pots and *dim sum* treats also help set the Palace apart from the masses. Cantonese, Hunan, and Szechuan dishes are served up in large portions. Even with three dining rooms, folks are usually standing in line on weekends, but the kitchen and help almost always take it in stride. Convenient to Highland Mall.

CHOPSTICKS
500-B Pampa
Northwest
458-2332
Tuesday through Sunday, lunch and dinner
$

The name is just a little misleading; you might expect to encounter MacMooshi, but what you actually get is a good, though limited, offering of Thai and Chinese dishes, as hot or as mild as you like. Devotees of jalapeño may, upon request, test their mettle here. A couple of cold Kirins will be necessary, though. While this is not a great Thai restaurant, it is a good, relatively cheap cafe.

And as long as you're here, you can do some shopping at the Oriental market next door.

CHUY'S FINE FOOD
1728 Barton Springs Rd. east of Zilker Park entrance
Southwest
474-4452
Open seven days, lunch and dinner
$; MC, V
W

Chuy's purposely pulls out every cliché in the Tex-Mex school of decor: pink and green walls; piñatas and crepe-paper festoons, black velvet Elvises, righteous low-riders flying through the sky, sandy-colored tile floors. Limited, trendy menu; customer favorites include taco salad, barbeque-chicken tacos, and blue-corn tortilla enchiladas. Favored prep hangout. Bar.

CISCO'S
1511 E. 6th
Central East
478-2420
Open seven days, breakfast and lunch
$
W

Tradition counts for as much around here as the food; the walls attest to that. LBJ and Darrell Royal were/are regulars here. Longhorns of all ages herd over on football weekends, grazing on *migas* or *huevos rancheros* and biscuits. Cisco's is the El Rancho of Mexican breakfasts.

Weekdays are considerably more sedate. Mexican lunches and a real chicken-fried steak can be yours at noon.

CITY GRILLE
401 Sabine
Central West
479-0817
Open seven days, dinner; weekend brunch
$$
AE, MC, V
W+
  Imagine your old summer camp dining hall gone high-tech. It works; so does the food. The grill is mesquite-fired. You can get your beef here, you can get your fish fresh: bluefish, tuna, swordfish, shark, salmon—fish that beg to be grilled. Bar.

CLARKSVILLE CAFE
1200 W. Lynn at W. 12th
Central West
474-7279
Monday through Saturday, dinner only
$-$$; MC, V
  SRO next door? No problem. In fact, there are those of us who prefer Jeffrey's younger sibling for its lighter, airy atmosphere. Lighter menu, too. Appetizers like hacked chicken and entreés like grilled rabbit with mustard sauce let you order dessert with, if not a clear conscience, at least an opaque one. Good wine list.

COPPER SKILLET
3418 N. Lamar
Central West
454-0457
Open seven days; breakfast, lunch, and dinner
$
  The burnt-orange chain-restaurant fitments of the Copper Skillet are deceptive. The food is definitely American, but prepared with the quality you would expect from a Green Pastures restaurant, which it is. Good breakfasts with some of the best biscuits in town. Nightly specials are a little more exotic—say, a stuffed flounder. The quality shows in such little extra touches as whipped real butter, leaf lettuce, homemade potato salad, and yeast rolls. Good chicken-fried steak. Bar.

COUNTY LINE
6500 W. Bee Caves Rd. about .3 mile west of Loop 360
Southwest
327-1742
Open seven days, dinner only
$-$$; MC, V
W
  What do you get when you cross a fern bar with a barbeque stand? The County Line. If you take your Haägen Dasz with whipped cream, you'll love the sauce here; otherwise, ask the waiter to have it left off.

Your wait—this place is very popular—is made easier by the beautiful Hill Country view. Everybody comes for the consistently good, lean brisket, meaty ribs, homemade bread, and tasty side dishes. You may have to ask for pickles and onions. The beer list—Coors and Michelob Light—speaks volumes. Steaks are also offered. Family-style service translates into "all you can eat" for most diners. Bar. Other location: 5204 FM Rd. 2222, .25 mile east of Texas Hwy. 360, Northwest, 346-3664, W.

DAN MCKLUSKY'S
419 E. 6th
Central West
473-8924
Lunch Monday through Friday; dinner seven days
$–$$; AE, MC, V
W

Many connoisseurs scoff when they hear anyone intimate that there are steaks comparable to Dan McKlusky's served anywhere in Austin. The waiter brings the beef out for your personal inspection before it is sent to the kitchen to be grilled to your specifications. The various side dishes and appetizers don't do anything to hamper the pleasure of the experience. Bar.

DAN'S HAMBURGERS
844 Airport Blvd.
Central East
385-2262
Open seven days; breakfast, lunch, and dinner
$
W

A longtime Austin hamburg institution, Dan's started serving breakfast several years ago; and now breakfast is as much an Austin mainstay as the burgers have been. Be prepared for a wait on Sunday morning, but the wait is worth it. If you order eggs sunny-side up or over easy, that's exactly how you'll get them; good hashbrowns. Although the biscuits look industrial, they eat homemade. When other Austinites are off at one of their favorite Sunday br016ncheries, Dan's mostly working-class crowd is enjoying biscuits and gravy and hotcakes with real butter, at cheap prices. And if you don't want breakfast proper at eight in the morning, you can always get a burger. Other breakfast location: 5602 N. Lamar, Northwest, 459-3239, W.

DIRTY'S/MARTIN'S CUMBACK
2808 Guadalupe
Central West
478-0413
Tuesday through Sunday, lunch and dinner
$
W

More has been said in print about Dirty's than about any other hamburger joint in Austin. They might as well hang a historical marker under the Coke sign, but it would probably be highjacked by one of Dirty's adoring patrons. We won't waste your time and ours with trifling descriptives. Just go. Eat inside, outside, or take advantage of Doc's curb service. For the full Dirty's experience, go for the O. T. Special, onion rings and/or fries, and a chocolate shake or a cold Shiner beer. Now do you see why the sign says "Since 1926"?

EATS
1530 Barton Springs Rd.
Southwest
476-8141
Open seven days, lunch and dinner
$–$$; MC, V
W+

Despite its tender age, Eats has managed to pull off a pretty good rendition of a classic Texas roadhouse cafe. The chicken-fried steak and mesquite barbeque shore ain't high tech, but you never ate no swordfish nor sharksteak back at the Chat 'N' Chew in Nockernutt, neither. Bar.

EL ARROYO
1624 W. 5th
Central West
476-4420
Tuesday through Sunday, lunch and dinner
Breakfast, lunch, and dinner Saturday and Sunday
$; MC, V
W

You dine here in the shadow of MoPac, serenaded by whistles and leaking mufflers on the banks of an authentic *arroyo* (ditch). Actually, it's not nearly as bad as it sounds, and if the ambience of the covered patio is not to your liking, you can always eat inside. Ice-cold beer and—if you order anything with barbeque chicken—good food. The barbeque-chicken enchiladas with white and yellow cheese are about the best in town. Chalupas, tacos, and plates can be ordered with the chicken as well. The rest of the nonchicken offerings are good, if not exciting. Hot sauce is some of the best in Austin, and everything is amazingly cheap. Beer.

EL RIO TORTILLAS
910 E. 6th
Central East
476-0945
Closed Sunday
W

Connoisseurs and smart party givers know that for the freshest chips and tortillas at the best prices, you have to go to the source. El Rio fries up chips and rolls out tortillas for many of Austin's popular restaurants. No doubt you've eaten them before. If you come to buy your chips here, you may have to wait for them to bag up some fryer-fresh ones; likewise the soft flour and corn tortillas. Come Christmas season, El Rio also does a healthy business selling the raw *masa* to the many holiday tamale makers in Austin.

EL TAQUITO CHEF
5849 Berkman in Windsor Village shopping center
Northeast
929-3492
Open seven days; breakfast, lunch, and dinner
$
W
The name may translate "King of the Little Tacos," but the chef reserves most of his bragging for the *fajitas* and *migas*. You may not call them the very best in town, but there are none better. The table *salsa* is finely grated fresh jalapeños and a dash of salt. Then there is the usual array of other Tex-Mex dishes.

G-M STEAKHOUSE
1908 Guadalupe
University/Central West
476-0755
Open seven days, lunch and dinner
$
W
The G-M cheeseburger—a heroic half-pound of beef flamebroiled and topped with Wisconsin cheddar—is acclaimed the best in town by many hamburger experts. The burger alone is enough to put most eaters under the table, but go ahead and go all the way with a platter, which is the burger with an equally overwhelming pile of wedge-cut fries. You probably won't be hungry for the rest of the day. Bus station decor. The ambience ranges from entertainingly brash to embarrassingly abrasive.

GALLERIA
Jefferson Square, W. 38th at Kerbey
Central West
452-5510
Open seven days, lunch and dinner
$–$$$; AE, MC, V
W
The Galleria provides one of Austin's most romantic dinner settings: cozy, candlelit, complemented by classic continental cuisine. Sunday brunch is a sit-down affair. Owner Bob Lowe is a wine connoisseur, and the wine list reflects that fact. Bar.

GIANNI'S
504 E. 5th near Neches
Central West
477-7497
Tuesday through Sunday, dinner only
No reservations taken
$$–$$$; AE, MC, V
W

Gianni's helped usher fine Italian cuisine into Austin, and ever since Basil's happened along, the two have been pitted in informal combat for the title of finest *ristorante* in Austin. Each has its adherents, and with good reason. Gianni's menu flirts with *la novella cucina* a bit more than Basil's does. The kitchen here goes out of its way to obtain the freshest meats and fish, like sea bass, trout, and their peers mussels and crawfish. The dining room is larger and more spacious than Basil's, if you lean toward the wide open spaces. Comfortable lounge makes the usual weekend wait easier. Extensive selection of California wines. Bar.

GREEN PASTURES
811 W. Live Oak
Southwest
444-4747
Open every day
Lunch and dinner; brunch only on Sunday
$$–$$$$; AE, MC, V
W

Royal peacocks strut about the manicured grounds fronting the great white Victorian home. The trend continues inside with both surroundings and service. This is vintage southern gentility as found nowhere else in Austin. Accompanying the gentility is a continental menu, à la southern aristocracy. The fare is not particularly innovative, but that would be rather uncomfortably at odds with the tone of the place, wouldn't it? The food is well executed, undeniably, especially the home-baked breadstuffs. If the praise heretofore has sounded just the slightest bit left-handed, let it be said here and now that the Sunday brunch, a Texas classic, is still the best in Texas.

HILL'S CAFE
4700 S. Congress
Southwest
442-1471
Open seven days, twenty-four hours
$; AE, MC, V
W

Hill's "sizzling steaks" have been part of the Austin lexicon for decades, since the days when this was the main drag south and Austin was miles away. Otherwise, the food is standard Tex-American food, whose chief virtue is being available twenty-four hours a day.

THE HOFFBRAU
613 W. 6th
Central West
472-0822
Tuesday through Saturday, lunch and dinner
$

What new and meaningful can we say about this Austin institution? Precious little, so we won't try. Don't be misled by the name; Austin's Hoffbrau is not a beer garden but a restaurant, serving up grilled steaks and a few simple side dishes in an absolutely unpretentious atmosphere. Neither the food nor the folks who bring it to you are put-ons. This is the original Hoffbrau, copied by the Dallas and Houston pretenders of the same name; original and put-ons all enjoy a land-office business. Beer.

HOUSE PARK BAR-B-Q
900 W. 12th
Central West
472-9621
Monday through Friday, lunch only
10:30–6
$
W

Most people seem to ignore this little barbeque stand on the banks of Shoal Creek, which is their misfortune, since House Park smokes the best barbeque in the university/west downtown area. Brisket, pork ribs, links, chicken, and *fajitas*, cooked by a slow oak fire. Portions are good for the price. Daily specials and good side dishes.

The heavenly smell from the pit is by far the most pleasant component of the physical trappings. Dine in the dark, spartan interior, enjoy the Lamar/12th Street traffic from one of the outdoor tables, or better yet, walk a few feet to the shaded Shoal Creek greenbelt.

HSIN YUAN
Balcones Woods, 11150 Research Blvd.
Northwest
345-9866
Open seven days, lunch and dinner
$–$$; AE, MC, V
W

Compared to many of Austin's Oriental restaurants, Hsin Yuan seems almost plush; maybe it's the rice-paper mural on the walls. The menu is both extensive and exotic. You can have your sea urchin and sea cucumber, as well as your squid, several different ways. Pork, chicken, beef, shrimp, and vegetable dishes run into the dozens. To sample the range of entire possibilities would run closer to a year than a month. *Dim sum* on Saturday and Sunday.

INN AT BRUSHY CREEK
IH 35 at Taylor exit, Round Rock
255-2555
Thursday through Saturday, dinner only; reservations required
$$–$$$; AE, DC, MC, V
W

The authentic restoration of this 1850s limestone house gives dinner a timeless quality here. The food is some of the finest to be found in central Texas. It's in a dry precinct, so bring your own bottle; free corkage. Desserts are intoxicating.

IRON WORKS BARBECUE
100 Red River at E. 1st
Central West
478-4855
Monday through Friday, lunch and dinner
$; MC, V
W

This tin shed first attained prominence as the Weigl Ironworks, and the Weigls' work is still in use all over town. These days barbeque is the hot item: brisket, sausage, chicken—but they have beef ribs as well, which aren't often found in this particular state or in Austin. There is actually a salad bar, too. It's big and breezy inside, even during the summer—an amazing feat, given the lack of air conditioning. The rest of the interior is equally rustic, down to the dozens of brands burned into the weathered wooden walls. Beer only.

JAIME'S SPANISH VILLAGE
802 Red River
Central West
476-5149
Monday through Saturday, lunch and dinner
$; AE, MC, V
W

Number two always tries harder: Jaime's plays Avis to Matt's (El Rancho) Hertz. The Old Mexico charm of the old Spanish Village has been retained; the food is improved. Supersonic attentive service; you're barely seated before chips and sauce are on the table. The chicken *mole*, while tasty, is not possessed of the traditional complexly spiced, slightly bitter taste. Otherwise, the menu is pretty close to El Rancho's, as are the margaritas. The food itself is often a little better. Bar.

JAKE'S
801 W. 5th
Central West
472-7443
Monday through Friday; breakfast, lunch, and dinner
$

With the exception of La Plaza and the Hoffbrau, Jake's is the last unreconstructed hangout on greater 6th Street, the closest thing to a family tavern for miles. The early 1940s decor is reminiscent of Louie's. An antique shuffleboard table is shoehorned in between tables and booths; portal windows add to the cozy feeling. Great ceiling neon. Jake's softball team's trophies clutter up one end of the long mirrored bar. Elsewhere, "Jake" is spelled out on a bulletin board with old pencils, pens, and erasers. Good old-fashioned hamburgers, fried oysters, and chicken-fried steak. One order of homemade fries is big enough for two people. Cheapest beer prices in the area of the strip. If you walk in feeling like you've crashed a private party, it's because everybody else tends to know everybody else. Don't let it stop you, though; just wade in. Beer.

JEFFREY'S
1204 West Lynn
Central West
477-5584
Monday through Saturday, dinner only
No reservations taken
$$–$$$; MC, V
To the ignorant or uninitiated, it's something of a mystery, all these cars parked in every conceivable space around the crossing of W. 12th and W. Lynn every evening. Nothing's open, except these two little buildings: Jeffrey's on the northwest corner, and Clarksville Cafe next door. Surely the passengers are not all crammed into these two little restaurants? No, not always. Sometimes they are cooling their heels in line outside the door. Why? No reservations. Hmph! Chow must be awful good.

Well, it is if you like chow such as redfish St. Malo, calf liver *moutarde*, paté of duck, or crab and artichoke soup. It's best to keep your plans for the rest of the evening pretty loose. Jeffrey's rivals Virginia's Cafe in this respect. Still, lots of folks say both places are worth it. Who are we to argue with them?

JULIO'S RESTAURANT
1005 W. Lynn
Central West
478-6516
Monday through Saturday; breakfast, lunch, and dinner
$
W
When talk of Austin's burgeoning culinary diversity crops up, Julio's is bound to come tripping off the tongue of trendy palates. This family-run hole in the wall dishes out Tex-Mex with a decidedly Carib accent. Patrons rant about Julio's beans and rice with fresh cilantro about as much as they rave about the roasted chicken and *fajitas*, which are actually *fajitas guisadas*.

KATZ'S
618 W. 6th at Rio Grande
Central West
472-2037
Open seven days, twenty-four hours
$; AE, MC, V
"Finally a real New York deli in Austin," Katz's ad claim. True or false? Let's put it this way: Katz's is to Austin what the Lone Star Cafe is to New York. The food is mostly good, though you'll wonder how a corned beef sandwich can cost so much. Once it's in front of you, you'll begin to understand. Katz's really comes into its own in those wee, postclub hours, when only a blintz will keep the edge on your finely tuned evening. Bar.

KERBEY LANE CAFE
3704 Kerbey
Central West
451-1436
Open seven days, breakfast and lunch
Dinner on Sundays
Open till 4 a.m. Tuesday through Saturday
$
W
Healthful food—not health food—with an emphasis on fresh is served here in spotless airy surroundings that could have been the product of a renegade Amish interior decorator. Local artwork occupies the walls, and you can request smoking or nonsmoking sections.

Tex–New Mex dishes are popular items here. Some might find them a trifle bland, but they perk up nicely with an infusion of the fresh table *salsa*. Veggies and carnivores can be perfectly happy at Kerbey Lane; the black beans are about the best in town. The cheeseburger comes on a whole-wheat bun, with Swiss cheese, leaf lettuce, Bermuda onion, and tomato. Good omelettes and desserts. Late-night hours make it popular; always crowded on Sunday morning.

KOREA HOUSE
2700 W. Anderson Lane
Northwest
458-2477
Open seven days, lunch and dinner (opens 2 p.m. Sunday)
$
W
This is an unabashed plea to Austin food enthusiasts: support your local Korean restaurant! And your local Thai restaurants. And while we're at it, why hasn't someone opened a Vietnamese restaurant? Or a real *dim sum* cafe?

Back to the local Korean restaurant: Korea House is hopelessly buried in back of the Village shopping center, with an advertising budget the wrong side of infinity. It serves delicious authentic dishes (right down to the *kim chee*) with great names like *bulgokki* and *doegee kalbi* and relies on word-of-happy-mouth to spread the good news. Well, we've been talking, have you been listening?

LAKEVIEW CAFE
3800 Lake Austin Blvd. south of Enfield intersection
Central West
476-7372
Open seven days, lunch and dinner
Brunch only on Sunday
$–$$; AE, MC, V
W partial
In keeping with Austin's tradition of recycling old landmarks (instead of tearing them down), this venerable lakeside beer joint has been transformed into a sun-decked restaurant and bar, one of those casual-chic places outfitted in rough wood and plants, peopled by designer khakis and Mexican embroidered dresses, serving *fajitas* and burgers and barbequed shrimp and spinach salads, and of course that priceless view of Lake Austin and the boat club. Bar.

LA PROVENCE
1800 Colorado
Central West
479-0011
Monday through Saturday, lunch and dinner
Reservations suggested
$$$–$$$$; cr.
W
Like we said in the beginning, it's pretty hard to spend $100 on dinner for two in Austin. It's possible here, but imported black bass and fresh wild mushrooms and all the other choice ingredients that go into your luncheon or dinner aren't cheap. Does the kitchen measure up to the quality of the ingredients and the tab? Generally so. Bar.

LAS MANITAS AVENUE CAFE
211 Congress
Central West
472-9357
Open seven days, breakfast and lunch
$
W
El Nuevo Wavo de la Cocina Texmexicana, from the trendy graphics on the walls to the grapefruit and melon garnishes on your plate, from the gold loop in your waiter's ear to the herbal teas on the menu. Breakfasts and lunches are at least semilegendary among young Tex-Mex connoisseurs. Interesting clientele makes it spiritual cousin to the Les

Amis of the early 1970s.

Huevos moltuleños are a refreshing alternative to the *migas* mania that has taken over Austin. Daily lunch specials are always worth a try. Hep yet homey food. Most all the selections from the limited menu will be less greasy than at other places, even the *menudo*. Beer.

LOUIE'S ON THE LAKE
2219 West Lake Dr.
327-8280
Tuesday through Sunday, dinner and Sunday brunch
$$
W

The Sunday champagne brunch and "Admiral's Ship Buffet" are popular draws, but what sets Louie's apart from the rest is its location, on the west shores of Lake Austin, just above Tom Miller Dam. You can drive to Louie's (by way of Redbud Trail or Bee Caves Road), but why bother? Not when you can ride the shuttle boat, which operates from Boat Town Marina on Lake Austin Boulevard, near Enfield. Bar.

MARTIN BROTHERS' CAFE
10th and Lamar (inside Whole Foods Market)
Central West
476-3363
Open seven days
W

Unless you enjoy dining in a crowded supermarket, you don't come to Martin Brothers for the atmosphere. Most of us come for two things: ice cream and vegetarian chili. The Brothers' ice cream is the closest thing to "organic" in town and often the most exotically flavored. Try avocado, or stick with tried-and-true favorites like carob-honey and vanilla. But first order your chili, which comes with tortilla chips. Ask for a side of grated Monterrey Jack, mix all three together, and *voila!* Frito pie *au naturel*. (You'll have to go to the 7-11 across the street for the Dr. Pepper and peanuts, though.)

MATT'S EL RANCHO
303 E. 1st at San Jacinto
Central West
472-5425
Wednesday through Monday, lunch and dinner
$–$$; AE, DC, MC, V
W larger building only

"King of Mexican food"? You bet. Matt Martinez was the first human being in Austin to make a million dollars off Mexican food. The pace has not slackened over the years. El Rancho is at least as well known as, say, the lieutenant governor, and generally more popular amongst its constituents. Why? Because it's "always good," just like Matt and the sign say. The food may be more exciting at other restaurants, and occasionally the margaritas more potent, but when you come here you can always count on a good meal and good service, especially when you order one of the specialties, like *chile relleno*, shrimp *a la Mexicana*, or even the Mexican pizza. One of the reasons for this admirable consistency is Matt himself. He still holds court every night, perched on his stool and sporting his bow tie, making sure everyone is happy. If it's good enough for Daddy D., it's good enough for you.

MEXICO TIPICO
1800 E. 6th; 1707 E. 6th
Central East
472-9389; 472-3222
#1 Thursday through Tuesday, breakfast and lunch
#2 Wednesday through Monday, lunch and dinner
$
W

Austin is full of good Tex-Mex cafes, and more specifically good Tex-Mex breakfasts. Anyone recuperating from a hard day's night knows the restorative powers of a plate of *migas con refritos y papas*, and maybe a cold Corona besides. The Tipico's *migas con queso*, refried beans (cooked with bacon grease), and *papas fritas* adorned with *salsa fresca* are bettered nowhere else in Austin. If you are really hungry and want the whole experience, request a spot of *carne guisada* on the side.

The rest of the breakfast and lunch offerings are good, too. Interesting eastside-westside mix of diners.

MIKE AND CHARLIE'S
1206 W. 34th
Central West
451-5550
Monday through Saturday, lunch and dinner
$
W

A westside institution, spiritual godfather to many of those upstart 6th Street bars and restaurants, with a correspondingly more mature crowd. Eclectic menu that has managed to retain the old favorites while keeping abreast of Austin's ever-changing culinary fads. (They haven't gone to mesquite yet.) The shaded courtyard is particularly nice on spring and fall days. Chicken salad is some of the best to be had anywhere in Austin. *Ceviche, tacos al carbon*, and *canasta de ensalada* are also among the tried-and-true favorites. Quite a bit of Austin memorabilia hangs on the walls. Mike and Charlie's also maintains a frontier deli down on Old Pecan Street (6th Street Emporium, 111 E. 6th, 478-4414) for those of you stranded downtown for lunch with an undeniable craving for chicken salad. Bar.

MILTO'S PIZZA PUB
2909 Guadalupe
Central West
476-1021
Open seven days, lunch and dinner
$
W

This is the popular university-area alternative to the barbaric pie. Sicilian or Neopolitan crust, whole wheat or white, varied choice of toppings. Milto takes a more traditional approach to pizza than many local parlors do, and the product is more consistently good here. If you're not in the mood for pizza, go for one of the sandwiches, Italo-Greek in nature. Try ordering double cheese, plus whatever else you want on top. Beer and wine.

MOTHER'S CAFE
4215 Duval
Northwest
451-3994
Monday through Saturday, lunch and dinner
$–$$
W

Never eat at any place called Mom's—a cardinal rule for itinerant eaters. Rules are made to be broken, of course, You know that this is no run-of-the-mill cafe when you walk in the front door and see the bicycles parked over in the far corner of the anteroom, and maybe somebody's bedroll and laundry bag next to the front door. This ain't the Quorum Club. A jazz trio plays off in another corner. Hippie types sit next to sorority types, eating wholesome vegetarian food with a healthy accent on the Tex-Mex and Italo-Mex. Healthful food can taste good, as the loyal following will attest. Most prefer to dine with the plants out on the covered patio. Pleasant service, no smoking. Once you're inside, it's hard to believe that this used to be a 7-11 store. Beer and wine.

NIGHT HAWK
336 S. Congress near Riverside
Southwest
478-1661
Open seven days; breakfast, lunch, and dinner
$–$$$; AE, MC
W

"When I want a good steak, I come here." That remark, overheard in the Number One room one night, sums up the reputation of this Austin institution, now fifty years old. None of the food is fancy; it's mostly fried or broiled, like oysters, catfish, and steaks—big and small. Big American breakfasts with biscuits and real butter lure many here on a daily basis. And the waitresses are always friendly. Consult phone book for other locations.

NOODLES
5416 Parkcrest
Northwest
459-7098
$

Along with taco salad, gourmet fast food looks to be a trend of the 1980s. Noodles is one of the latter places. Now you can *buy* fresh-daily spinach fettuccine for your special Alfredo, instead of having to make it. If you're in a hurry, you can take micro-ready veal tortellini or ravioli home with you. And if you just can't wait, you can eat it here.

NUEVO LEON
1209 E. 7th
Central East
479-0097
Open seven days, lunch and dinner
$
W

Other than the food, there is really no reason to dine at Nuevo Leon. Even with the help of neon *cerveza* signs and mirrored-over ex-windows, the interior manages to remain anonymous. You do not come here to see, or be seen. You come to eat, and perhaps to drink some of the coldest beer in town, served with a frosted mug. These brave Leones publicly disclaim the use of any family secrets in their kitchen. They don't need any. Some Austinites seem to board here, feeding on *fajitas*, *chiles rellenos*, and the various *carnes asadas*. Late, late weekend hours make it a best bet for hungry nightcrawlers. Beer and wine.

THE OMELETTRY
4811 Burnet
Northwest
453-5062
Open seven days; breakfast, lunch, and dinner
$

Some folks swear by this eatery; witness the weekend lines. Others swear at it. As the name implies, the Omelettry forged its reputation on the humble, versatile cackleberry, in the form of big fat omelettes and the legendary gingerbread pancakes. Pink Flamingo decor, help, and clientele. Food tends to be on the healthful side without being strident about it. Probably the best place in town for breakfast at four in the afternoon. The burger is as memorable as the BLT is forgettable. Other location: 2304 Lake Austin Blvd., Central West, 478-8645, W.

ORIENTAL GARDEN
208 W. 4th
Central West
Monday through Saturday, dinner only
$$

We have a man-of-the-world friend who lives in Houston and comes to Austin to eat *sushi*. Not bad for a town with one, year-old *sushi* bar. A lot of folks come here to eat rather unimaginative, cooked (though competently cooked, by and large) Japanese fare. But many of us come for the *magura*, *hamichi*, flying fish rolls, and lots of that sinus-searing *wasabi*. It's not exactly cheap, but it's fun to eat; and like Mom used to tell you, "Eat it! It's good, and good for you!" Your waitress may be a ringer for the girl next door, but she'll still be wearing a kimono. Bar.

PASTA CANATA
Research at Burnet in the Colonnade Shopping Center; second location 11643-B Research
Northwest
834-9977; 345-8267
Fresh pasta made daily, sauces, sausages, minestrone, and everything else you need to throw together a fine Italian meal at home in minutes. Convenient to the northwest suburban frontier.

THE QUORUM
United Bank Tower, 15th and Guadalupe
Central West
472-6779
Lunch Monday through Friday, dinner Monday through Saturday
$$$–$$$$; cr.
W
The Quorum is certainly one of *the* places to be seen—and to drink—in Austin. Fortunately it is also *a* place to eat, too. The kitchen and menu have had their peaks and valleys through the years, but over the long haul the Quorum's provender has usually been up to snuff. Bar.

RENE'S SOUTHERN DINING
4140 E. 12th at Springdale
Central East
926-7834
Monday through Saturday, lunch and early dinner
$
Fans of the old Southern Dinett on E. 11th are now enjoying this reincarnation several miles east. The food and help are the same; only the name and location differ. "We are the soul food specialists," Rene and company claim. They get our vote, for their smothered chicken, pork bones, meatloaf, pinto beans, cabbage, parsley-buttered potatoes, and last but not least, their peach cobbler. East Austin politicos lunch here on a regular basis.

SAM'S BAR-B-CUE
2000 E. 12th
Central East
478-0378
Open seven days, lunch and dinner
$
Well, okay, maybe the neighborhood isn't exactly polished. Neither

are Sam's outward trappings. Not much reason to stop, eh? Not if
you're in the habit of making judgments based on first impressions.
Others of us have discovered that Sam's puts out what may be the best
barbeque in town. The lineup: pork ribs, brisket, mutton, sausage,
chicken. One local restaurant reviewer publicly revealed this well-kept
secret a couple of falls ago, and it quickly became the darling of Austin's
hip media crowd. The result is the current slightly expanded Sam's,
which manages to maintain the flavor of the original tiny layout, thanks
in no small part to the oak-smoked scents that greet you at the door.
Side dishes are okay, too.

SAN MIGUEL
2330 W. North Loop
Northwest
459-4121
Open seven days
Lunch Monday through Friday; dinner; Sunday brunch
$$; DC, MC, V
W
    Funny thing: San Miguel aims to duplicate all the pleasures of dining
in one of Mexico's great "native" restaurants. And it succeeds. When-
ever I yearn for, say, the *guarache en liga* and *sopa de tortilla* at El Tapanco
in Saltillo, I can just get my fix here at San Miguel and save eighteen or
twenty hours in the process. It's all right here, down to the cool tile
floors and punched-tin light shades.
    La cocina Mexicana is blessed with many influences—French, Italian,
Chinese, and German among them—and San Miguel manages to pack
in both this flavorful heritage and adoring customers every night. Bar.

SCHOLZ GARTEN
1607 San Jacinto near E. 17th
Central West
477-4171
Monday through Saturday, lunch and dinner
$; MC, V
W
    As much history has been made under the trees of Scholz's beer gar-
den as inside the halls of state up the hill, and the garden-ers have
generally had more fun doing it. Elbows have been bending and jaws
flapping since August Scholz built the core building in 1866. In those
days Scholz brewed his own. The Saengerrunde Hall next door was
built a few years later, and the Austin Saengerrunde (a singing club)
has owned Garten and Hall since 1909. With the advent of liquor by the
drink in 1971, Scholz's lost some of its more conspicuous patrons, as the
dens of government multiplied many times over. That's okay; just leaves
more room for the rest of us. The burgers, nachos, chicken, etc., aren't
half-bad, either.

SHALIMAR
5451 N. IH 35 in Capital Plaza
Northeast
451-8085
Monday through Saturday, dinner only; Sunday lunch and dinner
$–$$; AE, DC, MC
W

As late as the early 1970s, Lim Ting and Lung's Chinese Kitchen were about as exotic as dining out in Austin got. And while we still cannot boast of any Abyssinian or Beylorussian provincial palaces of cuisine, we do have Indian food at Shalimar. Pan-Indian menu, with some concessions to American taste. The food is nonetheless quite tasty and reasonably authentic. Live bellydancing spices up the fare some nights; call ahead for schedule. Beer and wine.

SHANGHAI RESTAURANT
5555 N. Lamar, Suite E-125
Northwest
459-3000
Open seven days, lunch and dinner
Dim sum Saturday and Sunday
$–$$
W

Considering the competition, Shanghai's menu is not particularly exotic or particularly spicy (unless you throw a temper tantrum at your waitperson). Main dishes are pretty much confined to the beef, pork, chicken, duck, shrimp, vegetable, noodle, and rice categories; lovers of squid and sea cucumber and lion's head had best hunt elsewhere. But after nearly ten years in operation here, Shanghai is packing them in on weekends. They must be doing something right.

What they do is Cantonese and Hunanese, with some northern-style dishes thrown in. The Hunanese here is less spicy than in other restaurants, which makes it popular with those of mild palate. More important than the spiciness is the quality of the ingredients. Adventurers may deride the menu's calm, but the ingredients used are as fresh as you'll encounter anywhere else in town and are cooked requisitely.

SIAM GARDEN
9608 N. Lamar
Northwest
837-2483
Monday through Saturday, lunch and dinner
$–$$; AE, MC, V
W

Any restaurant that has the king and queen of Thailand looking benignly down upon customer and cash register has got to succeed, right? Siam Garden has some of the best food anywhere in town at reasonable prices. Try the red snapper for two, and we think you'll agree. Austin's appreciation for Asian cuisines is growing; small wonder, eating here. Bar.

SID'S
3501 N. Lamar
Central West
453-3321
Open seven days; breakfast, lunch, and dinner
$–$$; MC, V
W

The 1950s live on at Sid's, the turquoise capital of Austin: turquoise menus, chairs, booths, tables, carpet, couches, lunch counter, women's room floor, water pitchers, and baby seats. But you don't find vinyl of this quality anymore. Elvis's mother would have liked this place for Mother's Day dinner. The bill of fare is good old American food, right down the line, from the fluffy biscuits to the canned vegetables. Lunch and dinner specials; the drinks are cheap. The menu leans heavily toward fried, roasted, or baked. The food is comforting, as is the sight of old couples and old hippies eating side by side. Bar.

SPERANZA'S
318 Colorado
Central West
476-3469
Wednesday through Saturday, dinner only
$$–$$$; MC, V
W

We debated long and hard before including Speranza's in *Austin*. The Speranzas don't advertise because they have their hands (and tables) full enough already. They're small, and they like it that way. They need our plug like Austin needs another *fajita* restaurant. But we would be remiss in our guidely duties if we did not mention this delightful anomaly in Austin dining. To say that the Speranzas are devoted to *la cocina Italiana* is like saying that Barton Springs is all wet.

THE STALLION
5534 N. Lamar near Houston
Northwest
451-1626
Open seven days, lunch and dinner
$; AE, MC
W

The Stallion's chicken-fried steak and onion rings are local legends, deservedly so. But the fried chicken is the real star; forget the Colonel and his clones. Get a full (four-piece) order; that way, you'll have something to snack on tomorrow. Not for the fastidious or dieters. There are heresies like fried veggie things and crab-stuffed jalapeños on the menu now, and Michael McDonald on the jukebox, but the rest of the Stallion is pretty much the same as it was when it opened, back when Hank was still alive. Bar.

SWEETISH HILL
1202-B W. 6th at Blanco
Central West
472-7319
Open seven days, breakfast and lunch
$–$$; MC, V

The lives of some Austinites seem to revolve around croissants and Sunday brunch at Sweetish Hill. Why else would the adjoining Watson and Company bookstore find it worthwhile to be open at eight on Sunday morning?

The tree-shaded patio of this cafe is one of Austin's most pleasant breakfast-brunch-lunching spots, even in December. Your surroundings are neat and simple. The food, which runs from omelettes through *salades niçoise* to fresh seafood, is tasty and attractively presented. Even the mayonnaise on your sandwich is homemade. Yummy bread from the near-mythical bakery up front. Even the house wines are thoughtfully chosen to satisfy a variety of tastes. Regular menu and five or six daily specials. Beer and wine.

SWEETISH HILL DELICATESSEN
1200 W. 6th
Central West
472-7370
Monday through Saturday, lunch and dinner
W

Austin, specifically central Austin, has been waiting a long time for a place like this. Sometimes you want something truly gourmet for lunch, and either you're too lazy to make and pack it yourself, or the noon is too beautiful for spend inside a stuffy restaurant. What do you do? The recent opening of Sweetish Hill Deli has knocked the horns right off your dilemma. Perhaps a slice of *torta rustica*? Or mussels in dill sauce? Maybe just a chicken-salad sandwich, with homemade mayo and fresh herbs? Hearty eaters then have to choose between pasta salad, mushroom and artichoke salad, wild-rice salad, and such to accompany that sandwich. Sweetish Hill even provides the bag, along with fine groceries, beer, and wines from across the world.

TEXAS CHILI PARLOR
1409 Lavaca
Central West
472-2828
Open seven days, lunch and dinner
$; MC, V
W

Old-timers lament that the Chili Parlor is but a parody of its former outrageous self these days, but it nevertheless remains the best place in town to sample the national dish of Texas in all its classic deflections: straight, in chili pie, smothered over enchiladas and hot dogs, folded into flour tortillas, drizzled over salad greens. Choose X, XX, XXX heat. If you've never been here before, you'll enjoy taking in all the beer signs and sundry other junque covering the walls and ceiling. Beer.

THREADGILL'S
6416 N. Lamar
Northwest
451-5440
Open seven days, lunch and dinner
$; MC, V
W

Confidentially, this gas-station-turned-restaurant may just be an excuse for owner Eddie Wilson to show off his beer-sign collection. Wilson must have more vintage beer clocks and neon signs than anyone else in the world, and the best are hanging here. Probably the most neon between Times Square and Las Vegas.

After sitting in the new stainless-steel "diner" addition awhile—and with the help of a couple of beers—you might begin to think you're sitting in the Tic-Tock Diner, and Paterson, New Jersey, is lurking outside. Then the food comes and you remember that you're still down home: chicken frieds and liver and pork roast and chicken and dumplings and mashed potatoes and black-eyed peas and okra. Umm, umm. Their combination of a classic chicken-fried steak and vegetables *al dente* is practically unique in this town.

THUNDERCLOUD SUB SHOPS
Ten shops all over Austin
Open seven days, lunch and dinner
$
W

"French or whole wheat? Provolone or American? Would you like mayo and mustard on that sandwich, sir?" The submarine purist may sneer, but this is Austin, after all, not Philly or the Big Apple. Taste is what counts, and most versions of the Thundercloud—sixteen in all—get high marks. The offerings range from traditional cold cuts to chicken salad and seafood and hot meatball. The potato salad is homemade. Beer.

TORTILLERIA DOS HERMANOS
2730 E. 1st at Pleasant Valley
Central East
474-9655
Open seven days
$
W

Dos Hermanos is one of those mom-and-pop–type tortillerias—in this case a small, brother-and-brother affair. No chips, no flour tortillas, just thick, family-style corn tortillas, perfect for your heartiest enchilada filling. Dos Hermanos also dispenses food to go, like *barbacoa* and *carnitas* by the pound, and *taquitos* and *tortas* and *pan dulce*. Convenient to Longhorn Dam.

UDDER DELIGHT ICE CREAM FACTORY
5245 Burnet; 2604 Guadalupe
Northwest; University/Central West
452-1668; 473-2428

Forget Haägen Dasz, this is one of the new shrines for butterfat gluttons. There oughta be a law against places like this, especially if you like ice creams made (on the premises) with bits of your favorite snack bar or candy.

★★★
BAKERIES

BARBARA'S BAKERY
Rt. 1, Box 19, Hwy. 304, Rosanky 78953

Barbara bakes out of her home in Rockne, and her whole-wheat bread makes absolutely the best toast in town. Not available everywhere; mostly at Whole Foods Markets and smaller Austin and southeast Travis County groceries. Barbara also bakes up cookies, buns, coffee cakes, pies, carrot cakes, and anything else that strikes her fancy. These are definitely the closest to homemade baked goods commercially available in Austin. Two can split one cinnamon roll.

Barbara's is the best thing to come out of Rockne since 1932, when the town changed its name from Hilbigville in honor of the deceased football great.

HOT JUMBO BAGEL BAKERY
307 W. 5th
Central West
477-1137
Open seven days
W

Best bagels in town, several varieties, baked fresh here daily.

MRS. JOHNSON'S BAKERY
4909 Airport Blvd.
Northwest
459-5801
Open seven days, twenty-four hours

As is the case with barbeque and local color, to find the best donuts in town, you have to drive aways out of town, to Lone Star Bakery in Round Rock, or Red's Dough Shoppe in Georgetown. If you're willing to settle for merely delicious, head for Mrs. Johnson's Airport location. The Mrs. has been setting the standard hereabouts for decades.

SOUR DOUGH BAKERY
Whole Foods Market, 9070 Research at Burnet
Northwest
451-4377
Open seven days
W

The new kid on the block, operating out of the Whole Foods Market's
north store. European-trained baker and a fancy stainless-steel Swedish oven with controlled misting makes it a bakery to be reckoned with.
Its provender is healthful, innovative, and delicious for the most part,
definitely not of the white-flour-and-white-sugar school.

SWEETISH HILL BAKERY
1200 W. 6th
Central West
472-7319
Open seven days
MC, V
With the exception of Navarro's Federal, Sweetish Hill is Austin's
oldest westside custom bakery, and its most revered. Impressive, in-
clusive repertoire, year-round and seasonal, probably the most varied
in Austin. Enjoys an according reputation, though it sometimes is
guilty of coasting on it.

TEXAS FRENCH BREAD
3401 Guadalupe; 3213 Red River
Central West
458-3910; 478-8794
Open seven days, 6 a.m.–9 p.m.
Austin's darling of the 1980s, growing apace, rolling out hundreds
upon hundreds of baguettes, croissants, specialty whole-grain breads,
and other floury sweetmeats. Not always the *very* best in town, but the
most dependable.

FURTHER READING

Barkley, Mary (Starr). *History of Travis County and Austin, 1839–1899*. Austin, 1963.

Handbook of Texas, Vols. 1–3. Austin: Texas State Historical Association, 1952–1976.

Historic Austin. Austin: Heritage Society of Austin, 1981.

Jones, Joseph. *Life on Waller Creek*. Austin: AAR/Tantalus, 1982.

Olmsted, Frederick Law. *A Journey Through Texas*. Reprint of 1857 ed. Austin: University of Texas Press, 1978.

Owens, James. *Travis County in Stone, Bronze, and Aluminum*. Austin: Travis County Historical Survey Committee, 1972.

Pass, Fred, and Ruth Harris, eds. *Texas Almanac and State Industrial Guide*. 51st ed. Dallas: A. H. Belo Corporation, 1982.

Sharpe, Patricia, and Robert S. Weddle, eds. *Texas*. Austin: Texas Monthly Press, 1982.

Southwestern Historical Quarterly. Austin: Texas State Historical Association, 1898–   .

Waterloo Scrapbook. Austin: Friends of the Austin Public Library, 1968–   .

Williamson, Roxanne Kuter. *Austin, Texas: An American Architectural History*. San Antonio: Trinity University Press, 1973.